D0070923

Virginia
Government

CQ Press, an imprint of SAGE, is the leading publisher of books, periodicals, and electronic products on American government and international affairs. CQ Press consistently ranks among the top commercial publishers in terms of quality, as evidenced by the numerous awards its products have won over the years. CQ Press owes its existence to Nelson Poynter, former publisher of the *St. Petersburg Times,* and his wife Henrietta, with whom he founded Congressional Quarterly in 1945. Poynter established CQ with the mission of promoting democracy through education and in 1975 founded the Modern Media Institute, renamed The Poynter Institute for Media Studies after his death. The Poynter Institute (*www.poynter.org*) is a nonprofit organization dedicated to training journalists and media leaders.

In 2008, CQ Press was acquired by SAGE, a leading international publisher of journals, books, and electronic media for academic, educational, and professional markets. Since 1965, SAGE has helped inform and educate a global community of scholars, practitioners, researchers, and students, spanning a wide range of subject areas, including business, humanities, social sciences, and science, technology, and medicine. A privately owned corporation, SAGE has offices in Los Angeles, London, New Delhi, and Singapore, in addition to the Washington D.C. office of CQ Press.

Virginia Government

Institutions and Policy

Liliokanaio Peaslee and Nicholas J. Swartz
James Madison University

Los Angeles | London | New Delhi
Singapore | Washington DC

Los Angeles | London | New Delhi
Singapore | Washington DC

FOR INFORMATION:

SAGE Publications, Inc.

2455 Teller Road

Thousand Oaks, California 91320

E-mail: order@sagepub.com

SAGE Publications Ltd.

1 Oliver's Yard

55 City Road

London EC1Y 1SP

United Kingdom

SAGE Publications India Pvt. Ltd.

B 1/I 1 Mohan Cooperative Industrial Area

Mathura Road, New Delhi 110 044

India

SAGE Publications Asia-Pacific Pte. Ltd.

3 Church Street

#10-04 Samsung Hub

Singapore 049483

Printed in the United States of America

Library of Congress Cataloging-in-Publication Data

Peaslee, Liliokanaio.

Virginia government : institutions and policy / Liliokanaio Peaslee and Nicholas J. Swartz, James Madison University.

pages cm.
Includes bibliographical references and index.

ISBN 978-1-4522-0589-2

1. Virginia—Politics and government. 2. Public administration—Virginia. 3. Political planning—Virginia. I. Title.

JK3916.P43 2013
320.49755—dc23   2013016272

This book is printed on acid-free paper.

Acquisitions Editor: Charisse Kiino

Associate Editor: Nancy Loh

Editorial Assistant: Davia Grant

Production Editor: Jane Haenel

Copy Editor: Patrice Sutton

Typesetter: C&M Digitals (P) Ltd.

Proofreader: Rae-Ann Goodwin

Indexer: Michael Ferreira

Cover Designer: Edgar Abarca

Marketing Manager: Amy Whitaker

13 14 15 16 17 10 9 8 7 6 5 4 3 2 1

Contents

List of Tables, Figures, and Boxes   x

Preface   xiv

About the Authors   xvi

1. An Introduction to Government and Policymaking in the Commonwealth   **1**

One State, Many Virginias   2

    An Unparalleled Political History   4

    A Snapshot of Virginia Citizens   5

    The Economy   7

Plan of the Book   8

Key Concepts   9

Suggested Resources   9

Notes   9

2. A Framework for Governing: Exploring the Virginia State Constitution   **11**

Forms of Government   11

How and Why State Constitutions Vary   12

The Evolution of Virginia's Constitutions   13

    The 1776 Constitution   13

    The 1830 Constitution   15

    The 1851 Constitution   16

    1864: The War Constitution   16

    The 1870 Constitution   16

    The 1902 Constitution   17

    The Current System: The Constitution of 1971   18

Conclusion   23

Key Concepts   23

Suggested Resources   24

Notes   24

3. From Blue to Red and Back Again: Voting and Political Participation in Virginia **25**

Gaining the Right to Vote 26

Redistricting 30

Primaries and Elections 32

Voting in Virginia 33

Impact on National Politics 34

Direct Democracy 36

Other Forms of Political Participation 37

Conclusion 38

Key Concepts 39

Suggested Resources 39

Notes 39

4. Organized Interests: Political Parties and Group Politics in the State Capital **42**

The Purpose of Parties 42

Party in the Electorate 43

Party as Organization 44

Party in Government 44

Virginia's Political Parties 45

Interest Groups 49

Conclusion 56

Key Concepts 57

Suggested Resources 57

Notes 57

5. The Virginia General Assembly: Lawmaking in the Nation's First Legislature **60**

Structure of the General Assembly 61

Lawmaking Power 66

Constituent Services 68

Judicial and Executive Oversight 68

Impeachment Power 69

Apportionment of State Legislators 69

Legislative Leadership and Party Control   70

A Profile of Virginia's Legislators   71

Conclusion   73

Key Concepts   74

Suggested Resources   74

Notes   74

6. **Steering the Ship of the State: Executive Power in Virginia**   **77**

Virginia's One-Term Governor   78

Powers of the Office   80

The Governor as Party Head   82

    The Governor as Chief Budgeting Officer   83

    The Governor as Chief Appointer and Administrator 83

    The Governor as Spokesperson for the State   84

Life after Living in the Governor's Mansion   84

The Constitutional Executive Officers   84

The Office of Attorney General   87

Conclusion   89

Key Concepts   89

Suggested Resources   89

Notes   89

7. **Law and Order in Virginia: The State Court System**   **90**

Virginia's Court Structure   90

    Magistrates   91

    District Courts   92

    Circuit Courts   93

    Court of Appeals   94

    Virginia Supreme Court   95

    The Administration of Justice   96

The National Court System   96

Judicial Policymaking   97

State Judicial Selection   98

    Who Are Our Judges?   99

    Tenure and Compensation   100

Conclusion   102

Key Concepts   102

Suggested Resources   102

Notes   102

8. **Administering Government: Bureaucratic Power and Politics in Virginia**   **105**

Sources of Bureaucratic and Administrative Power in Virginia   106

The Virginia Merit System   110

Measuring Effectiveness and Improving Efficiency   113

Conclusion   117

Key Concepts   117

Suggested Resources   117

Notes   118

9. **Paying the Bill: Budgeting and Finance in Virginia**   **119**

The Biennial Budget   119

The Virginia Budget Process   120

Timeline   121

Where the Money Comes From   122

Where the Money Goes   126

Virginia's Fiscal Health and Solvency   127

How Is Virginia Doing?   128

Conclusion   130

Key Concepts   130

Suggested Resources   131

Notes   131

10. **Municipalities and Metropolitanism: Local and Regional Governance in Virginia**   **132**

Municipal Governments   133

Incorporation and the Growth of Local Governments in Virginia   136

County Governments   137

Local Government Revenue   140

Annexation and Governmental Consolidation in Virginia   143

Regionalism in Virginia   146

Conclusion   151

Key Concepts   152

Suggested Resources   152

Notes   152

11. Inside the Laboratory: Public Policymaking in Virginia   154

The Policy Process   155

K–12 Education Policy   157
  Funding for K–12 Education   159
  Academic Achievement in Virginia   159
  School Choice   163

Health and Human Services   165
  Poverty in Virginia   165
  Major Social Welfare Programs   166
  Accessing Health Care in the Commonwealth   169
  Major Health Policies   171

Energy and Environmental Policy   173
  How Virginia Uses Energy   174
  Virginia's Energy Policy   174
  How Does Virginia Stack Up?   177

Emergency Management and Homeland Security   180
  Federal Government Location and Impact on Homeland Security   182

Economic Development Policy   184
  Agencies Aiding Virginia Businesses and Workforce Development   186

Conclusion   187

Key Concepts   188

Suggested Resources   189

Notes   190

Index   193

List of Tables, Figures, and Boxes

Tables

Table 2.1   Articles of the Virginia Constitution   18

Table 4.1   Party Control of Virginia Government   48

Table 6.1   Term Limits by State   79

Table 6.2   Executive Orders   82

Table 8.1   Bureaucratic Agency Productivity in
Virginia from 2009–2012   114

Table 9.1   Annual versus Biennial
Budgets in the States   120

Table 9.2   Virginia Revenue Sources   124

Table 9.3   How Is Virginia Doing?   128

Table 9.4   Virginia Performs Program   130

Table 11.1   All Thirty-one High-Risk Areas for
Urban Areas Security Initiative (UASI)   183

Figures

Figure 1.1   Geographic Regions of Virginia   3

Figure 1.2   Virginia's People   6

Figure 1.3   Virginians by Age Cohort, 2010   7

Figure 1.4   Annual Household
Income in Virginia, 2010   8

Figure 3.1   Timeline: Black Civil Rights in Virginia   27

Figure 3.2   Gerrymandering in Virginia's
Congressional Districts   32

Figure 3.3   Voting Rates in Virginia and
the United States   35

Figure 4.1   The Growth of Lobbyists in Virginia   53

Figure 4.2	Comparison of Lobbyists by State, 2007–2011	54
Figure 4.3	Spending by Major Interest Group	55
Figure 5.1	How a Bill Becomes a Law in Virginia	67
Figure 5.2	How Educated Are Virginia's Lawmakers?	71
Figure 5.3	How Diverse Are Virginia's Lawmakers? Race, Ethnicity, and Gender in the General Assembly, 2013	72
Figure 6.1	Structure of the Executive	85
Figure 7.1	Virginia's Court Structure	91
Figure 8.1	Listing of Virginia's Executive Branch Agencies	107
Figure 8.2	The Organizational Structure of Virginia's Bureaucracy	108
Figure 8.3	Iron Triangle: Virginia General Assembly, Virginia Department of Motor Vehicles, and Mothers Against Drunk Driving (MADD)	110
Figure 8.4	Steps to Virginia's Hiring Process	111
Figure 9.1	Virginia's Budget Development Process	121
Figure 9.2	General Fund Money Collected in 2011	123
Figure 9.3	Virginia's Fiscal Year 2011 Revenues	123
Figure 9.4	Non-General Fund Revenues, 2012–2014	125
Figure 9.5	Virginia's Fiscal Year Expenditures, 2011	126
Figure 9.6	Virginia Performs Scorecard at a Glance	129
Figure 10.1	Map of Virginia Counties and Independent Cities	133
Figure 10.2	Growth in the Number of Virginia Governments	138
Figure 10.3	Growth in the Number of Governments in the United States	139
Figure 10.4	Local Government Revenue by Category and Jurisdictional Class for Counties and Cities in Virginia	140
Figure 10.5	Local Government Revenue for All Jurisdictions in Virginia	141
Figure 10.6	Operating Expenditures by Category for All Counties and Cities in Virginia	143
Figure 10.7	Metropolitan Planning Organizations in Virginia	148
Figure 10.8	Virginia's Metropolitan Statistical Areas Established in 1993	149
Figure 10.9	Virginia's Metro and Micropolitan Statistical Areas as of 2003	150
Figure 11.1	The Policy Process	156
Figure 11.2	Educational Attainment in Virginia	158
Figure 11.3	Gap in Percentage of Virginia Students Passing Reading/Language Arts Assessment	161

Figure 11.4	Gap in Percentage of Virginia Students Passing Mathematics Assessment	162
Figure 11.5	Poverty Rates by State	166
Figure 11.6	Virginia Poverty Rates by Selected Characteristics, 2010	167
Figure 11.7	Sources of Health Insurance Coverage in Virginia, 2010–2011	170
Figure 11.8	Virginians without Health Insurance, 2010	171

Boxes

Box 2.1	Virginia's Constitution as a Model	14
Box 2.2	Gay Marriage in Virginia and Other States	19
Box 3.1	Should Convicted Felons Have the Right to Vote?	30
Box 4.1	The Influence of Harry Byrd Sr. and the Byrd Organization	46
Box 4.2	Differences in Virginia Political Party Values	50
Box 4.3	Presidential Party Vote by Selected Voter Characteristics, 2012 Virginian Exit Polls	51
Box 5.1	The Virginia State Capitol	61
Box 5.2	Quick Facts about the 2012 Virginia General Assembly	63
Box 5.3	How Do They Do All That?	65
Box 5.4	Standing Committees in the General Assembly	66
Box 5.5	Breaking Barriers in the General Assembly: Senator Yvonne B. Miller	73
Box 6.1	The Country's Oldest Governor's Mansion	80
Box 6.2	Governor McDonnell's Executive Order No. 38	82
Box 6.3	Governor L. Douglas Wilder	86
Box 6.4	Duties and Powers of the Attorney General	88
Box 7.1	Drug Courts: Changing the Scope of Criminal Justice	100
Box 8.1	How Is It Done in New York?	112
Box 8.2	Virginia's Department of Motor Vehicles	116
Box 8.3	The Virginia Department of Health Measures Success	117
Box 9.1	Higher Education Revenues	122
Box 9.2	The Fifty-first State—NOVA vs. "Real Virginia"	125
Box 9.3	What Are States Doing with Their Surplus Money?	127
Box 10.1	Where Did All the Cities Go?	134
Box 10.2	Typical Powers Associated with Weak Mayor vs. Strong Mayor Town/City Councils	135

Box 10.3	Dillon's Rule vs. Home Rule States	136
Box 10.4	Arlington, Virginia	137
Box 10.5	The Last Town to Incorporate in Virginia	138
Box 10.6	Elaboration of Governmental Revenue Categories	142
Box 10.7	Elaboration of Governmental Expenditure Categories	144
Box 10.8	Fast Facts on Virginia's Local Governments	145
Box 10.9	What Are PDCs Required to Do?	148
Box 11.1	The Complexity of Assessing Poverty	168
Box 11.2	Did You Know That . . .	175
Box 11.3	Declaration of a State of Emergency	181
Box 11.4	Virginia Chief Jobs Creation Officer: Lieutenant Governor Bill Bolling	185
Box 11.5	Economic Development at the Local Level	186
Box 11.6	Did You Know That . . .	187

Preface

T idea for this book grew out of our own experiences in teaching undergraduate and graduate-level students at James Madison University (JMU).We were both frustrated with the lack of readily available and concise information on Virginia state government and policy. While there existed a number of texts dedicated to Virginia's rich political history and in-depth analyses of particular aspects of Virginia government, missing was a comprehensive overview of institutions and contemporary policy issues. This book is designed to fill that gap within our own classes as well as to meet the needs of a variety of other audiences. Beginning in 2011, Virginia now requires state and local government-specific competencies for teacher licensure (*SB 715: Civics Education: Teachers Training to Include Local Government and Civics Specific to State*). This book can easily be adopted for new and existing courses designed to satisfy the new specifications for teacher training. The text will also benefit Virginia citizens and government officials at the state and local levels who are interested in learning more about political institutions and policymaking in their state.

Virginia Government: Institutions and Policy is designed to serve as a companion text to introductory state and local government books, as well as to stand alone as a brief introduction to the topic. While the text provides an in-depth exploration of state-level institutions and actors in Virginia, it is grounded in the comparative method; throughout the text, we provide useful comparisons with governing institutions, political processes, and public polices in other states and localities. The book provides a mix of necessary background and historical analysis with current events and policy issues to make the information relevant and engaging to today's students and those interested in learning more about Virginia.

This book would not have been possible without the help of research assistants from JMU's undergraduate program in public policy and administration and master's program in public administration. We thank them for their hard work and dedication to this endeavor. We would also like to thank our friends and family who supported us throughout this process, particularly Jonas and Ben. Lastly, we would like to thank our reviewers Jerry Buschee, Mount Olive College; Mary Carver, Longwood University; and Roy Kirby, Roanoke College whose helpful comments and criticisms provided valuable feedback to strengthen this book.

About the Authors

Dr. **Liliokanaio Peaslee** is an assistant professor of Public Policy and Administration in the Department of Political Science at James Madison University. She has an undergraduate degree in political science, a master's degree in social policy, and a joint PhD in politics and social policy. Dr. Peaslee has published in the area of community policing, youth development, mentoring, rural education and employment policy, and university-community partnerships.

Dr. **Nicholas J. Swartz** is an assistant professor of Public Policy and Administration in the Department of Political Science at James Madison University. He is also the director of the Master in Public Administration program. He has an undergraduate degree in political science, a master's degree in public administration, and a doctorate degree in public policy. Dr. Swartz has published in the area of emergency management, city-county governmental consolidation, local government and nonprofit management succession planning, and university-community partnerships.

OUTLINE

One State, Many Virginias

An Unparalleled Political
History

A Snapshot of Virginia
Citizens

The Economy

Plan of the Book

CHAPTER 1

An Introduction to Government and Policymaking in the Commonwealth

> I know no safe depositary of the ultimate powers of the society but the people themselves; and if we think them not enlightened enough to exercise their control with a wholesome discretion, the remedy is not to take it from them, but to inform their discretion by education.
>
> —*Thomas Jefferson, 1820*

A s an introduction to government and policymaking in Virginia, in this book we attempt to answer the charge by Thomas Jefferson—perhaps one of Virginian's best known countrymen—to ensure a well-educated citizenry. Understanding our political structures and how state-level policy is made and being aware of resulting laws, regulations, and other political decisions are important for all citizens. There are numerous opportunities to participate in government at the state level and even more in local communities. Local governments, in particular, have been called "schools of democracy" where we can learn the art of citizenship. Unfortunately, we are often not as informed about what goes on close to home as we are with national issues, which tend to dominate media coverage. Institutions, like public policy, do not arise spontaneously, nor are they unable to be changed. Both the creation and modification of political

1

institutions are the result of political decisions (though many were made long ago) about how to best govern the polity. Whether you want to work in state or local government, are charged with teaching the next generation of Virginian citizens, or want to be able to better understand and contribute to political discourse, it is important to be informed about government and policymaking in the state.

While the focus of this book is on the state of Virginia, throughout the text we provide comparisons with the political institutions and policy choices made by other states. The Commonwealth shares many similarities with other American states; however, in many respects, Virginia is unique, with policies and governing procedures that differ significantly from those across the country. Examining these similarities and differences can help us better understand why Virginians have made the political choices that govern our lives. Using a comparative method also provides us with examples of other institutional arrangements and alternative policy solutions to public problems. Not only can state policymakers learn a great deal from their neighbors but national decision makers also look to the states for ideas about public policy. Solutions to many different policy problems—from welfare to education to job creation—are often first tried by state legislatures which act as "laboratories" for national public policy experiments.[1]

Virginia has a unique political history that has shaped the development of state and local political institutions and citizens' attitudes about government. The state is also marked by significant diversity—in geography and topography, demographics, the economy, and the politics of its citizens. Each of these characteristics frames the distinct choices about government and policy made by state-level political actors and provides an important context for governing the Commonwealth. These factors are each briefly explored below.

One State, Many Virginias

Situated in the Mid-Atlantic, halfway between New York and Florida, Virginia is often called the "gateway to the South." To its north, Virginia shares its borders with Maryland and with Washington, D.C., the nation's capital. To the south are North Carolina and Tennessee and to the west, Kentucky and West Virginia. The Atlantic Ocean runs along the Eastern Shore. This results in wide variability in topographical regions, which has given life to a variety of communities, traditions, and local economies: from coal mining towns in the heart of Appalachia to the mountainous west; from coastal and fishing villages on the Eastern Shore to the bustling D.C. suburbs (Figure 1.1). Virginia has traditions as distinct as car racing and Civil War heritage in the South and the living history of Colonial Williamsburg.[2] Each provides richness to Virginia's unique history and people. On the other hand, this diversity in land, resources, problems, and preferences can add complexity to governance.

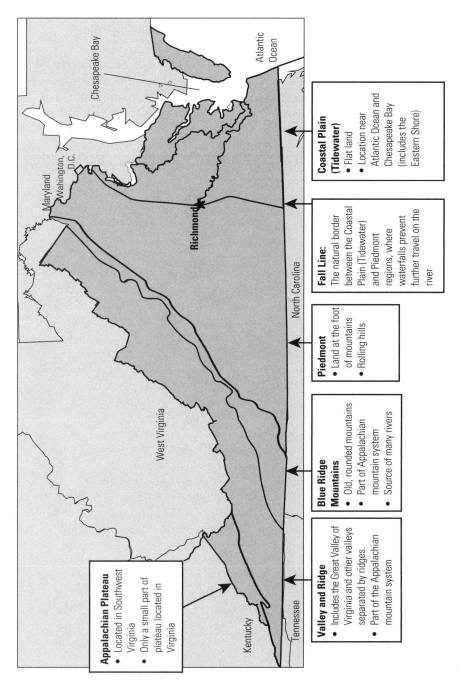

Coastal Plain (Tidewater):
• Flat land
• Location near Atlantic Ocean and Chesapeake Bay (includes the Eastern Shore)

Fall Line: The natural border between the Coastal Plain (Tidewater) and Piedmont regions, where waterfalls prevent further travel on the river

Piedmont
• Land at the foot of mountains
• Rolling hills

Blue Ridge Mountains
• Old, rounded mountains
• Part of Appalachian mountain system
• Source of many rivers

Valley and Ridge
• Includes the Great Valley of Virginia and other valleys separated by ridges.
• Part of the Appalachian mountain system

Appalachian Plateau
• Located in Southwest Virginia
• Only a small part of plateau located in Virginia

Chesapeake Bay

Atlantic Ocean

Maryland

Wahington, D.C.

Richmond

North Carolina

West Virginia

Kentucky

Tennessee

FIGURE 1.1

Geographic Regions of Virginia

Source: Virginia Department of Education.

An Unparalleled Political History

Of all the United States, Virginia has the deepest historical roots. The state is home to the first English colony; Jamestown was chartered in 1607—a decade before the Pilgrims steered the *Mayflower* onto Plymouth Rock. Unlike most of the other early colonies, Virginia was founded by the London Company and was predominantly a business investment by settlers seeking economic opportunities rather than a safe haven for Englishmen seeking religious freedom. This provides clear contrast to the Pilgrims in Massachusetts or Catholics in Maryland. However, the colony was not unreligious; the Anglican church was the official religion from 1607 to the American Revolution, with the King of England serving as head of both church and state.

The *state* of Virginia is technically a "**commonwealth**," though the two terms are used interchangeably. This designation is shared by just three other states: Massachusetts, Kentucky, and Pennsylvania. Meaning "common wealth" (or common good), a commonwealth is a state in which ultimate power is vested in the people and government is created to promote the welfare of its citizens. Reflecting the view of Virginia's founders that government is a contract between people who are created equally free and independent, the state was designated the Commonwealth when its first constitution was adopted on June 29, 1776.[3] Virginia is also sometimes referred to as the "Old Dominion State." Frank Atkinson explains that "Virginia's nickname . . . derives from colonial times. In the mid-17th century, King Charles II of England, who was especially fond of the colony, elevated Virginia to the 'dominion' status enjoyed by England, Scotland, Ireland, and France. The 'old' adjective was added by Virginians to reflect their status as the first of the King's settlements in the New World."[4]

Throughout its history, Virginia has also figured prominently in national politics. Eight of our country's presidents—George Washington, Thomas Jefferson, James Madison, James Monroe, William Henry Harrison, John Tyler, Zachary Taylor, and Woodrow Wilson—were all born here, more of them than in any other state. Many of these great men—along with countless other Virginia men and women—played a pivotal role in the American Revolution and in the nation's founding. During the Civil War—a darker time in American history—the Confederate Congress used the state capitol in Richmond as its home. Virginia's central place in the country's founding and its strategic location between the North and South, made the Commonwealth's decision to break with the Union especially significant for the cause of Southern succession.

Virginia's history and culture have played an important role in its **political culture**, which can be defined as the prevailing attitudes and beliefs about the proper size and scope of government. Political culture in Virginia has been identified as *traditionalist*, rather than moralist or individualist.[5] Because Virginia is so politically diverse, it can be hard to imagine a uniform political culture throughout the state. The term, however, refers not to citizens' political **ideologies** (such as liberal or conservative) but to the underlying political norms that shape the types of political structures and policies created by the Commonwealth. In traditionalist political cultures, politics is dominated by elites with limited political involvement by ordinary citizens. Government's primary role is to maintain social order, resulting in low spending on social services.[6] The Old Dominion has undergone many changes over the last four hundred years, and more recent demographic changes are slowly transforming state politics. However, as will be seen in the chapters that follow, compared with many other states Virginia's government still largely reflects traditional, conservative political values.

A Snapshot of Virginia Citizens

With just over eight million people, Virginia is the twelfth largest state in the United States. Although it has not experienced population growth as extreme as in the South and West, the state grew by 13 percent between 2000 and 2010 (nearly one million people in just ten years).[7] Most of this growth occurred in Virginia's metropolitan areas, especially northern Virginia and Hampton Roads. However, the population in Southside and the southwestern parts of the state declined slightly during the same period. While some of the overall population growth can be attributed to an increase in birthrates and life expectancy, importantly, it is also the result of in-migration. Nearly half of Virginia residents were born outside the Commonwealth. According to the 2010 Census, 38 percent of residents were born in another state and 11.4 percent were foreign born.[8]

The Commonwealth is also racially diverse. For the years 2007–2009, Virginia ranked fourteenth in the nation for the highest non-white population and sixteenth for the largest percentage of foreign born residents. Racial and ethnic diversity is greatest in northern Virginia, where the nation's capital draws citizens from across the country and around the world. The state has a significant black community: in 2010, 20 percent of Virginians were African Americans, compared with just 12.6 percent nationally. Projections by the state government's Council on Virginia's Future show that racial and ethnic diversity in Virginia will increase in coming years due to rising immigration, births to immigrant parents, and births to racially mixed couples. This growth is expected to be greatest among Asians and Hispanics (see Figure 1.2, Virginia's People).[9]

The demographic composition of the state will also shift as the baby boom generation grows older and the average age of citizens increases. In two decades, almost 20 percent of Virginians (one in five) will be 65 years or older. Since women live longer than men, seniors will be overwhelmingly female (see Figure 1.3 for a current age breakdown).[10] This changing age structure is likely to present new challenges for the Commonwealth in the years ahead. On the other hand, the state's strong public school system and an economy that attracts skilled workers have produced a well-educated citizenry. Thirty-four percent of Virginians have a bachelor's degree or higher, and an additional 27 percent have an associate's degree or attended some college. Nationally, just 28 percent of Americans have completed a four-year degree.

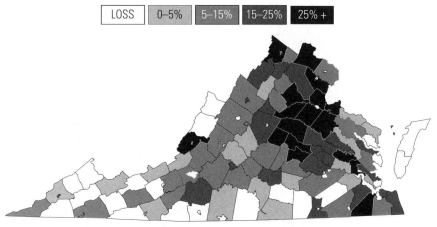

POPULATION CHANGE BY COUNTY: 2000–2010

| LOSS | 0–5% | 5–15% | 15–25% | 25% + |

STATE POPULATION BY RACE

PERCENT OF POPULATION	CHANGE 2000–2010
White alone — 68.6%	7.2% ⬆
Black or African American alone — 19.4%	11.6% ⬆
American Indian and Alaska Native alone — 0.4%	38.0% ⬆
Asian alone — 5.5%	68.5% ⬆
Native Hawaiian and Other Pacific Islander alone — 0.1%	51.5% ⬆
Some Other Race alone — 3.2%	83.1% ⬆
Two or More Races — 2.9%	63.1% ⬆

STATE POPULATION BY HISPANIC OR LATINO ORIGIN

PERCENT OF POPULATION	CHANGE 2000–2010
Hispanic or Latino — 7.9%	91.7% ⬆
Not Hispanic or Latino — 92.1%	9.2% ⬆

FIGURE 1.2

Virginia's People

Source: U.S. 2010 Census.

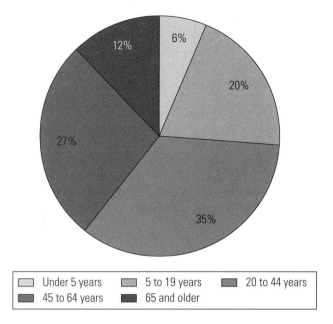

FIGURE 1.3

Virginians by Age Cohort, 2010

Source: U.S. 2010 Census.

The Economy

Economic contexts shape politics and policymaking in each state. A state's economic health impacts citizen needs, from social service provision to job creation initiatives. The size of the state budget also helps determine how much or how little policymakers are able to spend to solve social problems—though a robust economy on its own does not predict high levels of social spending.

Like other states around the country, Virginia was hit hard by the recent economic recession. Unemployment rose from a low of 2.3 percent in January 2001 to a high of 7.2 percent nine years later.[11] Although recently the number of Virginians out of work has been much higher than in the past, citizens still fare relatively well compared with workers in the rest of the country. In December 2012, just ten states had lower unemployment rates; unemployment around the country ranged from a low of 3.2 percent in North Dakota to a high of 10.2 percent in Nevada and Rhode Island (the national average was 7.8 percent).[12] Much of Virginia's economic success has been attributed to its responsible fiscal policies and strong government management. The Government Performance Project (a collaboration between the Pew Center on the States and *Governing* magazine) recently gave the state an A minus and rated Virginia as one of the best-governed states in the nation.[13] Many also point to Virginia's economic diversity as a major factor in the state's ability to weather economic downturns (see Chapter 11 for more on economic development in the state).

With the close proximity to Washington, D.C., a large number of Virginians work for the federal government or other complimentary sectors in the Capitol. Many workers are also employed by the U.S. military and private defense contractors in the Norfolk metropolitan area. These employers tend to be more insulated from economic downturns than those in the rest of the state. Northern Virginia, in particular, consistently has a lower unemployment rate and a much higher than average median household income (see Figure 1.4, Annual Household Income in Virginia). Southern Virginia, on the other hand, has felt significant strain from job loss. Not surprisingly, poverty rates are also higher in the south and lowest in the north. This is a result not only of employment rates but also of drastically different median wages across the state. Such economic diversity provides challenges for Virginia's representatives as they attempt to create policies to ensure the well-being of citizens throughout the Commonwealth.

Plan of the Book

This book is designed to accompany other state and local government textbooks or to read on its own as a short introduction to government and public policies in Virginia. We are particularly fond of Smith, Greenblatt, and Vaughn's *Governing States and Localities* and have designed this book to follow along with their chapters,

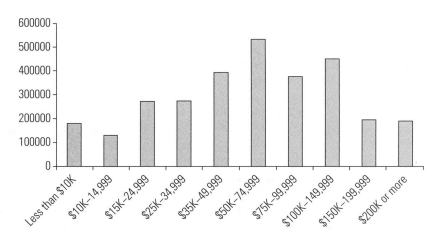

FIGURE 1.4

Annual Household Income in Virginia, 2010

Source: U.S. 2010 Census.

however, there are many others that can help you put state and local politics in a larger perspective. Throughout the book we will direct you to additional resources where you can learn about topics in more detail.

We begin the book with an overview of the Virginia Constitution, which provides a basic framework for the state's political institutions. From there we discuss voting and political participation by Virginia citizens, followed by a chapter on state-level political parties and interest groups. The next four chapters focus on the formal institutions of Virginia state government: the General Assembly, the governor's office, the judiciary, and the state bureaucracy. These are followed by a chapter on Virginia's budget and finances, and one on local and regional governance. Finally, we look at the policymaking process and discuss Virginia's approach to select policy issues: education, health and human services, emergency management and homeland security, energy and environmental policy, and economic development. Together, these chapters should give you a good sense of government and policymaking in Virginia. We hope you enjoy learning more about the Commonwealth!

Key Concepts

Commonwealth   Political culture
Ideologies

Suggested Resources

- http://www.virginia.gov: The **official website of the Commonwealth** provides a portal to visiting, living, and working in Virginia. Look for calendars of events and things to do in the Commonwealth.
- Kevin Smith and Alan Greenblatt, ***Governing States and Localities***, *fourth edition* (Washington, DC: CQ Press, 2014) provides a more extensive comparison of state government across the country.

Notes

1. Mark Carl Rom, "Taking the Brandeis Metaphor Seriously: Policy Experimentation Within a Federal System," in *Promoting the General Welfare: New Perspectives on Government Performance,* ed. Eric Patashnik and Alan Gerber (Washington, DC: Brookings Institution, 2006), 256–281.

2. For more on each of these different regions, see Virginia Tourism Corporation, "Virginia Map," http://www.virginia.org/VirginiaMap/.

3. Susan Clarke Schaar, "A Capitol Script: A Student Guide to Virginia's Legislative Process," (Richmond, VA: Senate Clerk's Office, October 2009), http://hodcap.state.va.us/publications/CapitolScript.pdf.

4. Frank B. Atkinson, "Virginia in the Vanguard," in *Governing Virginia*, ed. Anne Marie Morgan and A. R. "Pete" Giesen, Jr. (Boston, MA: Pearson, 2012), 256, n6.

5. Daniel Elazar, *American Federalism: A View From the States* (Cromwell, CT: Cromwell, 1972). See also Virginia Gray, "The Socioeconomic and Political Context of States," in *Politics in the American States,* ed. Virginia Gray, Russell L. Hanson, and Thad Kousser (Washington, DC: CQ Press, 2013).

6. In contrast to a traditionalist political culture, politics in moralist states attempts to advance the common good. As such, state government is much more active in policymaking. Conversely, in individualist political cultures, politics is seen as a venue for individual gain rather than for public problem solving.

7. U.S. Census Bureau. *Resident Population Data, 2010 Population Figures,* accessed September 17, 2011, http://www.census.gov/2010census/data/apportionment-pop-text.php

8. U.S. Census. *2010 American Community Survey* (Washington, DC: U.S. Government Printing Office). "Selected Social Characteristics in the United States," http://factfinder2.census .gov/faces/nav/jsf/pages/searchresults.xhtml?refresh=t.

9. Council on Virginia's Future, "A Profile of Virginia, 2012," Virginia Performs (2013), http://vaperforms.virginia.gov/extras/profileSummary.php.

10. Ibid.

11. U.S. Department of Labor, Bureau of Labor Statistics, *Local Area Unemployment Statistics,* http://data.bls.gov/timeseries/LASST51000003?data_tool=XGtable.

12. U.S. Department of Labor, Bureau of Labor Statistics. *Unemployment Rates for States* (Washington, DC: BLS, 2013), http://www.bls.gov/web/laus/laumstrk.htm. Note: This data is seasonally adjusted.

13. Katherine Barrett and Richard Greene, "Measuring Performance: The State Management Report Card for 2008," *Governing, March 2008.*

OUTLINE

Forms of Government

How and Why State
Constitutions Vary

The Evolution of Virginia's
Constitutions

The 1776 Constitution

The 1830 Constitution

The 1851 Constitution

1864: The War
Constitution

The 1870 Constitution

The 1902 Constitution

The Current System:
The Constitution of 1971

Conclusion

CHAPTER 2

A Framework for Governing

Exploring the Virginia State Constitution

Virginia, like every other state, has a constitution. Virginia's first constitution was enacted the same time as the U.S. Declaration of Independence in 1776. In fact, it was the first state to adopt its own constitution. Virginia's constitution serves as a framework for what the state and its officials can and cannot do to Virginia's citizens, institutions, and businesses. It sets forth the structure and organization of Virginia's government, limits the powers of government, and protects the rights of Virginia citizens. Virginia's constitution, like most state constitutions, is more detailed, specific, and longer than the U.S. constitution. This chapter provides a historical overview of the foundation of Virginia's first constitution and each subsequent constitution (1776, 1854, 1864, 1870, 1902, and 1971). The chapter further provides a more detailed look into Virginia's current constitution—the 1971 constitution. Subsequent chapters provide even more information on the state's distribution of powers as well as the rights and protections of Virginia's citizens.

Forms of Government

Federalism is a political system in which power is divided and shared between the national or central government and the states or regional units of government in order to limit the power one level of government has over the other. This is one of the major principles upon which the U.S. government is based. In contrast to a system of federalism, a **unitary system** concentrates most of its power in a single, central government. These systems typically have regional or local governments, but the central branch of government has the ultimate say and controls the actions of the subsidiary government. In a unitary system, local governments are by no means sovereign and are at the mercy of the central government, not the voters or local-level officials. There are more than 150 countries using the unitary system of government—countries such as France, Chile, Norway, and Turkey. In addition to federalist and unitary systems is a **confederacy**, a system defined as a voluntary association between independent, **sovereign** governments where power is concentrated with the smaller, regional governments. The United States operated under a confederate system twice. The Articles of Confederation was the United States' initial constitution, organizing the United States into a union of sovereign, independent states made up of the former British colonies. The second U.S. confederacy was during the Civil War when the Southern states seceded from the Union. This ended in 1865 at the end of the Civil War.

How and Why State Constitutions Vary

The principle of federalism outlined in the U.S. Constitution gives states a significant amount of power over state affairs. Each state in the United States has its own, unique **constitution**. Although many state constitutions are alike in many respects, they are drastically different in others. Some are long and require strong state intervention in community affairs and require full-time legislators, while others focus on the rights and roles of individuals and limited control over internal affairs. For example, Vermont has the second shortest state constitution with 10,286 words—the shortest constitution is New Hampshire's with 9,200 words. The primary role of the Vermont Constitution is to merely establish a framework for which its state government should operate. California, on the other hand, has a complex constitution that relies heavily on direct democracy and the input of its citizens. The California Constitution has approximately 59,500 words. The longest state constitution is Alabama's at 340,136 words. State constitutions vary beyond length, however; many states have different requirements for its legislatures and executives. They also differ when it comes to distribution of power among the various branches of state government. In the past, most states relied primarily on their legislatures for policymaking and governing, but in recent years, many states have shifted more and more power to their executives.

State constitutions vary greatly as a result of a number of factors. First, historical circumstances set the original blueprints that caused states to be formed differently. Second, political culture can mold the way a state models its constitution. For example, the Midwestern region with more of a moralistic political culture that views government as a way to help achieve a collective good[1] has constitutions allowing them to meet on a more regular basis, creating what are essentially full-time legislatures. This is a stark contrast to states such as Texas with more of a traditionalist political culture where politics and government are viewed as being dominated by the elite. These state constitutions establish a system whereby their legislatures seldom meet and rely primarily on limited government control of state issues, created because of their perception of activist governments after the Reconstruction that followed the Civil War. Geography also has an influence on state constitutions, most strongly in the Northeast. New England's short, framework-oriented constitutions mimic the small size of the states within. States with higher populations tend to have longer constitutions—for example, the New York Constitution has 51,700 words, the Florida Constitution has 51,465 words, and the Maryland Constitution has 46,600 words.

The Evolution of Virginia's Constitutions

The first settlers of the new world in Virginia did not own land but instead were merely occupants under King James I, who issued a charter concentrating ownership of property and its governance to the Virginia Company of London. Slowly, settlers began to receive political rights, and in 1618, the Virginia Company introduced English common law to the settlements—the same governing law that existed in England at that time. The governor was also instructed to create a representative assembly of settlers with authority to make laws, though these early laws were ultimately subject to the Virginia Company's approval. Modeled on English Parliament, this new legislative body, called the House of Burgesses, was the first legislative body in the new world. All males aged seventeen and older were given the right to vote, and what would become known as the General Assembly was completed when the governor created the Virginia Council, a six-member body appointed by the Virginia Company to advise the governor.

The concept of **representative democracy**, the principle that our elected officials represent a group of people and their interests, began to develop over time. In fact, it was never the intention, at least initially, to establish a representative democracy in the new colonies. Although the House of Burgesses had limited power, it established the foundation for future growth of the legislature. Outside of Iceland, no other colony and nation had a representative democracy before the nineteenth century. After 1623, when Virginia became a royal colony and the Virginia Company lost its charter, the House of Burgesses lost most of its power. It continued to represent Virginia citizens, but as time progressed, the British crown became more powerful. The House of Burgesses was never a powerful or significant legislative body, but at the very least, it embedded the idea of a representative democracy in Virginia. As a colony, every county in Virginia had two representatives, and even the cities of Jamestown, Williamsburg, and Norfolk were awarded a representative, along with the College of William and Mary.

The 1776 Constitution

The writing and adoption of the Virginia Constitution was during the same time period as the writing and adoption of the U.S. Declaration of Independence. Virginia was the first state to outline the rights and responsibilities of its citizens

BOX 2.1   **Virginia's Constitution as a Model**

The first Virginia Constitution was drafted during the same period as the Declaration of Independence that was being adopted by the thirteen colonies collectively. Virginia's constitution was the first of the thirteen state constitutions to be adopted, and the document was widely influential in both the United States and abroad. In fact, some of the key framers of the Virginia Constitution would go on to strongly influence the U.S. Constitution. Thomas Jefferson was also Virginia's representative at the Second Continental Congress, and his drafts of the Virginia Constitution strongly influenced his work on the U.S. Declaration of Independence. James Madison, another framer, used his work on the Virginia Constitution to help develop ideas and skills that he would later use as one of the primary architects of the U.S. Constitution.

and the proper role of government by adopting its first state constitution. The construction of the 1776 Virginia Constitution was handled by a large committee of appointed delegates that gathered at the first Virginia Constitutional Convention. They were instructed to prepare a declaration of rights and to plan a government that would maintain peace and order in the new colony and secure the equal liberty of the people. The 1776 constitution declared the separation of Virginia from the British Empire, accusing King George III of establishing an unsupportable tyranny. In its framework, the 1776 constitution established a bicameral (two-house) structure. It was accompanied by the **Declaration of Rights**, written primarily by George Mason. The Declaration of Rights guaranteed basic human rights, freedoms, and the essential purpose of government. Mason's influence on the Virginia Declaration of Rights also lent strongly to the U.S. Bill of Rights, as well as the foundation for a number of other state constitutions.

The 1776 constitution established the Virginia **General Assembly** to oversee legislative matters. The bicameral system housed a legislature divided into two separate houses—the House of Delegates and a Senate. The **House of Delegates** comprised two representatives from every state county plus one representative from the cities of Williamsburg and Norfolk who were elected on an annual basis. The **Senate** comprised twenty-four members who were elected on staggered terms so that six senators were up for election each year. Seeking to create balance, the Virginia Constitution also established an executive and judicial branch in addition to the legislative branch, proclaiming that the legislative, executive, and judicial branches should be separate and distinct and that neither could exercise the powers that were assigned to the others. While the framers sought to establish a balance of powers, the legislature ultimately controlled a majority of the power. Individuals at the time were extremely wary of executive power because of King George III and therefore wanting to limit the power of the executive, while granting certain powers more directly in the hands of the people. The governor's office was only a one-year term, and he was nominated by the General Assembly. The judges were also selected by the General Assembly. While the branches were separate on paper, the General Assembly had a lot of influence over the individuals in positions of power. The 1776 constitution established that the right to vote would only be granted to property owners and men of wealth. This effectively concentrated the power in Virginia in the southeastern parts of the state where a majority of landowners and aristocrats lived. The debate over voting rights established in the 1776 constitution would continue to dominate the political agenda in Virginia for well more than the next one hundred years.

The 1830 Constitution

Concerns over the first constitution began to emerge as the nineteenth century got under way. In fact, even prior to that, Thomas Jefferson aired some of his own concerns. In a book he released in 1775, Jefferson stated, "This constitution was formed when we were new and inexperienced in the science of government. It was the first too which was formed in the whole United States. No wonder then that time and trial have discovered very capital defects in it."[2] Jefferson again came out for reformation in 1816 when he noted that two thirds of those living at the time of the 1776 constitution were no longer alive and that the one third remaining had no right to impose their rule on the remainder of society. Jefferson believed that every constitution should be revised periodically so that each generation could leave its footprint on how they interpreted the law. Ultimately, the need for a convention and reformation of the constitution emerged from a growing level of discontent from western Virginians who did not approve of their level of representation in the legislature. By the 1820s, it was estimated that one third of Virginia's white males lacked the right to vote. Added pressure for reform began to emerge as the population in the western part of the state began to increase and was projected to surpass the eastern part of the state by 1830—remember that the individuals from the eastern part of Virginia dominated the legislature at the time. Many feared that one of two things would have to occur: (1) the creation of a new state constitution or (2) the separation of the eastern and western parts of Virginia into two separate states. The state remained intact, however, and plans were put in motion to create a new state constitution.

As it turned out, Jefferson would never see a new Virginia Constitution, but in 1830, four years after his death, delegates convened in Richmond to create a new constitution. Of those in attendance were two former presidents (James Madison and James Monroe) and a future president (John Tyler). Additionally, the chief justice of the U.S. Supreme Court (John Marshal), a number of former Virginia governors, future and past state legislators, and eleven future U.S. senators were present for deliberations. Still, the 1830 constitution was considered by many to be a failure overall. A frequent reapportionment scheme was adopted to appease the westerners. While it gave more representation to the westward region of the state, it further entrenched the ways of the easterners and guaranteed that the eastward region would always hold a majority of the power in the legislature. The problem of suffrage and representation was not solved. This allowed anger to build up, ultimately leading to the next convention in 1851.

The 1851 Constitution

The 1840 census revealed that the population of the western regions of Virginia had outgrown that of the eastern. The west's underrepresentation in the state legislature became an even more glaring issue. After the dissatisfaction with the 1830 constitution, western delegates tried and failed numerous times to win electoral reform in the Virginia legislature. Many began to openly discuss the abolition of slavery and secession of the western portion of the state from the rest of Virginia. These pressures eventually led those in the east to hold a new constitutional convention to help ease the growing tensions. By 1850, delegates were once again meeting in Richmond to discuss a new constitution.

Many significant changes emerged from the new state constitution, particularly issues that satisfied those in the west. The property qualifications considered obsolete by Thomas Jefferson were finally dropped and white male suffrage in Virginia became universal. This move gave more power to the western counties that had experienced significant population growth since the original 1776 constitution. Additionally, a new reapportionment scheme favoring western growth was adopted. This essentially guaranteed that the west would control both the House of Delegates and eventually the Senate (after the projected 1865 reapportionment). One of the most significant changes of the 1851 constitution was the elimination of the legislatively appointed governor. Instead, the governor would now be elected by the people of Virginia. While these significant changes eased tension due to misrepresentation, the Civil War would make the 1851 constitution a short-lived document.

1864: The War Constitution

Virginia's 1864 document was ultimately deemed illegal because it was drafted during the Civil War. When Virginia voted for secession from the United States in 1861, many of the western and several northern counties dissented. These counties succeeded from Virginia and established a new government creating the state of West Virginia and along with it a new constitution. The new Virginia Constitution abolished slavery, disenfranchised representatives that served the Confederate government, and adjusted the number and terms of office of members of the Virginia Assembly. Because the document was drafted during times of war, its legality is doubted, and the 1864 constitution is not listed in the forward of the 1972 constitution as one of the previous constitutions.[3]

The 1870 Constitution

The controversial post-wartime constitution of 1870, dubbed the "Underwood Constitution" and the "Negro Constitution," created a number of changes. These changes reflected the reconstruction mentality of the United States at the time. After the Civil War, Virginia came under a brief period of military rule by Union forces that had defeated the Confederacy under General John Schofield. In 1867, Schofield called for a new **constitutional convention** to meet in Richmond—a direct response to federal Reconstruction legislation. Provisions in the 1870 Virginia Constitution included extending the right to vote to *all* males over the age of 21—including African American males. Many of Virginia's conservatives refused to participate in the convention in protest of black suffrage. As a result, the convention was dominated by the Radical Republicans, led by Judge John Curtiss Underwood for which the constitution would receive its name.

The 1870 constitution created universal male **suffrage**, giving the right to vote to many males in Virginia aged twenty-one or over. Most significantly, the right to vote was extended to black males for the first time. Another significant addition to the constitution was the establishment of a statewide school system with state funding and mandatory attendance policies. Initially, the constitution also sought to disenfranchise most Virginians who had participated in the government of the Confederacy, but after the provision stalled the document's ratification, it was made a separate ballot issue. The constitution was approved by the voters and went into effect in 1870.

The 1902 Constitution

After Reconstruction, many southern states began implementing systems of racial disenfranchisement to reduce the new rights awarded to blacks granted after the Civil War. The era from 1876 to 1965 witnessed a wide array of state laws mandating racial segregation of public facilities. In Virginia, many conservative whites who boycotted the Underwood Constitution procedures felt they needed to go a step further—yearning for the years when the pool of registered voters was extremely selective and devoid of minorities and poor whites. In 1901, a call for a constitutional convention was approved.

The work of the 1901 convention is remembered primarily for its efforts to disenfranchise African Americans in the state. Convention leaders were very vocal and public that disenfranchisement was their primary goal. The convention succeeded, though not without consequence. In a twenty-one-section article, the state created a poll tax and a constitutional literacy test that aimed at limiting the number of African American voters. A grandfather clause exempted individuals from meeting the specified requirements if their fathers or grandfathers had voted in an election prior to the abolishment of slavery or if they or their fathers had been soldiers. This helped to account for poor, uneducated white voters, who may have been excluded through these voting restrictions. These provisions were effective in reducing the number of black voters; later elections revealed that the 1902 constitution essentially cut the Virginia electorate in half.

While the 1902 Virginia Constitution is best known for its disenfranchisement of African American voters, it also effectively segregated its public schools and abolished the county court system. Once abolished, the circuit courts took over the duties of the county courts. This occurred mainly due to the convention's being dominated by Democrats who wanted greater control over judges and local officials. By abolishing the county court system, they felt this would increase their authority and political clout. Proponents believed that county judges were operating as political machines. At the time, county judges appointed the local sheriff, clerk of court, and the Commonwealth's attorney—the judges themselves were appointed by the General Assembly. Progressives distrusted the county court officials and sought abolishment to rid the courthouse of corruption.[4] The constitution was ultimately ratified despite concerns that African American opposition would prevent its passing. The 1902 constitution was Virginia's longest-running constitution. Over the next sixty year, however, various U.S. Supreme Court rulings and amendments to the U.S. Constitution made many of the 1902 Virginia Constitution's elements illegal (more on segregation and political participation will be explored in Chapter 3).

The Current System: The Constitution of 1971

By the mid-1960s, many provisions of the 1901 Virginia Constitution had become outdated and in some cases unenforceable. Most of the 1901 constitution violated federal laws and Supreme Court rulings pertaining to the Fourteenth Amendment to the U.S. Constitution. In 1968, the General Assembly created the Commission on Constitutional Revision in response to growing discontent over the outdated 1901 constitution. The commission sought to appropriately balance tradition with change. As a result, the commission did not change the language of George Mason's philosophy of government found in the 1776 document—basic human rights, freedoms, and the essential purpose of government. Ultimately, four amendments were put up for a vote to the citizens of Virginia. The commission recommended shortening residency requirements for voting and deleting outdated provisions (such as provisions related to dueling), as well as making the obvious changes to guarantee against discrimination on the basis of race, sex, national origin, or religion.

An overview of the powers provided to the government of Virginia and her people are provided below. These principles continue to form the framework for our current government. Major provisions of the 1971 constitution are explored below (a complete list of articles can be found in Table 2.1). The constitution does not give

TABLE 2.1   Articles of the Virginia Constitution

Article I	Bill of Rights
Article II	Franchise and Officers
Article III	Division of Powers
Article IV	Legislature
Article V	Executive
Article VI	Judiciary
Article VII	Local Government
Article VIII	Education
Article IX	Corporations
Article X	Taxation and Finance
Article XI	Conservation
Article XII	Future Changes (Amendment and Constitutional Convention)

The U.S. government does not recognize same-sex marriage, but six states grant marriage licenses to same-sex couples. Massachusetts became the first state to grant marriage licenses to same-sex couples in 2004. Connecticut, New Hampshire, New York, Vermont, Iowa, California, and Washington, D.C., also grant marriage licenses to same-sex couples. The state of Maryland does not grant marriage licenses to same-sex couples but does recognize same-sex marriages granted from other states. Twenty-nine states prohibit same-sex marriage via their state's constitution while twelve states prohibit same-sex marriage via state statute.

The Commonwealth does not recognize gay marriage. In fact, in 2006, a constitutional amendment was passed that defined marriage as between one man and one woman. See below time line for state legislation and constitutional amendment pertaining to the issue of gay marriage in the Commonwealth.

- 1975: The Code of Virginia was amended to prohibit gay marriage.
- 1997: 1975 Code of Virginia prohibition of gay marriage is extended to voiding same-sex marriages from another state.
- 2004: 1975 Virginia Code is amended once again to ban civil unions and other similar arrangements between same-sex couples, while also not recognizing arrangements made in other states.
- 2006: A constitutional amendment limiting marriage to unions between one man and one woman passed the General Assembly and was approved 57 percent (1,325,668) to 43 percent (1,003,967) by a popular vote of the people and went into effect in 2007.

details on specific policy areas but is quite explicit on the state's role in and responsibility for education as outlined in Article VIII.

Bill of Rights

Article I contains the **Virginia Bill of Rights**. Many of the provisions found in the Bill of Rights remain from the original 1776 Virginia Constitution. Article I includes the entire section of the original Declaration of Rights, in addition to the federal-level provisions of due process, prohibition against double jeopardy, and the right to bear arms. Two recent amendments to the Bill of Rights have occurred. In 1997, a Victim's Rights Amendment was added. The need for this amendment was spurred by the crime victims' rights movement during the 1970s and other grassroots movements concerned with victims' rights. The overarching goal of the amendment is to give victims of crimes increased substantive rights and a greater voice in criminal proceedings. This would enable them to have greater standing in eventual court proceedings.[5] In 2006, voters approved an amendment already passed by the General Assembly prohibiting same-sex marriages or recognition of any union, partnership, or other legal status between unmarried people that tries to mimic the rights granted under traditional marriage.

Executive Branch

Article V of the Virginia Constitution establishes the executive branch. Three popularly elected officials encompass the executive branch. The highest ranking position of chief executive, or the state's governor, is filled every four years. Virginia is the only state in the United States that does not allow its governor to serve consecutive terms. In comparison, fourteen states as well as Puerto Rico and the District of Columbia mayor have unlimited terms. Citizens of Virginia also elect a lieutenant governor and attorney general through popular elections.

Article V grants the governor the power to sign legislation, veto bills (which can be overridden by a two-thirds majority in both houses of the Virginia General Assembly) and issue pardons. The governor has a number of administrative responsibilities, which are further explained in Chapter 6. The governor is also charged with ensuring the laws of the Commonwealth are faithfully executed and shall be commander in chief of the armed forces whose service can be used to repel invasion, suppress insurrection, and enforce the execution of laws. In addition, the governor has the power to fill vacancies in all offices of the Commonwealth for which the constitution and legislation make no other provisions. In order to qualify to become governor, an individual must be a citizen of the United States, a resident of Virginia for at least five years, and at least thirty years of age.

Article V contains only one sentence regarding the powers of the lieutenant governor. The individual in this position serves as the president of the Senate and is next in line should the governor be unable to perform the duties of office. The lieutenant governor is charged with making a tie-breaking vote in the Senate, which is the only time he or she is given a vote. The lieutenant governor must meet the same qualifications (age, Virginia residency, and U.S. citizenship) as the governor. There are no term limitations attached to this executive position.

The attorney general, second-in-line behind the lieutenant governor to succeed the governor should the governor become unable to perform the duties of office, is responsible for carrying out the duties prescribed to him or her by law. The attorney general and his or her staff provide legal advice to the governor, represent the legal interests of the state, represent the state in any constitutional challenges to state law, and represent the state in matters of appeal of criminal convictions. The attorney general must be a U.S. citizen, at least thirty years of age, and have the qualifications required for a judge of a court of record. There are no term limitations.

Legislative Branch

Article IV outlines the structure and responsibilities granted to the Virginia legislative branch. The structure establishes a bicameral legislature called the General Assembly. The two houses are called the House of Delegates and the Senate, with the House of Delegates having the larger body of the two. The General Assembly meets once a year, beginning on the second Wednesday in January, and can meet for no longer than sixty days during an even numbered year or thirty days during an odd numbered year.

The Senate is to consist of no more than forty and no less than thirty-three members. Any person may be elected to the senate who is twenty-one years of age, is a resident of any district that is seeking to be represented, and is qualified to vote for members of the General Assembly. Senators are to be elected quadrennially by voters of their respective senatorial districts on the Tuesday after the first Monday in November. Qualifications to run for senate are as follows: at least 21 years of age, resident of the senatorial district seeking representation, and qualified to vote for members of the General Assembly.

The House of Delegates may have no more than one hundred and no less than ninety members elected biennially by the voters of the respective house districts on the Tuesday following the first Monday in November.

Article IV prohibits any person holding a salaried office under the government of the Commonwealth, including judges, state attorneys, sheriff, treasurer, assessor of taxes, commissioner of the revenue, collector of taxes, or clerk of court, from becoming a member of the General Assembly.

Judicial Branch

Article VI outlines the laws guiding the state judiciary. The judiciary comprises the Supreme Court of Virginia and subordinate courts created by the General Assembly. Judges are appointed by a majority vote in the General Assembly to terms of twelve years for the Supreme Court of Virginia justices and eight years for all others. General jurisdiction trial courts, appellate courts, and others shall be designated by the General Assembly.

The Supreme Court of Virginia has the power to make rules governing the procedures and the practice of law in the Commonwealth's court system. The Supreme Court of Virginia, the court of final resort in Virginia, consists of a chief justice and six justices. Decisions made by the Virginia Supreme Court can be appealed to the U.S. Supreme Court if the case at hand involved a federal issue guaranteed right.

The General Assembly has the power to change that number with a two-thirds vote; however, the Supreme Court may have no fewer than seven and no more than eleven justices. The chief justice of the Supreme Court of Virginia is selected by a vote of the court's justices. The chief justice is considered the administrative head of the judicial system and may temporality assign any judge of a court of record to any other court of record except the Supreme Court of Virginia.

Education

Article VIII of the Virginia Constitution prescribes a mandatory and free primary and secondary public education for every child in Virginia. Funding for the education system is determined by the General Assembly. Costs are often apportioned between the state and local governments within the state. A state Board of Education is established to create school districts and implement overall education policies, though the actual supervision of individual schools is the direct responsibility of local school boards.

The General Assembly is permitted to provide for the establishment, maintenance, and operation of any educational institutions that are desirable for the intellectual, cultural, and occupational development for the people of Virginia. The General Assembly provides for the governance of and the status and powers of the Boards of Visitors of these institutions. Article VIII also establishes that no public funds can be directly paid to any school or institution of learning that is not owned or exclusively controlled by the General Assembly. (You can find more information on education policy in Virginia in Chapter 11.)

Local Governments

Article VII of the Virginia Constitution establishes the basic framework for local government in Virginia. A local government can be established for a town (with population of at least one thousand), city (with population of at least five thousand), county, and other regional bodies, such as a special district or public authority. While the General Assembly has the power to create laws for these political subdivisions, it cannot create a new regional government without the consent of the majority of the voters in that particular region. Section 4 of Article VII mandates that elections are to be held for the positions of a city or county treasurer, sheriff, attorney for the Commonwealth, a clerk of court, and a commission of revenue for each city and county.

Corporations

Article IX of the Virginia Constitution creates the Virginia State Corporation Commission responsible for the implementation of legislation that acts to regulate business activities. This three-person commission is charged with the issuance of business charters, amendments of domestic corporations, and all licenses for foreign corporations doing business in the Commonwealth. The commission is also charged with administering the laws made in pursuance with the Virginia Constitution for the regulation and control of corporations doing business in Virginia. The commission authorizes foreign corporations to conduct business in Virginia, but these businesses have only those rights and powers granted to domestic corporations.

Taxation and Finance

Article X of the Virginia Constitution establishes the framework for tax policies governed by the Commonwealth. All personal property in the Commonwealth is taxable at its fair market value, except for a list of exemptions (including churches, cemeteries, and nonprofit school property). A budget amendment, known as the "Lottery Proceeds Fund," went into effect in 1986, requiring all proceeds from the Virginia lottery system to directly support the state's education system. All taxes, licenses, and other Commonwealth revenues are collected by the proper officials and paid into the state treasury. The governor must ensure that no expenses should be incurred that exceed total revenues on hand and anticipated during a period not to exceed the two years and six-month period established in the Virginia Constitution.

Amending the Constitution

Changing or amending a constitution is not an easy process. The U.S. Constitution has been amended only twenty-seven times. The number of state constitutional amendments varies from state to state. The Alabama Constitution has been amended 766 times while the Rhode Island Constitution has been amended only eight times. The 1971 Virginia Constitution has been amended twenty-two times. In Virginia, individual amendments to the constitution may be proposed by the General Assembly and can be introduced in either the House of Delegates or the Senate. Once a proposal is approved by a majority in both houses of the General Assembly, it is put to a popular vote no sooner than ninety days prior to the General Assembly's passage. If an amendment garners the majority of the popular vote, it is added to the constitution. A second way to amend the constitution is by a constitutional convention, which can be called with a two-thirds vote from the General Assembly. The proposed changes are then put to a vote of the general population. Constitutional changes can be approved only by the general population through a popular vote, but voters do not have the power to propose an amendment or new constitution.

Conclusion

Virginia's constitution serves as a framework for what the state and its officials can and cannot do to the people, institutions, and businesses that call Virginia home. It is important for residents to have an understanding of the Virginia Constitution. This understanding enables you to not only know more about your state government, but it also enables you to know your rights and protections as a Virginia citizen. The chapters that follow provide more detail into each of the state's institutions and polices, including the Virginia General Assembly, the Virginia Executive Branch, the Virginia Judicial System, budgeting and finance in Virginia, Virginia's bureaucracy, and local government in Virginia.

Key Concepts

Confederacy

Constitution

Constitutional convention

Declaration of Rights

Federalism

General Assembly

House of Delegates

Representative democracy

Senate

Sovereign

Suffrage

Unitary system

Virginia Bill of Rights

Suggested Resources

- http://constitution.legis.virginia.gov: **Virginia State Constitution.**
- http://leg1.state.va.us/cgi-bin/legp504.exe?000+cod+TOC: **Code of Virginia.**
- http://www.iandrinstitute.org: **Initiative and Referendum Institute.**

Notes

1. Kevin B. Smith, Alan Greenblatt, and John Buntin, *Governing States and Localities,* 3rd ed. (Washington, DC: CQ Press, 2010), 12.

2. Thomas Jefferson, *Notes on the State of Virginia,* ed. William Peden (Chapel Hill: University of North Carolina Press for the Institute of Early American History and Culture, Williamsburg, VA, 1954).

3. Virginia, "Foreword," in *Constitution of Virginia* (Richmond: Dept. of Purchases and Supply, Commonwealth of Virginia 1971), n1.

4. Wythe W. Holt, Jr., "The Virginia Constitutional Convention of 1901–1902: A Reform Movement Which Lacked Substance," *Virginia Magazine of History and Biography* 76, no. 1 (1968): 78.

5. *Crime Victims' Rights, U.S. Code* 18 (2004), § 3771, Cornell University Law School Legal Information Institute, http://www.law.cornell.edu/uscode/text/18/3771.

OUTLINE

Gaining the Right to Vote

Redistricting

Primaries and Elections

Voting in Virginia

Impact on National
Politics

Direct Democracy

Other Forms of Political
Participation

Conclusion

CHAPTER 3

From Blue to Red and Back Again

Voting and Political Participation in Virginia

P olitical participation is the cornerstone of democratic societies. Virginia's designation as a "Commonwealth" at the state's founding—one in which power would be vested in the people and laws made for the common good—highlights the ideal of citizen engagement in public affairs. Voting plays a particularly important role in representative democracies where citizens elect officials to govern. Importantly, voting and other political behavior is the product of laws and regulations designed to either limit or expand political participation. In Virginia, these reflect the state's traditionalist political culture, where power is in the hands of political elite and public participation is limited. Securing political equality has also been greatly impacted by federalism, through the interplay of national and state politics and judicial rulings. This chapter provides a brief history of voting rights in Virginia, discusses the redistricting, primary, and election processes, and highlights key trends and barriers to political participation in the Commonwealth.

Gaining the Right to Vote

Voting may be the bedrock of political participation, but for many groups in Virginia, securing this right has been an uphill battle. Like many southern states, Virginia's commitment to political equality has been limited for most of its history. Virginia was just one of three original thirteen states (along with South Carolina and Georgia) that did not allow free black men to vote.[1] Laws that denied the **franchise** (the right to vote in elections) to Native Americans, women, and white men without property were also widespread throughout the states. Following the Civil War, congressional **Reconstruction** of former Confederate states gave black men the right to vote in 1867. At the same time, however, federal reformers also disenfranchised many men who had fought for the Confederacy. In Virginia, nearly 90 percent of black men voted in the subsequent elections. Changes to the Virginia Constitution in 1870 included provisions for universal male suffrage, and the Fifteenth Amendment to the U.S. Constitution prohibited states from denying men the right to vote based on their "race, color, or previous condition on servitude." Virginia, along with Texas, Mississippi, and Georgia, was required to ratify the Fifteenth Amendment as a condition of being readmitted to the Union and getting representation in Congress.*

Virginia's compliance with this provision did not signal a new commitment to political equality; that same year, the state began to enact a series of legislative statutes that would disenfranchise poor whites, blacks, and other minorities for the next one hundred years. This included separate voting books for whites and blacks so that the black vote could be limited through "technical delays." Racial **gerrymandering**—drawing electoral districts to purposefully dilute the voting power of minorities—was also widespread.[2] The adoption of the 1902 Virginia Constitution solidified legal enforcement of the state's **Jim Crow laws**, which sanctioned systematic racial segregation in government services, restaurants, and other establishments. In a convention dominated by conservative Democrats, the new state constitution—which was to govern Virginia until 1971—was amended to include literacy tests, property requirements, and poll taxes. In order to **register** to vote, a person was required to understand the Virginia Constitution and "make application to register in his own handwriting, without aid, suggestions, or memorandum."[3] A new poll tax ($1.50 in 1902, or around $40 in 2010 dollars) had to be paid six months prior to an election. Notes from the 1901 Constitutional Convention reveal that the new provisions, which exempted Civil War veterans and their sons, were designed to disenfranchise black voters without technically violating the Fourteenth and Fifteenth Amendments to the U.S. Constitution, which had abolished slavery and prohibited voting discrimination.[4]

---

*Between 1790 and 1850, however, the majority of states adopted constitutions that barred blacks from voting (only five New England states—Maine, Massachusetts, New Hampshire, Rhode Island, and Vermont continued to allow all men to vote).

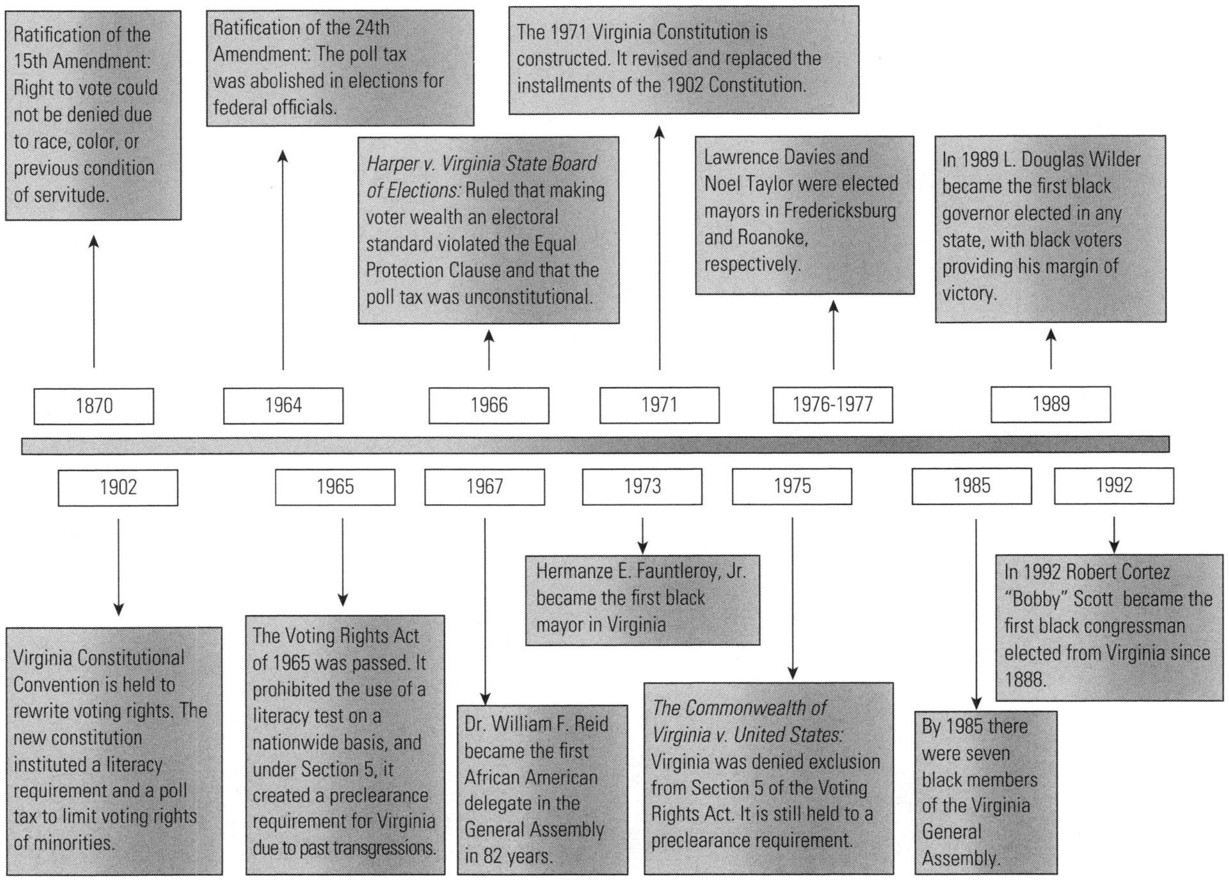

FIGURE 3.1

Timeline: Black Civil Rights in Virginia

Within three months after its adoption, more than 85 percent of black voters in Virginia had been removed from voter registration rolls. While African Americans felt the impact of voting restrictions the most, they were not the only targets for such laws. Nor was Virginia unique in circumventing the Fifteenth Amendment to disenfranchise citizens in the twentieth century. For example, Connecticut, the first state to adopt a poll tax, did so to keep Irish Catholics from voting. In Virginia, voting restrictions also limited the power of poor whites, liberals, and labor—those that primarily voted Republican or were Independent. Electoral participation plummeted over the next few decades, and by 1940, just 10 percent of Virginians over age 21 were going to the polls.[5] These restrictions were instrumental in strengthening the power of conservative Democrats—most notably the Byrd Regime, which supported the poll tax and literacy tests to rule the state from the 1920s to 1965 (see Chapter 4 for more thorough discussion of the Byrd Regime).[6]

The Twenty-fourth Amendment to the U.S. Constitution, ratified in 1964, banned poll taxes in federal elections, however, they continued to be used at the state and local levels, including in Virginia. Two years later, in a challenge to Virginia's poll tax in the 1966 case of *Harper v. Virginia State Board of Elections,* the Supreme Court ruled the use of poll taxes unconstitutional in all elections.* The 1965 federal Voting Rights Act (VRA) further expanded the franchise by banning literacy tests and gave the federal government oversight of voting procedures in Virginia and other southern states that had a history of suppressing poor and minority voters. Opposition to the VRA was widespread among Virginia's political elite, including almost all of the state's congressional delegation: both of Virginia's senators and nine of its ten representatives voted against it. Despite state-level opposition, these changes brought about by legislative and judicial rulings at the national level had tangible results in Virginia: the augmented voting power translated into increased electoral wins for African American candidates (see Figure 3.1 for a timeline of black civil rights successes in Virginia).[7]

Women also faced legal obstacles to political participation in Virginia, although gender discrimination was not as persistent or as violent as toward African Americans. Campaigns to give women the right to vote occurred later in the southern states than in the north, where a traditional political culture presented formidable barriers to what many feared would be a redefinition of gender roles. Many southerners also viewed attempts to expand the franchise as part of the "Reconstruction agenda being forced on the southern states by the Radical Republicans in the North."[8] Although some organizing occurred in the state as early as the 1870s, the creation of the Equal Suffrage League of Virginia in 1909 provided a vehicle for Virginians to join the national movement for women's **suffrage**. Virginia suffragettes used public education campaigns, protests, hunger strikes, and other means to push for constitutional amendments at both the state and federal levels

---

*In *Harper v. Virginia,* the Supreme Court held that the poll tax violates the fourteenth Amendment's equal protection clause; the decision overturned a previous ruling in *Breedlove v. Suttles* (1937).

that would grant women the right to vote. Even though Virginia women gained the right to vote when the Nineteenth Amendment to the U.S. Constitution took effect in 1920, Virginia was one of just nine states (all southern) whose state legislatures refused to ratify it. It would take over thirty more years before the General Assembly secured enough votes for ratification and until 1971 for the Virginia Constitution to officially remove gender qualifications for voting. While women made some early gains in the House of Delegates, the first woman was not elected to the Virginia State Senate until 1979, and not until 1992 did Virginia elect a woman to the U.S. Congress (there has still never been a female U.S. senator from Virginia).[9]

In 1972, the voting age was lowered from twenty-one to eighteen, and in 1976, residency requirements were shortened from six months to thirty days prior to an election. Still, while the state of Virginia has expanded voting rights over the past century, suffrage is not universal. Citizens who have been convicted of a felony cannot vote. Because the U.S. Constitution allows states to set voter eligibility requirements, this limitation applies not only to state and local elections but also to federal ones. In addition to Kentucky, Virginia is just one of two states that permanently disenfranchise felons unless they petition the governor to restore their civil rights.[10] Since African Americans and other minorities are disproportionally represented in our criminal justice system, many see this as an attempt to limit minority voting rights (see Box 3.1, Should Convicted Felons Have the Right to Vote?). Additionally, individuals who have been declared to be "mentally incompetent" cannot vote until their competency has been reestablished by the courts. Virginia is one of just five states that categorically denies voting rights to those with cognitive impairments.[11]*

Today, the reintroduction of bills to require voter identification in Virginia and elsewhere has led many critics—especially on the left—to worry that such requirements will effectively disenfranchise poor, minority, elderly, and student voters. Like many other Republican-controlled state legislatures around the country, conservative Virginia lawmakers have tried to strengthen voter identification requirements at the polls. Legislation passed in 2012 made voter identification mandatory, though Virginia does not currently require a photo ID (as in 15 states).[16]† For the past ten years, voters without proper identification have been able sign a sworn affidavit, attesting to their identity. Now, citizens can only fill out a provisional ballot until they can prove their identity.[17] The Virginia Black Caucus has criticized the bills as a way to discourage voting. Proponents, on the other hand, tout the requirements as a way to prevent voter fraud.[18]

---

*Other states' citizens with cognitive impairments either have no constitutional limitation on voting or have the explicit or implicit right to have courts specifically determine whether they should vote (as opposed to control of finances or other decisions).

†Valid sources of identification include a Virginia voter registration card, Social Security card, Virginia driver's license, any other identification card issued by a Virginia state, local, or U.S. government agency, or an employee identification card with a photograph. See Code of Virginia § 24.2-643. Qualified voter permitted to vote; procedures at polling place; voter identification.

BOX 3.1 Should Convicted Felons Have the Right to Vote?

More than 377,000 Virginians have been impacted by laws barring convicted felons from voting. According to the Sentencing Project, a national advocacy group that promotes sentencing reform, Virginia's laws are among the strictest in the country since the state does not automatically restore voting rights once a sentence is served (including prison, probation, or parole). In 2004, 6.8 percent of the state's total population was disenfranchised because of felony records. These rates were surpassed only by Florida (9 percent), Alabama (7.4 percent), and Mississippi (6.9 percent). In contrast, Maine and Vermont allow people with felony convictions to vote from prison. Not all Virginians are equally affected by these policies; because of disproportionate minority contact in the criminal justice system, nearly 20 percent of Virginia's African American citizens have lost the right to vote. In addition to the loss of voting rights, felons also lose the ability to run for and hold public office and to serve on juries.[12]

While Virginians can petition the governor to have their civil rights restored, the process has been criticized for being too arduous and bureaucratic. Nonviolent offenders can submit a two-page application to the secretary of the Commonwealth for a restoration of rights from three years after all court obligations have been served. Violent offenders and those convicted of drug manufacturing or sales must wait five years before they can submit a "cumbersome" twelve-page petition, that includes "a letter from your most recent probation or parole officer, copies of your pre- or post-sentence report, certified copies of every order of conviction and sentencing orders, three letters of reference and, to top it off, a personal letter to the governor explaining your convictions and how your life has changed."[13] In 2011, Governor McDonnell reinstated the voting rights of more than 1,100 felons, promising that his administration would have "the fastest and fairest civil-rights restoration process in modern history."[14]

Proponents of felony restrictions maintain that individuals should forfeit their civil rights when they commit a felony. For those who really want the privilege to vote, they can petition the government to have these rights restored. Opponents argue that once individuals have paid their debt to society, their rights should be automatically restored so that they can help shape the laws they live under. While the petitioning process exists, it takes a lot of time and resources, especially if the conviction took place many years ago or in another state. Virginians appear to be evenly divided on the topic, with slightly more people in favor of the status quo: in a 2010 poll, 49.5 percent of respondents said that the Virginia law should not be changed, while 45.8 percent thought that felons should have their rights automatically reinstated once they complete their sentence.[15]

What do you think?

Redistricting

Not only is *who* votes a contentious issue, but so too is *where* they vote. Elections in the United States, whether they are local, state, or national, are based on geography, with the ability to vote for a particular candidate tied to where you live. Virginia is divided into eleven electoral districts, whose boundaries are established by the

General Assembly. Although most of us do not think about the significance of where we vote, electoral boundaries are extremely important. How these lines are drawn can determine whether an **incumbent** (the existing office holder) will be easily reelected or there will be healthy political competition. This can shift the balance of power between Democrats and Republicans and determine how many state representatives each district gets, impacting the share of state dollars directed toward particular cities or towns.

In order to ensure the principle of "one-person, one-vote," district lines must be redrawn every ten years to make sure that voting districts have approximately the same number of people. This **redistricting** process is mandated by both the U.S. and Virginia Constitutions. Seats for the Virginia Senate and House of Delegates and the United States House of Representatives are **reapportioned**, or reallocated, to reflect changes in the state's population. Because of a history of systematic political discrimination, Virginia is one of seven states required to get U.S. Department of Justice approval for changes to electoral district boundaries and voting locations (Alabama, Alaska, Georgia, Louisiana, Mississippi, and South Carolina are also subject to the 1964 Voting Rights Act (VRA) provisions).*

Opponents have argued that such oversight is no longer needed and costs localities time and money to prepare and submit plans. Exemptions to VRA oversight are granted on the local level to communities who can prove that they have not discriminated for more than ten years. This proof includes having racially diverse election boards or city councils or having a majority of eligible adults registered to vote. In 1997, Fairfax City became the first jurisdiction in Virginia to get a "bailout," securing an exemption from Department of Justice requirements. Since then, a number of cities and counties in the state have successfully applied for exemption.[19†] Federal preclearance of Virginia electoral procedures continues to be a contentious issue. It is opposed by many on the right, including VA Attorney General Ken Cuccinelli, who has asserted that Virginia has "outgrown" the need for VRA oversight requirements. Proponents, however, argue that its elimination would threaten civil rights.[20] Unlike the original legislation in 1965, Virginia's congressional delegation unanimously voted to approve extensions the expiring provisions of the VRA in 2006.

While racial gerrymandering—the process of drawing district lines based on the racial makeup of a district—is unconstitutional, *political* gerrymandering is not. However, following the Supreme Court's ruling in *Reynolds v. Simms* (1964),

---

*The provision also covered political subdivisions in another four states (Arizona, Hawaii, Idaho, and North Carolina); revisions to the VRA extended federal oversight in 1970 to Texas and to parts of Alaska, Arizona, California, Connecticut, Idaho, Maine, Massachusetts, New Hampshire, New York, and Wyoming. In 1975 the VRA was further expanded to cover parts of California, Florida, Michigan, New York, North Carolina, and South Dakota.

†As of November 2011, twenty-five political jurisdictions in Virginia had bailed out of DOJ oversight under Section 4 of the Voting Rights Act. For a complete list, see "Section 4 of the Voting Rights Act," U.S. Department of Justice.

electoral districts must be based on the size of the population, rather than simply on partisan considerations. Some consequences of political gerrymandering include reducing political parties and electoral competition; strengthening incumbency, partisan bias, and gridlock in government; diminishing government accountability to the electorate, increasing voter apathy, and decreasing voter turnout.[21] The most recent redistricting occurred following the 2010 Census and was enacted in April 2011 after a lengthy and contentious process. After initial plans were vetoed by Governor McDonnell for being too partisan, the approved maps resulted in the addition of a second district in Virginia Beach, divided Prince William County into one fewer districts, and split the College of William and Mary from its existing district.

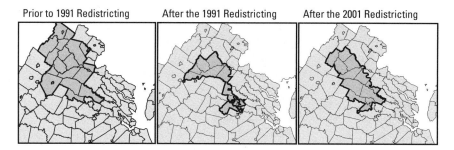

| Prior to 1991 Redistricting | After the 1991 Redistricting | After the 2001 Redistricting |

FIGURE 3.2

Gerrymandering in Virginia's Congressional Districts

Source: Kenneth S. Stroupe Jr., "Gerrymandering in Virginia: Will This Decade Mark the End?" *The Virginia News Letter* 85, no. 1 (2009): 1–10.

Primaries and Elections

Government in Virginia, like the United States as a whole, is considered a **representative democracy**, where citizens elect representatives to govern on their behalf. Elections, therefore, are one of the primary ways that citizens exercise political power and are held for local, state, and national positions. The number of statewide electoral offices is limited in Virginia and includes races for governor, lieutenant governor, and attorney general. In contrast, a number of other states also hold statewide elections for auditor, comptroller, secretary of state, commissioner of education/superintendent of public instruction, and treasurer. Others elect a commissioner of labor and commissioner of state lands. Just six states have fewer statewide offices: Hawaii, New Jersey, and Tennessee hold statewide elections only for governor and lieutenant governor; in Maine, New Hampshire, and Tennessee only the governor faces statewide election.[22] However, thousands more electoral races occur within Virginia's localities: city and town councils, county boards of supervisors, mayors, managers, city and county school boards, treasurers, clerks, and sheriffs. This large number of elections provides many opportunities for Virginians to vote, to elect their representatives, to run for office, and to participate in governing the Commonwealth. Unlike electoral contests at the national level, state-level elections are held in odd-numbered years. While this design helps disentangle national politics from state issues, it also results in low voter turnout for off-year elections. Low voter turnout reinforces the advantage of incumbents and results in low turnover among elected officials.

The Democratic and Republican parties in Virginia both use **primary elections** rather than caucuses (meetings of party supporters) to select candidates to run for state and national offices. Virginia has a hybrid primary system: any registered voter can vote in either the Democratic or Republican Party primary, though once they get to the polls, they need to declare in which one they will be voting. States with open primaries allow voters to cast a vote in either party's primary, regardless of their own political affiliation. States with closed primaries, on the other hand, exercise more control over the process by allowing only registered party members to cast a primary vote. In 2012, the Virginia State Republican Party contemplated requiring primary voters to sign a "loyalty oath" before voting at the party's presidential primary. The move was reconsidered after negative feedback from many members of the state Grand Old Party (GOP).[23] In many cities and counties in Virginia, local elections are nonpartisan; therefore, no primaries are held (in localities where parties nominate people for office and hold primaries, *ballots* are nonpartisan and do not indicate the candidate's party affiliation).

Voting in Virginia

Voting is one of the most common ways for citizens to participate in governance and plays a key role in selecting elected officials, providing access to those elected officials once in office, and impacting who is encouraged to run for office in the first place. The General Assembly is responsible for establishing voter and candidate qualifications as well as electoral procedures and regulations. The Virginia State Board of Elections, which is part of the executive branch, administers election laws and keeps track of electoral outcomes. Each independent city and county also has a three-member citizen board to administer local elections. Local electoral board members are nominated by the two major political parties—Republicans and Democrats—and selected by a local circuit court judge. The majority of board members (two of the three) represent the party of the governor, though electoral boards are supposed to be nonpartisan in the administration of election activities.

Despite its moniker as a Commonwealth where power is derived from the people, in recent years, Virginia has had relatively weak voter turnout. Over the past decade, Virginians have generally voted in numbers lower than the national average.

The exception to this was during the 2008 presidential election between John McCain and Barack Obama, when a greater proportion of eligible voters in Virginia cast their vote. This tendency was even more pronounced among minority voters. In years when there are no national elections, voter turnout is particularly low, a trend common in state and local elections nationwide. For example, 74 percent of *registered voters* (just 67 percent of the voting-age population in Virginia) cast votes in the 2008 election, a presidential election year. Yet just 30.2 percent of registered voters had voted the previous year, 40.4 percent in 2009, 44 percent in 2010.[24] Moreover, other groups—the poor, racial and ethnic minorities, and those with low levels of education—vote at significantly lower numbers (see Figure 3.3, Voting Rates in Virginia and the United States). Low voter turnout is especially severe at the local level. For those concerned about political participation, this is particularly troubling since local governments are often seen as schools of democracy, where citizens have abundant opportunities for political participation and learn the habits of citizenship.[25]

The timing of elections is a primary factor for driving voter turnout rates. Some analysts suggest that holding local elections concurrently with state or national elections could significantly boost local voter turnout.[26] Limited opportunities for direct democracy (a theme explored below) can also depress political participation. Others are concerned that the voter registration process creates barriers. In order to vote in local, state, or national elections, citizens must first register to vote. Voter registration deadlines in Virginia range from twenty-two days in advance of a general or primary election to thirteen days before a special election (and just seven if called by the governor). Still, many fear that this requirement stifles political participation. There have been a number of attempts to facilitate voter registration with federal Motor Voter laws that require states to register people at the Department of Motor Vehicles. Virginians can get registration applications at a range of other locations, including the State Board of Elections, local voter registration offices, state and local social service departments, armed forces recruitment centers, libraries, and online. Many political and civic organizations also hold voter registration drives to increase voter turnout. Although Virginia has not adopted same election day registration (which is currently allowed in just eight states and the District of Columbia), the state does allow early and absentee voting for residents who can document that they will be out of town or otherwise unable to vote on election day. Other reasons for not voting may include low levels of civic knowledge, political apathy, or dislike of electoral choices.

Impact on National Politics

Political culture and electoral institutions at the state level impact more than just the state of Virginia. In recent years, the political diversity of the electorate has made Virginia a key swing state in national elections. In 2008, Virginia's thirteen Electoral College votes went to Barack Obama, the second time a Democrat had secured the state's vote since the 1950s.* Obama again won the Virginia vote in

---

*The other was in 1964 when Lyndon Johnson beat Barry Goldwater.

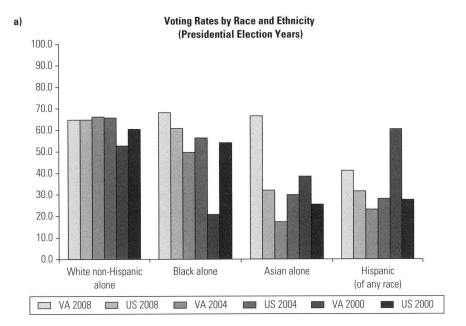

a)

Voting Rates by Race and Ethnicity
(Presidential Election Years)

Legend: VA 2008, US 2008, VA 2004, US 2004, VA 2000, US 2000

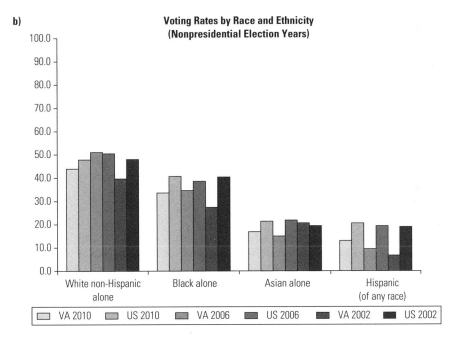

b)

Voting Rates by Race and Ethnicity
(Nonpresidential Election Years)

Legend: VA 2010, US 2010, VA 2006, US 2006, VA 2002, US 2002

FIGURE 3.3

Voting Rates in Virginia and the United States

Source: U.S. Census, Populations Characteristics Report, Voting by State (Sex, Race), http://www.census.org.

2012, but at just 2 percentage points, it was by a very narrow margin. Ballot access laws vary by state, sometimes leading to confusion among candidates running for national office. Traditionalist states tend to have tight ballot access, reflecting a traditional hierarchy between voters and the states' political elite. The 2012 primary election highlighted Virginia's strict primary ballot requirements, often considered "the most stringent in the nation."[27] In 2011, Newt Gingrich and Governor Rick Perry failed to gather the ten thousand signatures necessary for ballot access and were not included in Virginia's March 2012 primary.[28] Virginia also does not allow voters to write in candidates in primary elections. However, unlike early voting states, like New Hampshire and Iowa, that set the tone for subsequent primaries, Virginia's primary has less impact on shaping voting patterns across the county. Eleven other states will have already voted before Virginia, and nine other states vote on Super Tuesday each March. Still, in recent years, electoral results in Virginia have been a good predictor of political shifts throughout the country.[29]

Direct Democracy

Opportunities for direct democracy—the process by which citizens vote directly on policy issues and exercise more authority over public decision making—are limited in Virginia. Unlike half the states, Virginia does not allow *popular* **referendum** (where citizens petition to repeal an existing law), ballot **initiatives** (where citizens place issues on the agenda for popular vote), or constitutional amendment by initiative. However, all states allow *legislative* referendum—where the legislature puts a measure on the ballot for the voters to approve. In recent years, voters in Virginia have seen a variety of legislative referenda on their ballots. For example, in the 2010 general election, voters approved constitutional amendments to expand localities' discretion in granting property tax relief for the elderly, to grant property tax exemptions for disabled veterans, and to increase the state's "rainy day fund." In 2006, voters narrowly approved an amendment to the state constitution to limit marriage to a man and a woman, to delete a section of the Constitution that prohibited the state from granting the incorporation of churches, and to allow localities to grant partial exemptions from real estate taxes.[30]

Although Virginia does not allow direct **recall** of state officials, citizens can petition for a recall trial (rather than a direct recall *election* as in other states). The recall process occurs within the circuit court, where a judge determines whether there are grounds for removing the elected official prior to a recall election. Virginia is one of just eight states that specifies grounds for removal (eleven others allow recall for any reason). This includes "neglect of duty, misuse of office, or incompetence in the performance of duties when that neglect of duty, misuse of office or incompetence in the performance of duties has a material adverse effect upon the conduct of the office, or upon conviction of a drug-related misdemeanor or a misdemeanor involving a 'hate crime.'"[31] In 2010, voters in Portsmouth, Virginia, approved the recall of Mayor James Holley for having his assistants do personal tasks. Mayor Holley had been previously recalled from office in 1987, giving him notoriety as the only U.S. official to be recalled twice.[32]

Other Forms of Political Participation

While this chapter has focused primarily on voting, Virginians have a variety of ways that they can try to influence politics at the local, state, and national levels. This includes various forms of **conventional participation**: voting to choose candidates in primaries or to select representatives in general elections, trying to influence elected officials by writing them e-mail or signing petitions, working on a political campaign or donating money to candidates, or even running for office. Citizens can also express themselves through more **unconventional** forms of political participation, such as sit-ins, protest marches, or other kinds of demonstrations to convey dissatisfaction with government.

Unconventional participation has been an important strategy for groups traditionally shut out of conventional politics, particularly in expanding civil rights. In recent years, public demonstrations at the Virginia Capitol have included the Tea Party, the Occupy movement, and candlelight vigils and marches to protest state legislation limiting abortion access. State officials are not the only targets of political protests in Virginia. Opposition may be directed at the decisions of private

In March 2012, hundreds of citizens gathered outside the state capitol building in Richmond to protest a bill requiring women to undergo an ultrasound before receiving an abortion. More than thirty activists were arrested when they refused demands by Capitol Police to leave the area.

businesses—for example, attempts to get Dominion Virginia Power to invest in more renewable energy. In the aftermath of the Virginia Tech shooting, the Virginia Citizen Defense League organized a number of rallies on college campuses to try to convince administrators to allow students to carry concealed weapons.

Even when citizens are not actively trying to influence government, elected officials often pay attention to **public opinion**, though there is some disagreement as to how much and under what circumstances our opinions influence politics. While Virginia is known as a traditionally conservative state, there has been variation in public opinion over time and significant diversity of citizen opinion across the state. For example, in 2006, a majority of Virginia's voters (57 percent) approved a state constitutional amendment that prohibits same-sex marriage. Just five years later, however, a *Washington Post* poll found Virginians split on the issue, with 47 percent of respondents indicating that gay marriage should be legal in the state and 43 percent opposed.[33] There is also variation across the state, with more liberal citizens in northern Virginia and the Tidewater region and more conservatives in the central and western parts of the state. State laws often reflect the preferences of citizens; however, because Virginia is such a diverse state, it is difficult to enact legislation that pleases everyone.

Public opinion polls can be a valuable tool in giving representatives an idea of their constituents' preferences between elections. Although polls are more frequently conducted at the national level, even when public opinion is generally known, elected officials still have the ability to pass laws that diverge from majority preferences. Sometimes this is a reflection of lawmakers paying more attention to the active, rather than inactive, public. Not surprisingly, citizens who are more vocal in expressing their opinion are more likely to see their views reflected in state legislation. It may also reflect interest group activity (a topic that will be explored in more detail in the next chapter). In other instances, lawmakers and citizens may have different ideas about the best way to solve a problem. For example, the 2012 General Assembly repealed legislation that limited handgun purchases to one per month, despite polls that showed Virginians supported the law by more than two to one (66 percent to 31 percent). The legislature also passed a law that requires women seeking an abortion to first undergo an ultrasound, a move that was supported by just 36 percent and opposed by 55 percent of those polled.[34] Another issue where Virginians have seen clear divergence between citizen and legislator preferences is in state ownership of liquor stores. According to a 2010 statewide poll, 52 percent of respondents supported selling state-owned ABC stores, while only 38 percent were opposed.[35] Although legislation to privatize state liquor stores has been introduced in the General Assembly for the past few years, none have passed.

Conclusion

Over the past century, Virginia has come a long way in expanding democracy. However, we continue to see tension between the values inherent in a Commonwealth, where political authority is derived from the people, and Virginia's traditional political culture, where the few make rules to govern the many. Even with the removal of legal barriers to political participation, there still exist large differences in voting and political representation based on race, ethnicity, education, and income. Compared to many other states, Virginians have relatively limited opportunities to practice direct democracy. Declining voting rates, which mirror similar trends nationwide, present challenges to the legitimacy of our democratic political institutions. However, these trends also provide opportunity for Virginia in the twenty-first century to continue to expand opportunities for self-governance to citizens across the Commonwealth.

Key Concepts

Conventional participation	Recall
Franchise	Reconstruction
Gerrymandering	Redistricting
Incumbent	Referendum
Initiatives	Register
Jim Crow laws	Representative democracy
Primary elections	Suffrage
Public opinion	Unconventional participation
Reapportioned	

Suggested Resources

- http://www.sbe.virginia.gov: Find out where and when to vote, what's on your ballot, and more by visiting the **Virginia State Board of Elections** website.
- http://redistricting.dls.virginia.gov/2010/: Read more about Virginia's redistricting process at the **Division of Legislative Services.**
- http://www.quinnipiac.edu/institutes-centers/polling-institute/: **Quinnipiac University's Polling Institute** surveys citizens around the Commonwealth and across the country on a variety of policy and government-related topics.
- http://www.sentencingproject.org/template/index.cfm: To see how felony voting laws compare across the states, visit the **Sentencing Project.**
- http://www.rockthevote.com: **Rock the Vote** tries to empower young people through the voting process.

Notes

1. "Black Voting Rights: The creation of the Fifteenth Amendment," *HarpWeek*, http://15thamendment.harpweek.com/HubPages/CommentaryPage.asp?Commentary=03 Ratification.

2. Thomas R. Morris and Neil Bradley, "Virginia," in Quiet Revolution in the South: The Impact of the Voting Rights Act 1965–1990, ed. Chandler Davidson and Bernard Grofman (Princeton, NJ: Princeton University Press, 1994), 272.

3. *Virginia v. U.S.*, 420 U.S. 901 (1975). U.S. Supreme Court Center. http://supreme .justia.com/cases/federal/us/420/901/case.html.

4. "Virginia Constitutional Convention 1901," Virginia Center for Digital History, accessed October 19, 2011, http://www2.vcdh.virginia.edu/afam/politics/convention.html; *Encyclopedia Virginia*, "Virginia Constitutional Convention (1901–1902)," by Susan Breitzer, http://encyclopediavirginia.org/Constitutional_Convention_Virginia_1901-1902.

5. William Bryan Crawley, Jr., *Bill Tuck: A Political Life in Harry Byrd's Virginia* (Charlottesville, VA: University Press of Virginia, 1978), quoted in http://www.virginiaplaces .org/government/byrdorg.html.

6. Thomas R. Morris and Larry Sabato, "Politics: Stability and Change," in *Virginia Government and Politics: Readings and Comments* (Charlottesville, VA: Weldon Cooper Center for Public Service, University of Virginia, 1998), 44; V. O. Key, Jr., "Virginia: Political Museum Piece," in *Southern Politics in State and Nation* (New York: Alfred A., Knopf, 1949).

7. "Voting Rights," Virginia Historical Society, http://www.vahistorical.org/civilrights/ vote.htm.

8. Sandra G. Treadway, "A Lady's Place Is in the House (of Delegates): Virginia Women and Politics, 1909–2009," in *Governing Virginia*, ed. Anne Marie Morgan and A. R. "Pete" Giesen Jr. (Boston: Pearson, 2012), 85.

9. *Encyclopedia Virginia*, s.v. "Woman Suffrage in Virginia," by Jennifer Davis McDaid, accessed February 25, 2012, http://www.EncyclopediaVirginia.org/Woman_Suffrage_in_ Virginia.

10. Scott Weaver, "Voting Rights Elusive for Ex-Felons," *C-Ville Weekly*, May 20, 2008, accessed February 5, 2008, http://www.c-ville.com/Voting_rights_elusive_for_ex_felons/# .UQhBz7-B2W8.

11. See Sally Balch Hurme and Paul S. Appelbaum, "Defining and Assessing Capacity to Vote: The Effect of Mental Impairment on the Rights of Voters," *McGeorge Law Review* 38, no. 4 (2007): 931–1014.

12. "Number of People by State Who Cannot Vote Due to a Felony Conviction: State Felon Disenfranchisement Totals, 2010," *ProCon*, http://felonvoting.procon.org/view.resource .php?resourceID=000287; Christopher Uggen, Sarah Shannon, and Jeff Manza, "State-Level Estimates of Felon Disenfranchisement in the United States, 2010," The Sentencing Project, July, 2012, http://www.sentencingproject.org/doc/publications/fd_State_Level_Estimates_ of_Felon_Disen_2010.pdf.

13. Scott Weaver, "Voting Rights Elusive for Ex-Felons," *C-Ville Weekly*, May 20, 2008, accessed February 5, 2008, http://www.c-ville.com/Voting_rights_elusive_for_ex_felons/# .UQhBz7-B2W8.

14. Olympia Meola, "1,100 Felons Regain Right to Vote During McDonnell's First Year," *Richmond Times Dispatch*, March 9, 2011, http://www.timesdispatch.com/news/felons-regain -rights-in-mcdonnell-s-first-year/article_3af78d7d-16a5-52af-bc89-68073f89b6fc.html.

15. "Toplines," *CNU/Times Dispatch*, December 2010, http://cpp.cnu.edu/pdf/Dec2010_ VA_Statewide_Toplines.pdf.

16. See Va. Code § 24.2-643. Qualified voter permitted to vote; procedures at polling place; voter identification. National Council of State Legislatures. "Voter Identification Requirements." http://www.ncsl.org/?tabid=16602#2011.

17. Laura Vozzella and Anita Kumar, "New Virginia Voter ID Law Expected to Face Less Opposition From DOJ Than Others," *Washington Post*, March 15, 2012,

http://www.washingtonpost.com/local/dc-politics/vas-new-voter-id-law-expected-to-face
-less-opposition-from-doj-than-others/2012/03/13/gIQAhpyPES_story.html.

18. Julian Walker, "Black Legislators Blast Voter Suppression Bills," *PilotOnline*, January 11, 2012, http://hamptonroads.com/2012/01/black-legislators-blast-voter-suppression-bills; Amir Vera, "Democrats, Republicans Battle over Voter ID Bills," *Loudoun Times*, February 24, 2012, http://www.loudountimes.com/index.php/news/article/democrats_republicans_battle_over_voter_id_bills/.

19. See http://www.justice.gov/crt/about/vot/misc/sec_4.php#bailout.

20. Brian McNeill, "Governor May Intend to Form Redistricting Commission," *Daily Progress*, December 7, 2010, http://www2.dailyprogress.com/news/2010/dec/07/governor -may-intend-form-redistricting-commission-ar-701376/.

21. Kenneth S. Stroupe, Jr., "Gerrymandering's Long History in Virginia: Will This Decade Mark the End?" *Virginia News Letter* 85, no. 1 (2009): 1–10, http://www.cooper center.org/publications/gerrymanderings-long-history-virginia-will-decade-mark-end.

22. Council of State Governments, *Book of the States* (Washington, DC: Council of State Governments, 2009), 320–321.

23. Anita Kumar, "Virginia GOP Scraps Plans for 'Loyalty Oath' on Primary Day," *Washington Post,* January 17, 2012, http://www.washingtonpost.com/blogs/virginia-politics/post/virginia-gop-scraps-plans-for-loyalty-oath-on-primary-day/2012/01/17/gIQAqKev6P_ blog.html.

24. Zoltan Hajnal and Paul Lewis, "Municipal Institutions and Voter Turnout in Local Elections," *Urban Affairs Review* 38, no. 5 (2003): 645–668, http://www.sbe.virginia.gov/cms/Statistics_Polling_Places/Registration_Statistics/voting_statistics.html.

25. Alexis de Tocqueville, *Democracy in America*, trans. Harvey C. Mansfeld and Delba Winthrop (Chicago: University of Chicago Press, 2000).

26. Zoltan Hajnal and Paul Lewis, "Municipal Institutions and Voter Turnout in Local Elections," *Urban Affairs Review* 38, no. 5 (2003): 645–668.

27. Mark Guarino, "Virginia Primary: Was It So Hard for Gingrich and Perry to Get on the Ballot?" *Christian Science Monitor*, December 26, 2011, http://www.csmonitor.com/USA/Politics/The-Vote/2011/1226/Virginia-primary-Was-it-so-hard-for-Perry-and-Gingrich-to -get-on-the-ballot.

28. Katherine Q. Seelye, "Gingrich's Ballot Miss Could Shake Voters' Confidence," *New York Times,* December 24, 2011, http://www.nytimes.com/2011/12/25/us/politics/gingrich -falls-short-of-signatures-needed-for-spot-on-gop-primary-ballot-in-virginia.html?_r=1.

29. Frank B. Atkinson, "Virginia in the Vanguard," in *Governing Virginia*, ed. Anne Marie Morgan and A. R. "Pete" Giesen Jr. (Boston: Pearson, 2012), 7–13.

30. "Ballot Measures Database," *National Conference of State Legislatures,* http://www .ncsl.org/legislatures-elections/elections-campaigns/ballot-measures-database.aspx.

31. "Recall of State Officials," *National Conference of State Legislatures*, June 6, 2012, http://www.ncsl.org/legislatures-elections/elections-campaigns/recall-of-state-officials.aspx.

32. Dave Forster, "Voters Recall Portsmouth Mayor James Holley," *PilotOnline*, July 14, 2010, http://hamptonroads.com/2010/07/voting-begins-recall-election-portsmouth-mayor? cid=ltst.

33. "A Look Ahead: Virginia 2012," *Washington Post*, http://www.washingtonpost.com/ wp-srv/special/local/virginia-2012-elections/index.html.

34. Statewide Toplines, *CNU/Times-Dispatch*, February 2012, http://www.cnu.edu/cpp/ pdf/Feb2012_VA_Statewide_Toplines.pdf.

35. Statewide Toplines, *CNU/Times-Dispatch*, December 2010, http://www.cnu.edu/cpp/ pdf/Dec2010_VA_Statewide_Toplines.pdf.

CHAPTER 4

OUTLINE

The Purpose of Parties

Party in the Electorate

Party as Organization

Party in Government

Virginia's Political Parties

Interest Groups

Conclusion

Organized Interests

Political Parties and Group Politics in the State Capital

Public input into the political process often occurs through voting and other forms of individual participation; however, *organized* groups play an incredibly important role in political life. In Virginia and throughout the United States, two prominent types of organized groups are political parties and interest groups. While the three branches of government—the legislature, the executive, and the judicial—make up the *formal* political institutions in Virginia, political parties and interest groups are often considered *informal* political institutions, underscoring their significance to politics and policymaking. While political parties and interest groups have distinct functions, both serve as **intermediary institutions**, linking the people to government and the government to the people. This chapter describes the roles of organized interests, their structure, and major policies regulating how they function in Virginia.

The Purpose of Parties

Political parties have a long history in the United States, dating back almost to the founding of the country. They serve to aggregate, or bring together, a wide variety of interests in order to influence the political process and policy outcomes. Since political parties play a variety of roles, political scientists often divide the functions of parties into three distinct but interrelated categories: party in the electorate, party as organizations, and party in government.[1]

Party in the Electorate

One of the primary functions of parties—and the key characteristic that separates them from interest groups—is the role they play in voting and elections. Political parties simplify voting choices for citizens through two related processes. First, political parties nominate candidates for political office and hold primaries to narrow the field of candidates who will run in a general election. It is much easier for voters to find out information about two or three candidates in a general election than about dozens. Second, candidates who are nominated by a political party run for election on that party's label. Many citizens identify more closely with the **ideology**—the beliefs and values about the relationship between government, the economy, and society—of one political party than another.[2] Even when voters do not know a lot about a particular person on the ballot, a party label can act as a sort of shorthand, giving them a rough sense of the candidate's values and policy positions. Candidates nominated by political parties for national, state, or General Assembly elections must be identified by party affiliation on ballots. At the local level, however, ballots are nonpartisan, regardless of whether or not the person seeking office is supported by a local political party. A failed bill introduced in the 2012 legislative session sought to require local ballots to include party labels.[3]

Political parties in Virginia (like in the United States) are "umbrella" organizations. They must try to appeal to a wide variety of citizens if they are to win elections. That is because most elections rely on a **single member plurality** system, where only one member is elected from a geographic area, and the person with the most votes wins. This system, also referred to as first-past-the-post, creates an incentive for people to organize themselves into two main parties—today the Democrats and the Republicans—and makes it difficult for third parties to play more than a minor role in government. In Virginia, citizens do not have to indicate their party preference when they go to vote. Voters are free to vote for one party for national office and another for state or local positions, commonly known as **split-ticket** voting. Voters can also cross over from one political party to another between elections and are a key target of party organizers who try to woo these "swing voters."

Some political scientists argue that American political parties are too weak and should follow a **responsible party model**. According to this view, "For the great majority of Americans, the most valuable opportunity to influence the course of public affairs is the choice they are able to make between political parties in the principal elections."[4] As such, parties should present clear choices to voters, voters should make decisions based on the substantive choices between parties, and parties should follow through with campaign promises by enacting these policies once elected and be held accountable by voters for their policy choices in subsequent elections.[5] How do our parties compare to this model? The majority of individuals running for public office do identify themselves as either Republicans or Democrats (at the state level only a small handful run as Independents; this is much greater at the local level because local elections—or at least local ballots—are nonpartisan). However, elections tend to be "candidate-centered," with office-seekers running as individuals rather than closely aligning themselves with party platforms. Once in office, representatives may also diverge from party platforms when making policy decisions. Finally, as shown in Chapter 3, voting rates are very low and citizens have limited knowledge about parties' policy decisions.

Party as Organization

Political parties in Virginia, as in the United States, are very decentralized, with national, state, and local representative organizations. Each has a good deal of discretion over how they organize and select key decision makers. State party committees define the party platform and determine what kind of mechanism—a primary or caucus—will be used to nominate candidates for *state* political office (see Chapter 3 for more on Virginia's primary structure). National committees make similar decisions about the organization of national elections, and county and city party committees determine the structure of local elections. While parties themselves used to nominate candidates for general elections, this role is now given to voters. Parties at all levels play a key role in helping raise money for candidates, organizing volunteers, and recruiting more would-be voters. State parties also hold meetings known as **party conventions**. There, delegates (nominated by local party organizations) meet to adopt the party's platform and to nominate candidates to the national convention.*

Party in Government

Political parties also help organize government so that elected officials can enact policies. Within the General Assembly, party leadership makes committee appointments and holds caucuses to build consensus among party members (see Chapter 5 for more on the committee structure and legislative party leadership). Additionally, new laws have to pass through both the House and Senate and be signed by the

---

* For example, in June 2012 the State Convention of the Republican Party of Virginia met in Richmond to elect thirteen at-large delegates and thirteen at-large alternate delegates to the Republican National Convention; nominate two electors at-large to be voted for in the November presidential election; elect a state party chairman; nominate a national committeeman and national committeewoman; and conduct other party business. Since state political parties can structure their party organizations as they see fit, there are differences in the party convention and nominating structures. The Democratic Party of Virginia's Party and Delegate Selection Plan calls for the election of fourteen pledged party leaders and elected official delegates, twenty-three at-large delegates, two at-large alternates to the Democratic National Convention, two Democratic electors, and chose four members (two men and two women) to represent Virginia in the Democratic National Committee.

governor. Parties in government can act as a bridge between these different political institutions. Communication between branches is important in unified government (when the same party holds power in the General Assembly and the governorship) but especially to build bipartisan consensus when there is **divided government**. This occurs when one party controls the legislature and another controls the executive. One consequence of affording political parties such a key role in government is heightened partisanship, which can result in policy deadlock. Many people—citizens and elected officials alike—express frustration with the divisiveness that comes from opposition factions within government, both in Virginia and at the national level.

Virginia's Political Parties

Political parties in Virginia have largely reflected national-level parties. Those historically successful parties found across the country—the Whigs, Democrats, Republicans, Libertarians—also took root in the state. However, others are unique to Virginia and reflect the state's particular history. For example, the Readjuster Party (also called the Readjuster-Republicans) developed in the aftermath of the Civil War to try to compel creditors of war (and prewar) debt to reduce the amount owed by the state (and therefore by taxpayers). Primary opposition to the Readjusters came from the Funders Party, which argued that the taxpayers had a responsibility to repay the state's debt. The Readjustment Party also sought progressive taxation policies, expanded access to education, and extended universal suffrage and other rights for black Virginians. The party gained significant power in state government between 1879 and 1883, winning the governorship and, through a coalition of black and white Republicans and white Democrats, controlled the General Assembly. Readjusters even won two U.S. Senate seats and a majority of U.S. congressional districts.[6]

As the Readjuster Party broke down, the Democrats rose to power. Between the turn of the century and the mid-1960s, the Democratic Party completely controlled Virginia politics. In the first half of the twentieth century, the state had seventeen Democratic governors in a row. At the national level, a majority of Virginians voted for the Democratic candidate in twelve of thirteen presidential elections, and Democrats won all twenty-five races for the U.S. Senate during the period.[7] At the beginning of the 1960s, not only was the governor a Democrat, but there were only six Republicans in the entire General Assembly, and they made up just two of Virginia's twelve members of Congress.[8]

Democratic Party success in Virginia was maintained through the Byrd Organization, a highly successful **political machine**—a group that controls the party activities—that dominated state politics for more than half a century. While most states had prominent political machines, V. O. Key wrote, "Of all the American states, Virginia can lay claim to the most thorough control by an oligarchy."[9] The Byrd Organization controlled voting through voter suppression

BOX 4.1 The Influence of Harry Byrd Sr. and the Byrd Organization

Governor Harry F. Byrd

Harry F. Byrd (1887–1966) was a Virginia politician who headed the state's Democratic political machine that dominated state politics for nearly half a century. Byrd was first elected chairman of the Virginia Democratic State Central Committee in 1922, served as governor from 1926 to 1930, and served as a U.S. senator from 1933 until 1965. His influence on Virginia politics remains unparalleled.

The Byrd Organization, which got its name from the vast political network headed by Byrd, was not the first of its kind in the state. It was preceded by the Martin Organization, named after U.S. Senator Thomas Martin. Martin helped create the Democratic Party machine in Virginia that wrested state political control from Republican and Readjuster Party dominance. Like its predecessor, the Byrd Organization emphasized fiscal conservatism and limited voting rights. It largely drew its support from white, conservative voters, who were attracted to Byrd's commitment to low taxes and strong opposition to issuing state bonds to fund road construction projects (a system referred to as "pay as you go"). However, Byrd is perhaps best known for spearheading the policy known as "massive resistance," actively opposing racial integration in the aftermath of the 1954 *Brown v. Board of Education* decision.[10]

Unlike many other urban political machines of the era, the Byrd Organization did not rely as heavily on **patronage** (exchanging goods, services, and jobs for political support) or on political corruption for personal financial gain. Byrd himself referred to the party as a "loose organization of friends." This network of "friends," which was strongest in the rural areas of Virginia, relied on "courthouse cliques" that often included the sheriff, Commonwealth attorney, clerk of court, county treasurer, and commissioner of revenue. The General Assembly appointed county judges, who reserved local political appointments to those loyal to the Byrd Organization. Appointed and elected officials made sure there was high voter turnout among party faithful by helping them register to vote and paying their poll taxes. While governor, Byrd also ushered through constitutional amendments that reduced the number of statewide elected officials from eight to three (governor, lieutenant governor, attorney general). This change centralized political control and reduced the ability of potential political challengers to develop statewide political bases of their own.[11]

In the late 1950s and 1960s, U.S. Supreme Court rulings overturned many of the mechanisms used by the Byrd organization to suppress the franchise, weakening the regime's hold over the electorate (see Chapter 3). Support for the organization's platform also waned with population growth, especially from the impact of people moving from out of state to northern Virginia. Many of these new voters wanted the government to invest in infrastructure, health care, and public schools, which were incompatible with the Byrd Organization's fiscal policies.[12] However, the Byrd legacy continues to be felt in Virginia in the twenty-first century. Economic and political disparities persist from prolonged racial segregation. Changes to the state constitution under Byrd's governorship influence state politics by limiting the power of the electorate and making it more difficult to cultivate candidates for national office.[13] Finally, the conservative philosophy embraced by the Byrd Organization—especially a low tax rate and relatively limited spending on social services—continues to resonate with many Virginians today.

and controlled political appointments. Box 4.1 describes the Byrd Organization in more detail.

Under the guidance of Harry Byrd, Virginia Democrats pursued an agenda committed to low taxes and opposed to deficit financing and labor unions. The party attempted to maintain racial segregation throughout society and adopted a policy of "massive resistance" in the face of judicial rulings that ordered public school integration.[14] Byrd criticized the national Democratic Party for being too liberal especially on issues of civil rights, labor unions, taxation, and social service provision. The distinction between state and national party politics was evident in voting patterns, with many Virginias continuing to support Virginia Democrats but shifting allegiance to Republican candidates at the national level, which was quickly becoming the more conservative party. Between 1948 and Obama's victory in 2008, a majority of Virginia voters had supported the Republican candidate for president in all but one election (the 1964 contest between Johnson [D] and Goldwater [R]). In fact, the design of the Virginia ballot intentionally encouraged split-ticket voting. State law prohibited listing a candidate's party affiliation, making it easier for voters to choose Democrats for state and local office and a Republican for the presidency. Virginia was the last state to eliminate party identification bans, and by the time a Republican-controlled legislature did so in 2000, state and national party ideology had aligned.[15]

The Virginia Republican Party experienced resurgence after World War II. National legislation and judicial ruling that strengthened black civil rights hastened the dissolution of Democratic Party dominance. In particular, the repeal of the poll tax and literacy tests incorporated not just blacks but also poor whites into the active electorate.[16] As the party splintered over whether to try to recast themselves to attract these new voters, many white conservatives abandoned the Democrats in favor of the Republican Party, while the Democratic Party shifted to the left (though it was not until the late 1980s that a clear majority of southern whites identified with the Republican Party).[17] This **party realignment** (when popular support switches from one party to another) mirrored a similar trend throughout the South. Republicans gained new voters from both shifts in party loyalty and new conservative voters moving to Virginia.[18]

In the 1970s, the Republicans became the majority party in the state, and in 1980, "the Democratic Party had attained the dubious distinction of having the worst continuous record of defeats of any state Democratic Party in the nation."[19] However, during the next decade, Democrats gained back some of their power, and beginning in the 1990s, serious competition between the two parties began. Today, Virginia has a strong and competitive two-party system. The state was a battleground for the Obama-McCain presidential race in 2008 and again in 2012 when Obama beat Romney by just 2 percentage points. According to a 2011 Gallup Poll, Virginia and Mississippi were "the most balanced states politically" (evenly divided between Republicans and Democrats).[20] Still, in state-level elections that same year, Virginia swung to the right, with the state Grand Old Party (GOP) gaining an even larger majority in the House of Delegates and control of the state Senate (see Table 4.1, Party Control of Virginia Government).

TABLE 4.1 Party Control of Virginia Government

| | Executive | | General Assembly | |
| | Governor | Lieutenant Governor | State Senate | House of Delegates |
Year				
1992	Democrat	Democrat	Democrat (22 D, 18 R)	Democrat (52 D, 47 R, 1 I)
1994	Republican	Democrat	Democrat (22 D, 18 R)	Democrat (52 D, 47 R, 1 I)
1996	Republican	Democrat	Split (20 D, 20 R)	Democrat (51 D, 48 R, 1 I)
1998	Republican	Republican	Republican (21 R, 19 D)	Republican (52 R, 47 D, 1 I)
2000	Republican	Republican	Republican (22 R, 18 D)	Republican (64 R, 34 D, 2 I)
2002	Democrat	Democrat	Republican (23 R, 17 D)	Republican (52 R, 47 D, 1 I)
2004	Democrat	Democrat	Republican (24 R, 16 D	Republican (61 R, 37 D, 2 I)
2006	Democrat	Republican	Republican (23 R, 17 D)	Republican (58 R, 38 D, 3 I)
2008	Republican	Republican	Split (20 R, 20 D)	Republican (54 R, 44 D, 2 I)
2010	Republican	Republican	Democrat (22 D, 18 R)	Republican (58 R, 39 D, 2 I)
2012	Republican	Republican	Republican (split 50-50 but Lieut. Governor can break tie)	Republican (67 R, 32 D, 1 I)

In recent years, the emergence of the **Tea Party** in Virginia has influenced state party politics. While not a formal party (i.e., its candidates for office generally run as Republicans or Independents), "Tea Party Patriots" have helped to secure the electoral success of more conservative candidates and moved Republican policies further to the right. However, this has not been without cost to party unity, adding to the tension between those on the right endorsing limited government and those who want to use government to support a particular view of morality.

While there may be some division *within* state parties, there are even more significant differences *between* the two major political parties. The Republican and Democratic Party platforms diverge over both political values and policy objectives. According their 2011 platform, the Republican Party of Virginia is dedicated to "common-sense conservative values and principles." This includes lower taxes, less and smaller government, personal responsibility, protection of life, empowering families, and defending freedom and liberty.[21] The state's Democrats, on the other hand, are committed to restoring economic security for Virginia's families, ensuring affordable, quality health care for all, preserving Virginia's world-class public education system, preserving Virginia's natural resources, celebrating diversity and community, ensuring fair elections, and finding solutions to transportation needs.[22] More on the parties' ideological positions can be found in Box 4.2.

Not surprisingly, the two major political parties attract different kinds of citizens. An examination of 2012 polling data reveals that Virginians who voted for Obama were younger and more liberal than those who voted for Romney. Democrats were also the more likely choice for voters who are minority, urban, or lower income. Conversely, citizens who are older, white, wealthy, and evangelical were more likely to cast their vote for the Republican Party. Box 4.3 provides a more detailed look at differences in voter characteristics.

Interest Groups

Similar to political parties, interest groups are groups of like-minded individuals who join together to try to influence government. Unlike parties, however, interest groups do not nominate people to run for office, nor do candidates run on an interest group label. While political parties look to a broad base for support and seek to incorporate diverse interests under the party umbrella, interest groups generally represent more narrowly defined concerns. Although much more attention is paid to the activities of interest groups at the national level, they also play a prominent role in Virginia politics and policymaking.

Interest groups perform a number of tasks central to democratic societies and provide a means for connecting citizens to government. While they are not always politically active, interest groups provide a vehicle for political participation. As associations of like-minded citizens, they magnify the voices of individuals so that government will respond to their interests. Interest groups also play an important role in educating citizens about the issues facing the Commonwealth, and many help organize people for political action. During elections, interest groups often mobilize voters to go to the polls. Finally, interest groups can act as a watchdog by following government activities and monitoring public programs.

While all of the above are *indirect* ways of influencing government, the role citizens most associate with interest groups is **lobbying**, when interest groups try to *directly* influence government action. According to Virginia law, lobbying involves (1) influencing or attempting to influence executive or legislative action through oral

BOX 4.2   Differences in Virginia Political Party Values

How do the two major political parties differ in Virginia? The Virginia Republican Party "Creed" states:

> We Believe: That the free enterprise system is the most productive supplier of human needs and economic justice, that all individuals are entitled to equal rights, justice, and opportunities and should assume their responsibilities as citizens in a free society, that fiscal responsibility and budgetary restraints must be exercised at all levels of government, that the federal government must preserve individual liberty by observing Constitutional limitation, that peace is best preserved through a strong national defense, that faith in God, as recognized by our Founding Fathers is essential to the moral fiber of the Nation.[23]

Key Republican Party policy positions include supporting the Constitutional right to keep and bear arms, establishing English as the official language of the United States, strengthening immigration and border control, improving science and math education, providing tax credits for alternative energy sources, increasing oil drilling and refineries in the United States, eliminating the death tax, lowering corporate tax rates, and expanding public private partnerships.[24]

The Virginia Democratic Party's "Statement of Common Purpose" reads:

> The Democratic Party of Virginia is united in its efforts to elect Democratic leaders of character, integrity, ability, vision, and commitment to delivering results for Virginians. The Democratic Party of Virginia is the party that commits to delivering fiscal responsibility, ensuring excellence in education, reinvesting in our infrastructure, preserving a social safety network, providing accessible healthcare and creating economic opportunity for all Virginians. We are dedicated to protecting our inalienable rights and constitutional freedoms that provide us the opportunity to improve the lives of others. We will work to elect leaders that will provide change through leadership that is both commonsense and results-oriented. As Democrats we know there is more that unites us rather than divides us. Working together, we make this Commonwealth and nation a stronger and better place for all.[25]

Some policy positions linked to the Democratic Party platform include creating jobs, advancing early education, improving infrastructure, reducing fraudulent mortgage brokers and lenders (by providing accurate disclosure to homebuyers), supporting the right of workers to form bargaining units and equal pay for equal work, fulfilling No Child Left Behind and supporting fair compensation for teachers, preserving natural resources and farmland, investing in new energy, promoting equal rights for women, expanding services and funding for disabled Virginians, supporting domestic partnership benefits, expanding use of alternative modes of transit and smart growth initiatives.[26]

Which party better represents your beliefs?

BOX 4.3 Presidential Party Vote by Selected Voter Characteristics, 2012 Virginian Exit Polls

Not surprisingly, decisions about who to vote for vary by party identification and ideology. But did you know that voting patterns are also associated with gender, age, race, education, income, religious identification, geography, and a voter's policy priorities?

Voter Characteristics	Party Identification		
Vote by Sex	**Democrat**	**Republican**	**Independent**
Male	47%	51%	2%
Female	54%	45%	1%
Vote by Age	**Democrat**	**Republican**	**Independent**
18–29	61%	36%	3%
30–44	54%	54%	1%
45–64	46%	53%	1%
65 +	46%	54%	N/A
Vote by Race	**Democrat**	**Republican**	**Independent**
White Men	34%	64%	2%
White Women	40%	59%	1%
Black Men	91%	9%	–
Black Women	95%	4%	1%
Latino Men	–	–	–
Latino Women	–	–	–
All Other Races	63%	36%	1%
Ideology	**Democrat**	**Republican**	**Independent**
Liberal	92%	7%	1%
Moderate	56%	42%	2%
Conservative	11%	87%	2%
Vote by Party Identification	**Democrat**	**Republican**	**Independent**
Democrat	94%	6%	–
Republican	5%	94%	1%
Independent	43%	54%	3%

(Continued)

BOX 4.3 (Continued)

Voter Characteristics	Party Identification		
Vote by Education	Democrat	Republican	Independent
HS Grad	49%	50%	1%
Some College	47%	51%	2%
College Grad	48%	50%	2%
Postgrad	57%	42%	1%
Vote by Income	Democrat	Republican	Independent
Under $50,000	60%	38%	2%
$50–100,000	46%	53%	1%
$100,000 +	47%	51%	2%
"White Evangelical/ Born Again"	Democrat	Republican	Independent
Yes	17%	83%	N/A
No	64%	35%	1%
Size of Place	Democrat	Republican	Independent
Urban	64%	35%	1%
Suburban	49%	50%	1%
Rural	45%	54%	1%
Most Important Issues	Democrat	Republican	Independent
Foreign Policy	N/A	N/A	N/A
Deficit	28%	69%	3%
Economy	46%	52%	2%
Health Care	78%	22%	N/A

Source: http://www.cnn.com/election/2012/results/state/VA/president.

or written communication with an executive or legislative official, or (2) solicitation of others to influence an executive or legislative official.[27] Although lobbyists work to benefit their clients and their members, lawmakers also benefit from lobbying and often rely on interest groups for information. This is particularly the case in citizen legislatures like the Virginia General Assembly, where legislators are in office for a limited time and have few staff. Lobbyists can provide information about the scope and magnitude of problems as well as analysis of how proposed polices will impact their constituents. They may even help draft new proposals for consideration before the General Assembly.

The number of registered lobbyists in Virginia has grown dramatically over the past two decades. The ratio of lobbyists to state representatives is now 52:1 in the Virginia Senate and 21:1 in the House of Delegates (see Figure 4.1, The Growth of Lobbyists in Virginia). This proliferation in lobbying reflects the large growth in interest groups across the United States over the last half century. However, Virginia has a relatively high number of registered lobbyists when compared with other states (Figure 4.2). In part, this could be due to the diversity of the Commonwealth, where citizens have a wide variety of needs and competing ideas about government and public policy. Variation in lobbying can also reflect differences in state laws regarding interest group activities.

States have unique lobbying regulations concerning registration costs, disclosure of activities and expenses, giving gifts to public officials, campaign finance donations, and more. Such laws are designed to make the influence of lobbyists more transparent in order to balance their particular goals with the public interest. In Virginia, all lobbyists must register with the Virginia secretary of state, who maintains a database of registered lobbyists. Unlike a number of states, Virginia does not require lobbyists to wear name badges to distinguish them at the state house (fourteen states currently require name badges, and four states encourage the practice). Lobbyists represent a wide variety of interests in the Commonwealth, including business and corporate interests, unions,

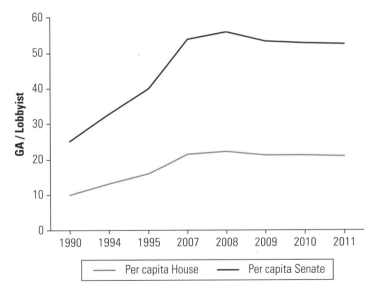

FIGURE 4.1

The Growth of Lobbyists in Virginia

Source: Data obtained from Secretary of Commonwealth, Lobbyist Registration Database, http://www.commonwealth .virginia.gov/stategovernment/Lobbyist/lobbyist.cfm.

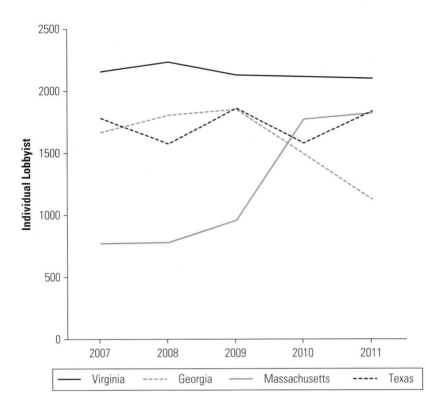

FIGURE 4.2

Comparison of Lobbyists by State, 2007–2011

Source: Virginia: Secretary of the Commonwealth of Virginia, Lobbyist Registration Database, http://www.commonwealth
.virginia.gov/stategovernment/Lobbyist/lobbyist.cfm; Massachusetts: Secretary of the Commonwealth of Massachusetts,
Public Records Division, Lobbyist Registration Database, http://www.sec.state.ma.us/LobbyistPublicSearch; Georgia:
Georgia Government Transparency and Campaign Finance Commission, Lobbyist Reports, http://media.ethics.ga.gov/
search/Lobbyist/Lobbyist_ByName.aspx; Texas: Texas Ethics Commission, Lobby List and Reports, http://www.ethics
.state.tx.us/dfs/loblists.htm.

environmental groups, civil rights advocates, and consumer and public interest
groups. The Virginia Municipal League lobbies state officials on behalf of cities, counties, and towns throughout the state. Interest groups representing health
care (hospitals, nursing homes, insurance) and other businesses greatly outspend
other lobbyists (see Figure 4.3).

Elected officials are not the only target of interest group action. Some groups also
try to influence the rules and regulations issued by public agencies. Political scientists have referred to the relationship between interest groups, administrative agencies, and lawmakers as an iron triangle, with interest groups attempting to benefit
from the policies being passed and implemented by government. Similarly, interest
groups also lobby the governor's office in order to influence favorable policy and

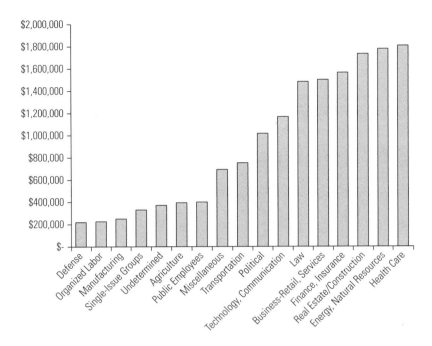

FIGURE 4.3

Spending by Major Interest Group

Source: "Top Donors," Virginia Public Access Project, http://www.vpap.org/donors/top_industries1?cmte_type_1=all &page=1&cmte_type_2=default.

funding decisions. Last, interest groups may seek to shape judicial rulings by sub-mitting *amicus curiae* (friends of the court) briefs in favor of one side of a case. For example, the Virginia Farm Bureau has submitted briefs in a variety of cases involving agricultural or environmental regulation. Additionally, a number of important civil rights cases have been filed and funded by groups such as the National Association for the Advancement of Colored People (NAACP).

Many citizens view these relationships suspiciously and are concerned about their influence in the political process. This is not a new concern; at the founding of the country, James Madison commented that such factions have interests "adversed [*sic*] to the rights of other citizens, or to the permanent and aggregate interests of the community."[28] Today, many people continue to be worried about the impact of interest groups, especially the uneven influence of groups with more money and resources. Others (including Madison himself) argue that such associations are the building blocks of diverse, pluralist democracies, where citizens have many interests and a belief in self-governance. Madison and others have also asserted that various groups will balance one another, so that no one group dominates political discourse. This argument has not, however, dampened criticism of interest groups.

The discomfort with interest group influence is perhaps greatest concerning the role of **political action committees** (PACs). A PAC is a committee formed by an interest group to raise money on behalf of a political candidate. Donations to political candidates are regulated by campaign finance laws, and states set their own policies for state and local elections. These include campaign contributions, spending by candidates, and disclosure of the funds they raise. Unlike at the national level, Virginia does not limit contributions to individual candidates, PACS, or political parties. However, groups cannot solicit or give money during the legislative session. Only three other states—Missouri, Oregon, and Utah—allow unlimited contributions. Businesses can make campaign contributions, but nonprofits and local governments cannot (employees can still make donations as private citizens).[29]

Although there are no limits on campaign contributions or spending by candidates, Virginia has strong state **disclosure** laws. The Commonwealth received an A minus from the Campaign Disclosure Project, ranking it number four in the nation.[30] David Poole, executive director of the Virginia Public Access Project, explains the rationale behind Virginia's campaign finance laws: "Contribution limits . . . tend to drive money into unregulated channels and make it more difficult for the public to understand who is underwriting campaigns."[31] Instead, if it is over $100, candidates, PACs, and parties have to say who they received money from and how they spent the money.

Candidates must raise a lot of money to have a competitive campaign. Even at the state level, it is expensive to run for office. In 2011, Ward Armstrong (D) and Charles Poindexter (R) each spent over a million dollars trying to win District Nine in southwestern Virginia. While not all races in the state cost this much, candidates still need to raise large sums of money to compete. To make running for office viable for more individuals, many states provide **public financing** in elections. Ten states provide public funding to candidates in statewide elections, and Hawaii, Minnesota, Nebraska, and Wisconsin also have provisions for funding state legislative elections. Virginia does not do either; however, citizens can donate up to $25 on their income tax forms to finance the political party of their choice and will receive an income tax credit for half of their contribution.[32]

Conclusion

In democratic societies, where public action is supposed to be linked to the will of its citizens, interest groups and political parties play an important role in connecting people to the government and government to the people. Though political parties have a more formalized role in governing, both help to keep citizens and politicians informed about public decisions, support and raise money for candidates, and attempt to influence policymaking to reflect the interests of their members. Interest groups and political parties have been criticized for being too divisive and for representing the interests of the few at the expense of the many. In the coming years, Virginians will continue to struggle with how to best balance competing interests in order to achieve compromise and effective governance.

Key Concepts

Disclosure

Divided government

Ideology

Intermediary institutions

Lobbying

Party conventions

Party realignment

Patronage

Political action committees (PACs)

Political machine

Public financing

Responsible party model

Single member plurality

Split-ticket

Tea Party

Suggested Resources

- http://www.vademocrats.org/: **Democratic Party of Virginia;** http://rpv.org: **Republican Party of Virginia**: Learn more about the two major political parties in Virginia.
- http://www.vpap.org/: The **Virginia Public Access Project** has a wealth of resources concerning lobbying regulations and the role of money in politics.
- http://www.campaigndisclosure.org/: Search for candidates and current issues and compare state campaign disclosure laws.

Notes

1. These categories were developed by V. O. Key Jr. in his 1962 *Politics, Parties, and Pressure Groups*, 4th ed. (New York: Crowell, 1962).

2. This is a very simplified definition; for a more nuanced view of political ideologies, see John Gerring, "Ideology: A Definitional Analysis," *Political Research Quarterly* 50, no. 4 (1997): 957–994.

3. VA House Bill 769, which was introduced by Delegate R. Steven Landes (R), was defeated 12–10 by the Committee on Privileges and Elections; Wesley P. Hester, "Voter ID Bills Decried by Democrats Advance," *Richmond Times-Dispatch*, January 28, 2012, http://www2.timesdispatch .com/news/2012/jan/28/tdmain05-voter-id-bills-decried-by-democrats-advan-ar-1645850/.

4. "Toward a More Responsible Two-Party System: A Report of the Committee on Political Parties," *American Political Science Review* 44, no. 3 (1950): 15, http://www.apsanet .org/~pop/APSA1950/APSA1950_Part2.pdf.

5. Austin Ranney, *The Doctrine of Responsible Party Government: Its Origins and Present State* (Urbana: The University of Illinois Press, 1954).

6. Charles Chilton Pearson, *The Readjuster Movement in Virginia* (New Haven, CT: Yale University Press, 1917); Harry Kollatz, Jr. "The Readjuster Party," *Richmond Magazine*, April, 2007, http://www.richmondmagazine.com/?articleID=96e5f9f789c1bc27c5913067badbc0a8.

7. Philip A. Grant, Jr., "Eisenhower and the 1952 Republican Invasion of the South: The Case of Virginia," *Presidential Studies Quarterly* 20, no. 2 (1990): 285–293. See also Thomas R. Morris and Larry Sabato, "Politics: Stability and Change," in *Virginia Government*

and Politics: Readings and Comments (Charlottesville, VA: Weldon Cooper Center for Public Service, University of Virginia, 1998), 44.

8. Thomas R. Morris and Larry Sabato, "Politics: Stability and Change," in *Virginia Government and Politics: Readings and Comments* (Charlottesville, VA: Weldon Cooper Center for Public Service, University of Virginia, 1998), 44.

9. Ibid., 44. Quote is attributed to Key as quoted in Stephen K. Medvic's, "Forging 'Debatable Ground': The Transformation of Party Politics in Virginia," in *Government and Politics in Virginia: The Old Dominion at the 21st Century*, ed. Quentin Kidd (Needham Heights, MA: Simon & Schuster, 1999), 83.

10. *Encyclopedia Virginia*, s.v. "Thomas Staples Martin (1847–1919)," by Ronald L. Heinemann, http://encyclopediavirginia.org/Martin_Thomas_Staples_1847-1919; ibid., s.v. "Byrd Organization," by Brent Tarter, http://encyclopediavirginia.org/Byrd_Organization.

11. Ira M. Lechner, "Massive Resistance: Virginia's Great Leap Backward," *The Virginia Quarterly Review* 74, no. 4 (Autumn 1998): 631–640; Frank B. Atkinson, *The Dynamic Dominion: Realignment and the Rise of Two-Party Competition in Virginia, 1945–1980* (Lanham, MD: Rowman & Littlefield, 2006); "The Byrd Organization," Virginia Places, http://www.virginiaplaces.org/government/byrdorg.html.

12. Ira M. Lechner, "Massive Resistance: Virginia's Great Leap Backward," *The Virginia Quarterly Review* 74, no. 4 (Autumn 1998): 631–640; Anne Marie Morgan and A. R. "Pete" Giesen Jr., eds., *Governing Virginia* (Boston: Pearson, 2012).

13. Vivian J. Paige, "The Byrd Machine's Continuing Influence," *PilotOnline*, February 16, 2011, http://hamptonroads.com/2011/02/byrd-machines-continuing-influence.

14. Ira M. Lechner, "Massive Resistance: Virginia's Great Leap Backward," *The Virginia Quarterly Review* 74, no. 4 (1998): 631–640.

15. "From a 'Museum of Democracy' to a Two-Party System in Virginia: The End of the Byrd Machine," Virginia Places, http://www.virginiaplaces.org/government/museum2party.html.

16. Thomas R. Morris and Larry Sabato, "Politics: Stability and Change," in *Virginia Government and Politics: Readings and Comments* (Charlottesville, VA: Weldon Cooper Center for Public Service, University of Virginia, 1998).

17. Wattenberg, Martin, "The Building of a Republican Regional Base in the South: The Elephant Crosses the Mason-Dixon Line," *Public Opinion Quarterly* 55 (1991): 425.

18. Stephen K. Medvic, "Forging 'Debatable Ground': The Transformation of Party Politics in Virginia," in *Government and Politics in Virginia: The Old Dominion at the 21st Century*, ed. Quentin Kidd (Needham Heights, MA: Simon & Schuster, 1999), 91.

19. Thomas R. Morris and Larry Sabato, "Politics: Stability and Change," in *Virginia Government and Politics: Readings and Comments* (Charlottesville, VA: Weldon Cooper Center for Public Service, University of Virginia, 1998), 39–40.

20. Jeffrey M. Jones, "State of the States: D.C., Hawaii Most Democratic, Utah Most Republican State in '11," Gallup Poll, August 11, 2011, accessed October 3, 2011, http://www.gallup.com/poll/148949/Hawaii-Democratic-Utah-Republican-State.aspx.

21. Republican Party of Virginia, "About RPV," accessed September 25, 2011, http://rpv.org/about.

22. Democratic Party of Virginia, "Party Platform," accessed September 25, 2011, http://www.vademocrats.org/party-platform.

23. Republican Party of Virginia, "RPV Creed," para. 1, accessed September 25, 2011, http://rpv.org/ node/269.

24. Ibid., "2008 Party Platform," http://www.rpv.org/node/272.

25. Democratic Party of Virginia, "Party Platform," Statement of Common Purpose section, para. 1, accessed September 25, 2011, http://www.vademocrats.org/party-platform.

26. Ibid., "Party Platform."

27. Virginia State Code § 2.2–419. http://leg1.state.va.us/cgi-bin/legp504.exe?000+cod+ 2.2-419.

28. James Madison, "Federalist, No. 10: The Union as a Safeguard Against Domestic Faction and Insurrection," *Daily Advertiser,* November 22, 1787, http://www.constitution .org/fed/federa10.htm.

29. David Bailey and Tom Hyland, "A Closer Look: The Role and Ethics of the Lobbyist" in *Governing Virginia*, ed. Anne Marie Morgan and A. R. "Pete" Giesen Jr. (Boston: Pearson, 2012), 107–111.

30. "The State of Disclosure in Virginia," *Grading State Disclosure 2008,* http://www.cam paigndisclosure.org/gradingstate/va.html.

31. David Poole, "Money in Virginia Politics," in *Governing Virginia*, ed. Anne Marie Morgan and A. R. "Pete" Giesen Jr. (Boston: Pearson, 2012), 221.

32. National Council of State Legislatures, "Public Financing of Campaigns: An Overview," January 6, 2010, http://test.ncsl.org/legislatures-elections/elections-campaigns41/ public-financing-of-campaigns-overview.aspx.

OUTLINE

Structure of the General Assembly

Lawmaking Power

Constituent Services

Judicial and Executive Oversight

 Impeachment Power

 Apportionment of State Legislators

Legislative Leadership and Party Control

A Profile of Virginia's Legislators

Conclusion

The Virginia General Assembly

Lawmaking in the Nation's First Legislature

Virginia's state legislature is the oldest representative body in the United States, tracing its founding to the House of Burgesses in Jamestown when it was still a young colony. Although it has undergone a number of changes—including its size, scope, and even location—since it was first established in 1619, the General Assembly remains a citizen legislature and is the seat of lawmaking in Virginia. Public opinion polls show that citizens tend to look more favorably upon lawmakers at the state level than those who work for the federal government. This is a trend that is certainly apparent in the Commonwealth. In fact, Virginians report more satisfaction with their state representatives than do citizens in many other states. In a 2011 poll conducted by Quinnipiac University, 47 percent of Virginians surveyed said that they approved of the job being done by the legislature (compared with 35 percent who expressed disapproval), making the General Assembly the only state legislature in the survey to get a positive approval rating![1] Still, others have criticized the part-time nature of the Virginia legislature, arguing that they do not have enough time, resources, or staff to function effectively.[2] This chapter takes a closer look at the structure, purpose, and composition of the nation's first legislature, the Virginia General Assembly.

BOX 5.1 The Virginia State Capitol

The General Assembly has met in its current location in Richmond since 1788, making it the second oldest working capital in the country (Maryland has the oldest). In addition to the legislature, the Capitol building, designed by Thomas Jefferson, initially housed a church, a courtroom, and the governor's office. From 1861 to 1865, the state legislature shared its home with the Congress of the Confederate States, which represented the thirteen southern states that had seceded from the Union.[3]

Structure of the General Assembly

The Virginia General Assembly is **bicameral**, meaning that it is divided into two lawmaking bodies: the Virginia House of Delegates and the Virginia Senate. Originally established as a unicameral institution, the legislature has been divided into two chambers since 1650. This is a feature shared by the U.S. Congress and by all state legislatures except Nebraska, which continues to have a unified body. This division of authority allows one house to act as a check on the other's power, so neither gets too strong. This is a consideration that has been important in a state like Virginia where many residents are wary of strong government. Although the Virginia Constitution stipulates that there must be a minimum of thirty-three state senators and ninety delegates, there are currently forty senators and one hundred delegates. There is a lot of variation in the number of representatives serving in state legislatures across the country. This difference is not just because of state population. For example, New Hampshire, a state with fewer residents, has 424 state legislators (twenty-four senators and four hundred House members!). Each of Virginia's one hundred state delegates represents 77,000 constituents, while each of the forty senators represents 193,000.[4] Decisions about legislative size involve a trade-off: a small body can more thoroughly discuss complex issues without everyone fighting to be heard. On the other hand, having more members enables each one to represent a smaller geographical area, thus, allowing them to better get to know their **constituents** (the citizens from the district that elected them). Differences in legislative size also partly reflect competing ideas about representation. Smaller legislatures often embody a view of elected officials as **trustees**, who should use their experience and wisdom to make decisions in the best interest of the public. In larger chambers, members can act like **delegates**, making decisions that are more closely tailored to preferences of those they represent. To some degree, we can still see these ideas inherent in the design and membership of the General Assembly's two chambers today, with the House clearly embodying the delegate model and the Senate resembling the trustee model.

The minimum qualifications for running for office in state legislatures are less restrictive than they are to run for Congress. Candidates to the House and Senate must be twenty-one years old, must be eligible to vote in Virginia, and must live in the district that they are representing. In order to avoid a conflict of interest, the Virginia Constitution also bars sitting judges, sheriffs, tax collectors, and U.S. government officials from holding legislative office.[5] Members in the Virginia House of Delegates serve two-year terms, while Senators hold their seats for four years. Virginia does not have legislative **term limits**; representatives can hold office as long as voters keep sending them back to Richmond. Sen. Charles J. Colgan currently holds the record for the longest serving senator in the state's history. In 2012, the eighty-five-year-old Democrat from Prince William County began his thirty-sixth year in the Virginia Senate.[6] That same year, eighty-four-year-old Del. Lacey Putney began his fifty-first year in the House.[7]

Unlike professional legislatures, where lawmaking is a full-time job, the General Assembly is a **citizen legislature**: representatives serve part-time and meet in Richmond to deliberate and craft Virginia's laws just a few months out of the year. The legislature convenes on the second Wednesday each January and meets for sixty days in even-numbered years and thirty days in odd-numbered years. The short session can be extended for an additional thirty days if approved by two thirds of the members of each house. Alternatively, the governor can also reconvene the legislature for a special session to consider bills that he has vetoed or returned for amendment.[8]

Number of Representatives

House: 100

Senate: 40

Salary

House: $17,640

Senate: $18,000

Members also get a stipend for food and expenses while in Richmond

Legislative Session

Odd years: 30 days

Even years: 60 days

Electoral Terms

House: 2 years

Senate: 4 years

No term limits

Partisan Makeup

House: 32 Democrats; 67 Republicans; 1 Independent

Senate: 20 Democrats; 20 Republicans

While this seems really short—especially compared with many other state legislatures—until 1971, the Virginia General Assembly met only for two months every two years! As the population of Virginia increased and society became more complex, the legislative session was extended. Lawmakers now meet on an annual basis in order to tackle the large amount of legislation they face.[9] Proponents of short legislative sessions assert that a condensed schedule helps to prevent lawmakers from passing significant amounts of legislation. Others like that it gives representatives more time to spend with constituents in their home districts, allowing them to be better connected with those they represent than in professionalized legislatures. Stressing cost savings and arguing that more qualified candidates might be willing to serve if the session was even shorter, Del. Frank Hall (a Democrat from Richmond) tried unsuccessfully in 2003 to further reduce the sixty/thirty-day sessions. However, critics of such short session lengths worry that lawmakers do not have enough time to study and to fully address the large number of bills before them. A more extensive legislative calendar would give lawmakers greater ability to check the power of the governor, who serves year round.[10]

In addition to a short legislative session, two other aspects common to part-time legislatures are relatively low pay and limited staff. Once these characteristics are taken into account, the Virginia General Assembly looks more like a **hybrid** of citizen and professionalized legislatures. Members of the Virginia House of Delegates earn a salary of $17,640 while Senators are paid $18,000. While this may seem low, remember that legislators are in session for just a month or two and most either have full-time jobs or are retired. Members also receive a per diem for lodging, meals, and other expenses while in Richmond. The speaker of the House receives additional compensation, with an annual salary of $36,321, and Virginia Senate leaders get an extra daily allowance for business-related expenses. In a number of states with part-time legislatures, compensation is much lower. In Utah, for example, state House and Senate members make $130 a day—$5,850 for a forty-five-day session—plus reimbursement for daily expenses. New Hampshire representatives earn just $200 for serving a similar term (forty-five days annually). While they get reimbursed for mileage, they are not given a per diem during the session. Compare this to professionalized, full-time legislatures in states, such as Pennsylvania and New York, where lawmakers earn nearly $80,000 plus expenses. At just over $95,000 plus a per diem, California legislators command the highest salaries in the country.[11]

Each member can also hire a year-round legislative aide to assist them in Richmond while in session and back in their home district office. Legislative leaders are given funding for extra staff support in order to help them with the complexities of their jobs (a discussion of these positions can be found at the end of this chapter). Committees are also assigned a staff person. Much of the administrative work in the Virginia House of Delegates and in the Virginia Senate is overseen by a clerk, who is elected by the members of each body. The clerks and their staff in the House and Senate clerks' offices are responsible for keeping records of legislative business (committee schedules, bill statuses, legislative histories, etc.), processing and preparing legislation, and much more.[12] The General Assembly's policymaking capacity is enhanced by the Virginia Division of Legislative Services, whose staff conducts legal research and drafts legislation (see Box 5.3, How Do They Do All That?). These abilities are further enhanced by work in legislative committees and year-round commissions.

Like most lawmaking bodies in the United States, the Virginia House of Delegates and Virginia Senate are further decentralized to committees and subcommittees, smaller bodies that examine the details of proposed legislation. Committees have a lot of power in shaping policy in Virginia. Once a bill is introduced in either chamber, it is referred to a committee based on subject area to hold hearings and debate and amend legislation. Bills must be referred out of committee before they can be voted on by the whole body. Committees have discretion over whether or not they report out or **table** (postpone) legislation; many bills die in committee, never making it to the House or Senate floor for a vote.

The Virginia General Assembly has four types of committees:

- *Standing committees* are permanent bodies that meet regularly while the legislature is in session (see text box for a list of current standing committees).
- *Joint committees* are made up of members from both the Virginia House of Delegates and the Virginia Senate.

BOX 5.3 **How Do They Do All That?**

Have you ever wondered how Virginia's delegates can know so much about so many different kinds of policies? They have help! Such assistance is particularly vital given the General Assembly's status as a citizen legislature. With such short legislative sessions and limited personal staff, having policy researchers to help analyze and craft Virginia laws is incredibly important.

Although most state legislatures have nonpartisan policy-research organizations that they rely on for policy-related information and advice, Virginia's **Division of Legislative Services (DLS)** is one of the oldest in the country. The DLS was first established in 1914 as the Legislative Reference Bureau (LRB) (thirteen years after the creation of the first LRB in Wisconsin), and placed within the office of the Virginia Attorney General.[13] The LRB was charged with drafting the legislation that delegates introduced into the General Assembly. As its mission grew to include the provision of legal services to support the General Assembly, the Virginia DLS was moved from the attorney general's office to the legislative branch and renamed the Division of Statutory Research and Drafting. In 1973, it was renamed once more, becoming the DLS.

Today, its staff provides legal and research support for the members of the Virginia House of Delegates and Virginia Senate, standing committees, and legislative commissions. When a legislator wants to introduce a new bill, staff at the DLS look at existing laws to avoid duplication, make sure that the proposal is constitutional, and then draft the bill for introduction in the legislature. The DLS also provides information to lawmakers, citizens, and the media about public records and the legislative redistricting process.

Legislators also rely on more than one hundred bipartisan **legislative commissions** that have been charged with studying a wide variety of issues that face the Commonwealth. A quick glance at some of these commissions reveals the diversity of the General Assembly's policymaking responsibilities. In 2012, for example, these included the Virginia Commission on Energy and Coal, the Virginia Foundation for Healthy Youth, the Small Business Commission, the Forensic Science Board, the Civics Education Commission, and the Military Advisory Council. Some commissions are primarily comprised of state delegates and senators while others include citizens appointed by members of the House and Senate.

- *Conference committees* are established on an ad hoc basis to work out differences between House and Senate bills.
- *Interim committees* work on important policy matters prior to the start of a legislative session.

Each legislator is assigned to more than one legislative committee. This division of labor enables lawmakers to get more done, develop expertise in particular policy areas, and to serve the interests of their constituents. In the Virginia House of Delegates, committee membership is decided by the Speaker of the House, while Senate committee assignments are determined by a majority vote of its members. Assignments are supposed to mirror the partisan makeup of the legislature as well as reflect the demographics and geographical distribution of congressional districts.

BOX 5.4 Standing Committees in the General Assembly

Standing Committees in the Virginia House

Appropriations

Agriculture, Chesapeake and Natural Resources

Commerce and Labor

Courts of Justice

Education

Health, Welfare, and Institutions

Finance

General Laws

Counties, Cities and Towns

Privileges and Elections

Rules

Transportation

Science and Technology

Militia, Police and Public Safety

Standing Committees in the Senate

Agriculture Conservation and Natural Resources

Commerce and Labor

Courts of Justice

Education and Health

Finance

General Laws and Technology

Local Government

Privileges and Elections

Rehabilitation and Social Services

Rules

Transportation

Lawmaking Power

As the state's legislative branch, the Virginia House of Delegates and the state Virginia Senate must work together to create laws that govern the lives of Virginians. Under the state's first constitution in 1776, only the Virginia House of Delegates had the power to originate legislation; the Senate would then approve, reject, or amend House proposals. The Senate's power over revenue bills was even more limited: it could approve or reject spending bills but could not offer revisions. In 1971, the Virginia Constitution was revised to allow both chambers to originate legislation.[14] Virginia's legislators have the power to enact any laws not specifically prohibited by the Virginia Constitution and to levy taxes to pay for these policies. One additional limitation facing all state representatives is that they cannot pass laws that conflict with powers granted to the federal government by the U.S. Constitution.

Despite a short legislative session, the General Assembly has a lot to accomplish. At the start of the 2012 session, more than 1,500 bills were introduced in the House of Delegates and 780 in the Senate. Many of these policies are examined in more detail in Chapter 11. Only a fraction of the proposals introduced each year will become law. With so many competing ideas and interests represented in the

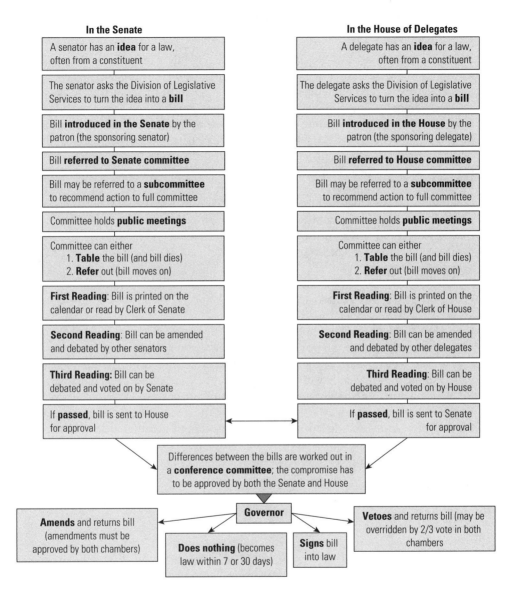

In the Senate

A senator has an **idea** for a law, often from a constituent

The senator asks the Division of Legislative Services to turn the idea into a **bill**

Bill **introduced in the Senate** by the patron (the sponsoring senator)

Bill **referred to Senate committee**

Bill may be referred to a **subcommittee** to recommend action to full committee

Committee holds **public meetings**

Committee can either
1. **Table** the bill (and bill dies)
2. **Refer** out (bill moves on)

First Reading: Bill is printed on the calendar or read by Clerk of Senate

Second Reading: Bill can be amended and debated by other senators

Third Reading: Bill can be debated and voted on by Senate

If **passed**, bill is sent to House for approval

In the House of Delegates

A delegate has an **idea** for a law, often from a constituent

The delegate asks the Division of Legislative Services to turn the idea into a **bill**

Bill **introduced in the House** by the patron (the sponsoring delegate)

Bill **referred to House committee**

Bill may be referred to a **subcommittee** to recommend action to full committee

Committee holds **public meetings**

Committee can either
1. **Table** the bill (and bill dies)
2. **Refer** out (bill moves on)

First Reading: Bill is printed on the calendar or read by Clerk of House

Second Reading: Bill can be amended and debated by other delegates

Third Reading: Bill can be debated and voted on by House

If **passed**, bill is sent to Senate for approval

Differences between the bills are worked out in a **conference committee**; the compromise has to be approved by both the Senate and House

Governor

Amends and returns bill (amendments must be approved by both chambers)

Does nothing (becomes law within 7 or 30 days)

Signs bill into law

Vetoes and returns bill (may be overridden by 2/3 vote in both chambers

FIGURE 5.1

How a Bill Becomes a Law in Virginia

Source: "How a Bill Becomes a Law in Virginia," The Virginia General Assembly, Capitol Classroom, http://capclass.virginia generalassembly.gov; Susan Clarke Schaar, "A Capitol Script: A Student Guide to Virginia's Legislative Process," The Senate Clerk's Office, October 2009, http://hodcap.state.va.us/publications/CapitolScript.pdf.

legislature, consensus on how to best solve our public problems can be difficult to achieve. The Virginia legislature generally relies on a process of majority rule; that means that fifty-one of the one hundred delegates and twenty-one of the forty senators must vote to pass a bill. Certain scenarios, however, require a **supermajority**: To override a governor's **veto** (rejection of a bill), two thirds of the members in each house must assent. New laws usually take effect July 1 of each year. However, some problems cannot wait that long for a solution. Legislators can pass emergency legislation that will go into effect as soon as it is signed by the governor. To do so, however, requires a four-fifths vote (eighty delegates and thirty-two senators)—even more agreement than overriding a veto.[15] Not only must a majority of the members in each chamber agree, but both the House and the Senate also have to pass bills with the exact same language. Halfway through each legislative session on crossover day the Virginia House of Delegates sends its bills to the Virginia Senate, and the Senate to the House, for consideration. Only once differences are resolved can a bill be sent to the governor to sign it into law or veto it. Even when the governor approves a policy, the Supreme Court of Virginia still has the power to overturn legislation if they think it conflicts with the state constitution (see Chapter 7). It's no wonder that the legislative process seems so complicated!

Constituent Services

Even though the General Assembly meets in Richmond for just a few months each year, legislators are busy at work in their **home districts** (the areas from where they are elected) for most of the year. Many hold town hall meetings, attend hearings, and meet individually with their constituents. Delegates and senators play a problem-solving function not just through lawmaking but also by helping citizens navigate state government. Such **casework** might include acting as a liaison with the Department of Taxation, answering questions about legislation, helping citizens navigate the voting process, or assisting former prisoners who are trying to secure a gubernatorial pardon. Casework inquiries can also provide impetus for elected officials to introduce new legislation.

Judicial and Executive Oversight

Although the powers of state government are separated into three branches—legislative, executive, and judicial—each has some overlapping responsibilities that allow them to check and balance the others. The General Assembly has some oversight of the state court system and administrative agencies in the executive branch. Legislators select judges, including to the Virginia Supreme Court (though when the legislature is not is session this responsibility falls to the governor). The General Assembly can also make laws regarding judicial compensation and plays a role in deciding court jurisdiction (this will be explored in more detail in Chapter 7).

Under the 1776 Virginia Constitution, the General Assembly appointed the governor. Today, the governor is independently elected by voters, but the legislature still has to confirm all positions appointed by the governor (see Chapter 6). Moreover, the power to approve the state's budget and funding for administrative agencies gives the legislature continuing influence over how laws are administered. The General Assembly's influence over the state's fiscal matters also comes from its election of the auditor of public accounts. The auditor, who is part of the legislative branch, provides oversight of state spending through the Joint Legislative Audit and Review Commission (JLARC). JLARC helps the General Assembly oversee policy and program implementation in the Commonwealth. The bipartisan commission's main purpose is to make sure that state and local agencies are using funds efficiently and effectively. It plays a primary role in government oversight and accountability by reviewing whether laws are working as intended and recommending ways to save money. JLARC membership includes nine members of the Virginia House of Delegates (at least five must be members of the House Appropriations Committee) and five members of the Virginia Senate (two from the Senate Finance Committee).[16]

Impeachment Power

The General Assembly has the power to impeach state officials for "offending against the Commonwealth by malfeasance in office, corruption, neglect of duty, or other high crime or misdemeanor." This includes the governor, lieutenant governor, attorney general, judges, members of the State Corporation Commission, gubernatorial appointees, and officials elected by the General Assembly. As at the national level, impeachment charges are levied in the House and prosecuted by the Senate.[17]

Apportionment of State Legislators

Members of the Virginia General Assembly are elected geographically from separate legislative districts. Each district corresponds with an electoral seat: one hundred in the Virginia House of Delegates, forty in the Virginia Senate, and eleven to choose members to the U.S. House of Representatives. Since the number of delegates and senators has been fixed by law, legislative districts must be redrawn every ten years to reflect changes in the state's population. Following the Supreme Court's ruling in *Reynolds v. Simms* (1964), electoral districts must be based on the size of the population in order to ensure the principle of "one man, one vote."[18] While racial **gerrymandering**—the process of drawing district lines based on the racial makeup of a district—is now unconstitutional, political gerrymandering still occurs. The **redistricting** process is extremely controversial. How district lines are drawn affect the nature of politics in the state by redistributing power among different political parties. Since the state legislature is responsible for drawing district maps in Virginia, new districts usually favor the party that holds the most power in the General Assembly.

Just like with bills, governors can veto redistricting plans with which they disagree. If the two elected branches cannot come to a consensus, district lines could be decided in state or federal courts. Because of a history of racial discrimination, Virginia's redistricting plans also have to be approved by the U.S. Department of Justice. The most recent redistricting occurred following the 2010 Census, which showed that Virginia's population had grown by 11.4 percent between 2000 and 2009. As a result, new districts were added in northern Virginia and representatives **reapportioned** to reflect demographic trends. In 2011, Governor Bob McDonnell appointed an independent redistricting commission to help facilitate a bipartisan agreement and to try to ensure public input in the redistricting process. Nevertheless, the legislature's redistricting maps were still subject to partisan stalemate, delay, and a failed citizen lawsuit before they were finally approved by the General Assembly in 2012 just in time for that year's elections.[19]

Legislative Leadership and Party Control

House and Senate leadership play the important role of coordinating the votes of the rank and file and organizing day-to-day activities in the legislature. Leadership positions are determined by political party control, with the majority party (the party with the most members) filling those that are most important. The most powerful of these positions is the **speaker of the Virginia House**, who is selected every two years by the majority party **caucus** (a meeting of legislative party members). The speaker serves as the presiding officer of the Virginia House of Delegates and also appoints members to the chamber's fourteen standing committees. An elected majority leader assists the speaker of the House in securing legislative support for the party's policy preferences. Similarly, the minority party caucus also elects a **minority leader** to organize members in pursuit of their own legislative agenda.[20]

The majority and minority leaders in the House have similar counterparts in the Senate. However, here, the roles of presiding officer and party leader are split in two. The president pro tempore governs daily procedures and is elected every four years by the majority party. The president pro tempore must be a senior senator and is typically the longest serving member in the chamber. The lieutenant governor serves as the presiding officer but can vote on bills only when there is a tie. After the 2011 election, the even split between Republicans and Democrats drew attention to this role, highlighting that it is not one that is well understood. Lt. Governor Bill Bolling, a Republican, argued that through his tie-breaking vote, he had the authority to give the GOP power to organize the Virginia Senate—including the appointment of committee members. Hoping to force a power-sharing arrangement between the two parties, Democratic caucus chairman Senator Donald McEachin filed a lawsuit to clarify the lieutenant governor's power over organizational issues.[21] Since the lawsuit was later withdrawn, the scope of his tie-breaking power remains unresolved. It is clear, however, that the lieutenant governor is not allowed to vote on the budget, taxes, election of judges, or constitutional amendments.[22] In the 2012 session, Lt. Governor Bolling cast twenty-eight tie-breaking votes (more than the total votes he made during his previous six years in office).[23]

A Profile of Virginia's Legislators

Potential candidates for the General Assembly must have the resources necessary to run and hold office, including adequate money and time to campaign, and, flexible schedules that allow them to be in Richmond two months a year. These factors provide informal constraints on the kinds of people who can run for and hold office. As a result, more than half of all state representatives in Virginia hail from just two occupations: 30 percent are lawyers, 18 percent are business executives, and 9 percent are retired.[24]

In 2011, the state of Virginia ranked thirty-eighth in the nation for the percent of female state legislators, with just eight women serving as state senators and nineteen as delegates.[25] For the 2013 session, these numbers declined to just six women in the Virginia Senate and eighteen in the Virginia House of Delegates. Ethnic and racial

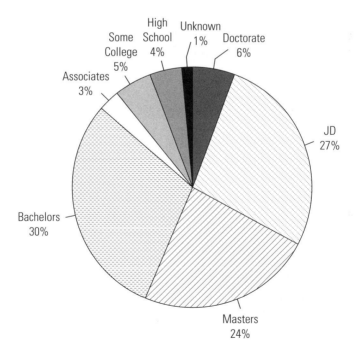

FIGURE 5.2

How Educated Are Virginia's Lawmakers?

Source: http://dela.state.va.us/dela/MemBios.nsf/MWebsiteTL?OpenView.

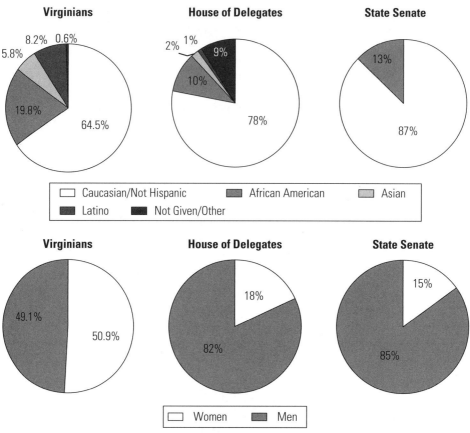

FIGURE 5.3

How Diverse Are Virginia's Lawmakers? Race, Ethnicity, and Gender in the General Assembly, 2013

Source: National Conference of State Legislatures, "Legislator & Legislative Staff Information," accessed January 22, 2013, http://www.ncsl.org/legislatures-elections.aspx?tabs=1116,113,782.

minorities are also underrepresented in both bodies, though the Senate is particularly homogenous. Compared with the demographic makeup of the state, Virginia's lawmakers do not seem very representative of the constituents they serve (see Figure 5.3, How Diverse Are Virginia's Lawmakers?). Does it matter? Many argue that **descriptive representation**—having elected officials who are similar to the people they serve in terms of gender, race, and socioeconomic status—is not as important as **substantive representation**—electing officials with similar policy views, regardless of their demographic profile. Others, however, worry that this gap could lead to policies that are out of touch with citizens needs and that the underrepresentation of women and minority groups results from persistent discrimination.

A Democrat from District Five (which includes parts of Chesapeake City, Norfolk City, and Virginia Beach City) in 1984, Yvonne Miller was the first African American woman to be elected to the Virginia House of Delegates. Then in 1988, she was the first African American women elected to the state Senate. Eight years later Senator Miller became the first woman to chair a committee in the Virginia Senate. She currently chairs the Transportation Committee and serves on the Commerce and Labor, Finance, Rehabilitation and Social Services, and Rules committees.

Conclusion

The General Assembly has gone through many changes since its beginnings four centuries ago. Still, the legislative branch maintains a primary role in state government. Virginia's delegates and senators are responsible for making the policies that impact citizens every day and represent their constituents when governing. Lawmakers can have a difficult job, representing people in a state as diverse as Virginia. Knowing more about what the General Assembly looks like, how the legislative process works, and the varied roles that our representatives play cannot only help you understand this important institution but also help citizens take a more active role for influencing the laws which govern the Commonwealth.

Key Concepts

Bicameral

Casework

Caucus

Citizen legislature

Constituents

Delegates

Descriptive representation

Division of Legislative Services (DLS)

Gerrymandering

Home districts

Hybrid legislature

Legislative commissions

Minority leader

Reapportionment

Redistricting

Speaker of the Virginia House

Substantive representation

Supermajority

Table

Term limits

Trustees

Veto

Suggested Resources

- http://virginiageneralassembly.gov: Discover who represents you in the Virginia General Assembly.
- http://lis.virginia.gov; or Richmond Sunlight: http://www.richmondsunlight .com: Track the status of bills and learn about new legislation through Virginia's Legislative Information System.
- http://capclass.virginiageneralassembly.gov/Middle/HowABill/HowABill .html: Examine more on how a bill becomes a law.
- http://www.ncsl.org: Compare state legislative structures and procedures across the country at National Council of State Legislatures.
- http://dls.virginia.gov/index.html: Find out more about the Virginia Division of Legislative Services.

Notes

1. "Virginia Voters Satisfied with State, but Not U.S., Quinnipiac University Poll Finds; Voters Support Nuclear Power Plants, Oppose I-95 Tolls," Quinnipiac University, October 12, 2011, http://www.quinnipiac.edu/institutes-and-centers/polling-institute/virginia/release -detail?ReleaseID=1659.

2. Catherine M. Banks, *The Commonwealth: A History of the Government and Politics of Virginia* (Boston: Pearson Learning Solutions, 2008), 91.

3. Susan Clarke Schaar, "A Capitol Script: A Student Guide to Virginia's Legislative Process," The Senate Clerk's Office, October 2009, http://hodcap.state.va.us/publications/CapitolScript.pdf.

4. Ibid.

5. Virginia Constitution, Article IV, Sec. 4.

6. "Colgan Is Virginia's Longest-Serving Senator: Prince William County Democrat Begins 36th Year of Service in General Assembly," NBC Washington, January 11, 2012, http://www.nbcwashington.com/news/politics/Colgan-Is-Virginias-Longest-Serving-Senator-137149338.html.

7. Anita Kumar, "John Warner Honors Del. Lacey Putney for 50 years of Service," *Washington Post, Post Local*, January 18, 2012, http://www.washingtonpost.com/blogs/virginia-politics/post/john-warner-honors-del-lacey-putney-for-50-years-of-service-i/2012/01/18/gIQAOS4Z8P_blog.html.

8. Virginia Constitution, Article VI, Sec. 6.

9. Thomas R. Morris and Larry Sabato. *Virginia Government and Politics: Readings and Cases* (Charlottesville, VA: The University of Virginia Weldon Cooper Center, 1990), 130.

10. Kathleen Murphy, "Legislatures Vary in Session Lengths," *Pew Charitable Trusts, Stateline,* January 9, 2003, http://www.pewstates.org/projects/stateline/headlines/legislatures-vary-in-session-length-85899393435.

11. "General Assembly of Virginia (101)," Virginia's General Assembly, Legislative Information System, http://lis.virginia.gov/cgi-bin/legp604.exe?111+bud+11-1+pdf; National Conference of State Legislators, "2012 State Legislator Compensation and Per Diem Table," 2013, http://www.ncsl.org/legislatures-elections/legisdata/2012-ncsl-legislator-compensation-data.aspx.

12. "Clerk of the Virginia House of Delegates and Keeper of the Rolls of the Commonwealth," n.d., http://house.state.va.us; "Clerk of the Senate of Virginia," 1995–2013, http://sov.state.va.us.

13. John A. Hird, *Power, Knowledge, and Politics: Policy Analysis in the States* (Washington, DC: Georgetown University Press, 2005).

14. Quentin Kidd and Connie Jorgensen, "The General Assembly: Coping with Change and Tradition," in *Government and Politics in Virginia: The Old Dominion at the 21st Century*, ed. Quentin Kidd (Needham Heights, MA: Simon & Schuster, 1999), 31.

15. Andrew Cain, "Va. Unlikely to Change Law to Allow Gingrich Write-In," *Richmond Times Dispatch*, December 26, 2011, http://www.timesdispatch.com/archive/va-unlikely-to-change-law-to-allow-gingrich-write-in/article_54f232d7-553f-5d09-a0ab-8118ed313b14.html.

16. Commonwealth of Virginia, Auditor of Public Accounts, "About the Auditor of Public Accounts," n.d., http://www.apa.virginia.gov/about_us.aspx; Joint Legislative Audit and Review Commission, "About JLARC," n.d., http://jlarc.virginia.gov/about.shtml.

17. Virginia Constitution, Article IV, Section 17.

18. While the Reynolds decision applied to legislative districts, the Supreme Court also ruled in *Avery v. Midland County* (1968) that the requirement for equal legislative representation also applied to local electoral districts. See *Avery v. Midland County*, 390 U.S. 474 (1968), *Justia, U.S. Supreme Court Center*, http://supreme.justia.com/cases/federal/us/390/474.

19. "Judge Dismisses Virginia Redistricting Suit," CBS, February 28, 2012, http://washington.cbslocal.com/2012/02/28/judge-dismisses-virginia-redistricting-suit; Anita Kumar, "Justice

Dept. Approves Virginia's Congressional Redistricting Plan," *Washington Post, Post Local*, March 14, 2012, http://www.washingtonpost.com/blogs/virginia-politics/post/justice-dept -approves-virginias-congressional-redistricting-plan/2012/03/14/gIQAXW1pCS_blog.html.

20. Council of State Governments, *Book of the States* (Washington, DC: Council of State Governments, 2009), 94.

21. Todd Allen Wilson, "Lt. Gov. Bolling Breaks Tie to Give GOP Senate Control: Dems Fail to Get Power Sharing Agreement, Issue in Courts," January 11, 2012, http://www.dailypress .com/news/politics/dp-nws-g.a.-2012-session-opens-20120111,0,5633723.story.

22. Jim Nolan, "Fight to Control Senate Highlights Start of Session," January 11, 2012, http://www2.timesdispatch.com/news/news/2012/jan/11/2/tdmain01-fight-to-control -senate-highlights-start–ar-1602333.

23. Josh Goodman, "Contention and Compromise in Virginia, Oregon Tied Chambers," *Pew Charitable Trusts, Stateline*, April 6, 2012, http://www.stateline.org/live/details/story?content Id=643855.

24. Other occupations include Consultant/Professional/Nonprofit (7.9 percent), K–12 Educators (5.7 percent), Medical (5.0 percent), Real Estate (4.3 percent), Business Owner (3.6 percent), Engineer/Scientist/Architect (2.9 percent), Business: Nonmanager (2.1 percent), College Educator (2.1 percent), Insurance (2.1 percent), Agriculture (1.4 percent), Accountant (0.7 percent), and Clergy (0.7 percent). See National Conference of State Legislatures, "Legislator Demographics: State-by-State," n.d., http://www.ncsl.org/default.aspx?TabId=18248.

25. "CAWP, Fact Sheet: Women in State Legislatures 2013," Center for American Women and Politics, Rutgers, State University of New Jersey, January 2013, http://www.cawp.rutgers .edu/fast_facts/levels_of_office/documents/stleg.pdf.

CHAPTER 6

OUTLINE

Virginia's One-Term Governor

Powers of the Office

The Governor as Party Head

   The Governor as Chief Budgeting Officer

   The Governor as Chief Appointer and Administrator

   The Governor as Spokesperson for the State

Life After Living in the Governor's Mansion

The Constitutional Executive Officers

The Office of Attorney General

Conclusion

Steering the Ship of the State

Executive Power in Virginia

Executive power in a state typically focuses on the right to managerial control, **appointment**, and fiscal power, as well as the right to issue executive orders. Executive power in a state is dependent upon the state's constitution. The scope of power authorized to governors must be in accordance with the state's constitution and is also influenced by tradition. As chief executives and state managers, governors use their power to serve as leaders of their state. They are responsible for implementing state law and controlling their state's executive branch. Virginia's governor shares many things in common with chief executives in other states but also elements of office that are quite unique.

Article V of the Virginia Constitution establishes the state's **executive branch** of government. There are only three officials elected statewide in Virginia beyond the positions for U.S. senator and U.S. president. These include the state's governor, **lieutenant governor,** and **attorney general**. Collectively, these positions and their agencies make up Virginia's executive branch of government. The governor serves as Virginia's **chief executive officer**. The lieutenant governor serves as the president of the Virginia Senate and is next in line should the governor be unable to perform the duties of the office. The attorney general and its office basically serves as the state's law firm. This chapter provides an overview of the structure, powers, and responsibilities of Virginia's executive branch.

Governor Bob McDonnell, the seventy-first governor of Virginia (*bottom right*), is pictured here shaking the hand of state delegate Scott Garrett (R-Lynchburg) at a press conference. He is accompanied by Lieutenant Governor Bill Bolling (*center right*) and Attorney General Ken Cuccinelli (*top right*). These three positions—governor, lieutenant governor, and attorney general—are the only elected statewide offices in the Commonwealth.

Virginia's One-Term Governor

The highest-ranking position of chief executive, or the state's **governor**, is filled every four years. Article V of the Virginia Constitution requires that to become governor an individual must be a citizen of the United States, a resident of Virginia for at least five years, and be at least thirty years of age.

Virginia is the only state in the United States that does not allow its governor to serve consecutive terms. In comparison, fourteen states as well as Puerto Rico and the Washington, D.C., mayor have unlimited terms. There is no constitutional restriction against serving nonconsecutive terms in Virginia; a sitting governor must sit out for four years before running again for office. See Table 6.1 below for a comparison of term limits by state.

During colonial times, the governor of Virginia was appointed by the King of England and served as the king's substitute, running the colony and serving until his retirement or death.[1] The "royal" governor was able to veto and automatically kill any measure of law, dispense land as he saw fit, enforce and interpret the royal policy of England, and appoint members of the General Assembly.[2] For well over a century, the governor of Virginia was able to exhibit considerable power and control over the colony. It was not until Virginia adopted its first constitution on June 29, 1776, that the structure of the Commonwealth's governance began to change.

The new constitution supported a one-year term for its governor, not to exceed three term years. According to the constitution at that time, the governor of Virginia "shall not continue in that office longer than three years successively, nor be eligible,

TABLE 6.1 Term Limits by State

States with *four-year terms* and *no restrictions* on reelection	Connecticut, Illinois, Iowa, Massachusetts, Minnesota, New York, North Dakota, Texas, Utah, Washington, Wisconsin, Wyoming
States with *four-year terms* and *restrictions* to serve only *two terms*	Alabama, Alaska, Arizona, Arkansas, California, Colorado, Delaware, Florida, Georgia, Hawaii, Idaho, Indiana, Kansas, Kentucky, Louisiana, Maine, Maryland, Michigan, Mississippi, Missouri, Montana, Nebraska, Nevada, New Jersey, New Mexico, North Carolina, Ohio, Oklahoma, Oregon, Pennsylvania, Rhode Island, South Carolina, South Dakota, Tennessee, West Virginia
States *with four-year terms,* but *consecutive reelection* is *prohibited*	Virginia
States *with two-year terms* and *no restrictions* on reelection	New Hampshire, Vermont

until the expiration of four years after he shall have been out of that office."[3] The governor was required to work alongside an eight-member Council of the State, elected by constituents and "shall, with the advice of a Council of State, exercise the executive powers of government, according to the laws of this Commonwealth; and shall not, under any pressure, exercise any power or prerogative, by virtue of any law, statute or custom of England."[4] This marked the end of England's tyranny over the colony and initiated the start of a great and independent Commonwealth, the Commonwealth of Virginia.

Today, the Virginia Constitution continues to support limiting the power and influence of its governor. The governor "shall be ineligible to the same office for the term next succeeding that for which he was elected and to any other office during his term of service."[5] Virginia remains the only state to not permit its governor to serve consecutive terms in office. In its early history, before the governorship took on the role it has today, the state had a number of multi-term governors. Patrick Henry held office from 1776 to 1779 and again between 1784 and 1786. Future U.S. president James Monroe served from 1779 to 1802 and again in 1811. George William Smith served twice, both for mere months, in 1811. William Smith served 1846 to 1849 and again from 1864 to 1865. James Monroe served in between Smith's terms. Multiple-term governors have become incredibly rare in modern times, though, with only Mills E. Godwin Jr. serving more than one term in the modern era (1966–1970 and 1974–1978).

Limiting the governor to a single consecutive term can severely limit the size and scope of the governor's agenda. While the term limitation restrains the ability of the governor to make a large policy footprint, the Virginia legislature meets for just

BOX 6.1 **The Country's Oldest Governor's Mansion**

Did you know that Virginia's "First House" is the oldest occupied governor's mansion in the United States? In 2013, the Executive Mansion will celebrate its 200th anniversary. The mansion was built during the War of 1812 and has served as the residence for all sitting governors since it opened its doors in 1813. Fifty-four families have called the mansion home since its completion. Open to the public at certain times throughout the year, the mansion also serves as a place for public and private events.

The Virginia governor's mansion, better known as the Executive Mansion.

Source: http://www.executivemansion.virginia.gov.

sixty days during even years and thirty days during odd years. This in turn gives the governor significant power, during the periods in which the state legislature is out of session, despite a limited term in office.

Powers of the Office

The governor of Virginia performs a variety of important functions. He or she is given the power to sign legislation, administer the state's **bureaucracy** including appointing cabinet secretaries and the heads of all state agencies, veto bills (which can be overridden by a two-thirds majority in both houses of the General Assembly), prepare the biennial state budget, and issue pardons. The governor has a number of administrative responsibilities. The chief executive is charged with ensuring that the Commonwealth's laws are faithfully executed; he or she acts as commander in chief of the armed forces and can use their services to repel invasion, suppress insurrection, and enforce the execution of laws. The governor is also charged with dealing with the state's foreign affairs and has the power to fill vacancies in all offices of the Commonwealth for which the Virginia Constitution and legislation make for no other provisions.

Although primarily tasked with the administration of government, the governor also plays an important policymaking role. However, it is sometimes difficult for the state's chief executive to carry out policy plans since the position is limited to one consecutive term. The governor does, however, have extensive power over appointments, legislation, and budgetary issues. Additionally, the short-term legislative period in the Commonwealth gives the governor more control over state issues year-round. One area, though, where the governor may actually lose some power is with the election of the lieutenant governor. In some states, the lieutenant governor is elected on the same ticket as the governor, but in Virginia, they are elected independently—meaning, they do not run on the same ticket. If the lieutenant governor hails from a different party, his or her role to oversee the state legislature may make it more difficult to negotiate on policy issues. If the lieutenant governor is of the same party, though, it can increase the power of the governor and his party in enacting policy.

Once legislation is introduced and passes through the General Assembly, the governor has numerous options. First, he or she may sign the bill into law or simply allow the bill to become law without his or her signature, assuming the legislature is in session. Second, if the legislative body is not in session, any unsigned bills are automatically vetoed. When the General Assembly is in session, the governor can **veto**, or reject, an entire bill. The governor's role in the budgetary process is significant—specifically the use of the **line-item veto** in appropriations bills. This grants the governor the power to remove certain appropriations to which he or she objects. The governor's veto can be overridden by a two-third majority vote in the General Assembly. According to the National Conference of State Legislatures, forty-four states give their governors some form of line-item veto power. Governors without veto power include the governors of Indiana, Nevada, New Hampshire, North Carolina, Rhode Island, and Vermont. Virginia's gubernatorial veto power with respect to major budget bills include vetoes for funding for a particular line item, funding for an entire program or agency, language accompanying an appropriation, language in a footnote or following an appropriation that explains how money should be spent, and provisions or contingency language on appropriation expenditure.

According to the Code of Virginia, the Virginia governor shall issue **executive orders** as the governor deems necessary. An executive order is not law per se but does have the "force and effect of law" and the violation of an executive law can be punishable as a Class 1 misdemeanor. As of spring 2012, Governor Bob McDonnell

BOX 6.2   **Governor McDonnell's Executive Order No. 38**

On August 23, 2011, a rare 5.8 magnitude earthquake and a series of aftershocks struck in central Virginia. According to the release by Governor McDonnell, the earthquakes constituted a disaster wherein human life and public and private property were imperiled, in which the health and general welfare of the citizens required the state to take action to help alleviate the situation.

The executive order allowed the state to allocate resources to areas in need of assistance. A number of other technical maneuvers were implemented to ease communication between agencies (the establishment of the Virginia Emergency Operations Center and the Virginia Emergency Response Team), provide funding assistance for restorations, and provide guidelines for carrying out certain elements of the relief plan.

Executive Order No. 38 was to run from August 23, 2011, until June 30, 2012, unless otherwise amended or rescinded by further executive order. The order was signed by the governor on August 31, 2011.

Source: http://www.governor.virginia.gov/PolicyOffice/ExecutiveOrders/viewEO.cfm?eo=38&pdf=yes.

had issued forty-three separate executive orders. See Table 6.2 for a comparison of number of executive orders issued by Virginia's most recent governors. Governor McDonnell's executive orders range in topic from declaring a state of emergency after the rare August 23, 2011, earthquake that affected localities throughout Virginia (see Box 6.2 for more information) to promoting efficiency in government.

TABLE 6.2   Executive Orders

Governor	Number of Executive Orders Issued While in Office
Bob McDonnell	57*
Timothy Kaine	110
Mark Warner	102
James Gilmore	88
George Allen	61

*As of January 2013.

The Governor as Party Head

The governor in most states is typically the most prominent leader of his or her political party. This is especially the case if the governor's party also is in control of the state's legislature.

During the first half of the twentieth century, state politics in Virginia were basically dominated by Harry Flood Byrd and his political organization. From the time he served as governor in 1923 until his resignation from the U.S. Senate in 1965, the governorship in Virginia was dominated by the Byrd-led Democratic Party. Byrd's opponents preferred to refer to this organization as a political machine, but as experts point out, the Byrd machine was founded on a set of principles, comprising like-minded individuals who believed in frugal fiscal management of the state governor and provided purpose-laden incentives. Byrd died in 1966, a year after his resignation from the U.S. Senate. A leader for Byrd's successful and long-running organization failed to step forward.

Following the decline of the Byrd machine, Linwood Holdton, elected governor in 1969, was the first Republican governor to be elected in Virginia since 1880. The fractionalization between Byrd's former conservative Democrats (Fred G. Pollard), a more centrist nominee (William Battle), and a liberal (Henry Howell) and changing party alignment at the national level led to a brutal primary that ultimately damaged the party and allowed for the election of a Republican. In fact, former Democratic governor Mills E. Godwin Jr. (1966–1970) ran as a Republican and was reelected to office in 1974 (1974–1978). Former Byrd Democrats eventually began to side with the more conservative Republican Party. The identity problems within the Democratic Party in Virginia continued throughout the 1970s. Finally, in 1981, Chuck Robb was able to bring together the numerous factions and won the governorship with a conservative campaign. The Democrats swept into office again in 1985, winning all three offices of governor, attorney general, and lieutenant governor. History was made in 1989 when Virginia citizens elected former lieutenant governor L. Douglas Wilder to the governorship, making him the first African American governor in the United States.

The Governor as Chief Budgeting Officer

The governor has significant power and influence over the state's budget. The Executive Budget Act of 1922 gave the governor the power of preparing the biennial budget to submit to the General Assembly. While the General Assembly can amend the proposed budget, the governor still holds the veto and line-item veto powers to help shape the budget he wants. This influence allows the governor to have significant influence over state programs and policies. For more information on the governor as chief budgeting officer see Chapter 9.

The Governor as Chief Appointer and Administrator

The Virginia executive branch has the sole authority and responsibility for the operation and administration of the state's bureaucracy, or the agencies and their rules and regulations that are used to carry out and implement the state's policies and programs. As Virginia's chief administrator, the governor appoints many key positions throughout the state. These include state agencies, the Board of Trustees or Board of Visitors for all state colleges and universities, as well as regulatory commissions and advisory boards. For more information on the governor's role as chief administrator see Chapter 8, Administering Government: Bureaucratic Power and Politics in Virginia. The current structure of the governor's executive office can be found in Figure 6.1.

The Governor as Spokesperson for the State

Though the Virginia governor has many formal roles, the governor has many informal roles and powers as well. Some may view these as the governor's ceremonial duties. Ceremonial functions include events such as proclaiming special days or weeks in honor of a particular person or event; dedicating new highways, buildings, or bridges; ribbon cutting ceremonies for new or expanding businesses; and greeting and hosting distinguished visitors of the state in Richmond. The governor of any state is typically the most visible officeholder in the state as they represent the state in times of crisis and celebration. The governor in this capacity acts as the official spokesperson for the state and its citizens. The governor serves as chief economic advocate for Virginia, spending significant energy and time attempting to attract or retain businesses both from domestic and international corporations. See Chapter 11 for more information on Governor McDonnell and his role as Virginia's chief economic advocate.

Life after Living in the Governor's Mansion

Virginia's list of governors, especially in the early years of this country's existence, reads like a list of American Revolutionary patriots, founding fathers, and future presidents. Virginia's first governor was Patrick Henry (1776–1779, 1784–1786). He famously shouted "Give me liberty or give me death" in a pro-revolutionary speech. He was followed by Thomas Jefferson (1779–1781), the father of the U.S. Constitution and third president of the United States. Also on the list of early governors are future presidents Benjamin Harrison (1781–1784), James Monroe (1799–1802, 1811), and John Tyler (1825–1827). More recently, the country's first African American governor, Douglas Wilder, held office from 1990–1994. For more information on former governor Douglas Wilder, see Box 6.3. George Allen (1994–1998) and Mark Warner (2002–2006) both went on to represent the state in the U.S. Senate, while Jim Gilmore (1998–2002) also sought a U.S. Senate seat but lost. Tim Kaine (2006–2010) served as the fifty-first chair of the Democratic National Committee from 2009–2011. In 2012, he defeated former senator and governor George Allen in the state's open U.S. Senate seat formerly held by U.S. Senator Jim Webb.

The Constitutional Executive Officers

While the governor plays the primary role in the administration of government, this power is also shared with the lieutenant governor. According to the Virginia Constitution, the lieutenant governor serves as the president of the Virginia Senate and is next in line should the governor for whatever reason be unable to perform the

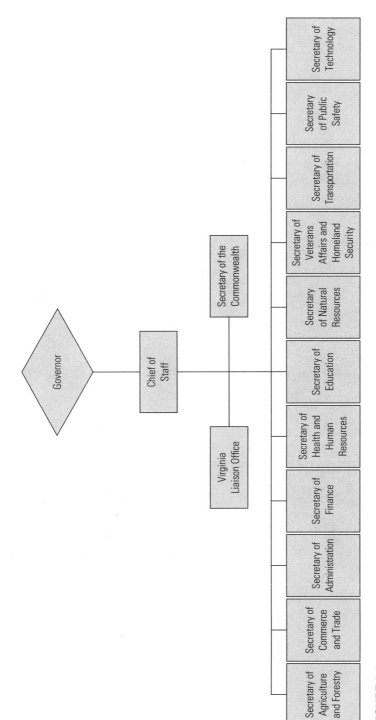

FIGURE 6.1

Structure of the Executive

BOX 6.3   **Governor L. Douglas Wilder**

Wilder became the first African American elected to statewide office in Virginia when he was elected as Virginia's lieutenant governor in 1986. Wilder ran a successful campaign for governor in 1990 and served the state as its first African American governor from 1990–1994. He ran a slightly conservative campaign in comparison to his predecessors and won favor with the media. The issue of abortion was prominent in the election cycle, and Wilder's pro-choice stance won him the election by garnering most of the votes in the more liberal northern Virginia and Tidewater areas of the state, winning by a narrow margin over Republican candidate Marshall Coleman. He was the state's first African American elected to statewide office in Virginia, but he was also the nation's first African American governor! Wilder was commended for his sound fiscal management and balancing the state's budget, during difficult economic times. *Financial World* magazine ranked Virginia as the best managed state in the United States for two consecutive years under his administration. Wilder later served as the mayor of Richmond, Virginia's state capital, from 2005–2009. In 2004, Virginia Commonwealth University named its School of Government and Public Affairs in honor of Wilder.

Governor L. Douglas Wilder

Source: http://www.wilder.vcu.edu/faculty/wilder.html.

duties of the office; however, no governor has died in office since Virginia adopted the 1851 constitution. The 1851 constitution called for the popular election of the lieutenant governor. The lieutenant governor in forty-two other states is first in line of succession to the governor.

The lieutenant governor is charged with making a tie-breaking vote in the Senate, which is the only time he or she is given a vote. Unlike the state's chief executive, the Virginia Constitution does not prohibit the lieutenant governor from serving consecutive terms. The constitution requires the lieutenant governor to meet the same qualifications as the governor: must be a citizen of the United States, a resident of Virginia for at least five years, and at least thirty years of age. The lieutenant governor does not run on the same ticket as the governor as the positions are elected separately. As previously mentioned, the lieutenant governor and governor may be from separate political parties. This can increase the strain on negotiations, especially if the legislature is politically divided. In addition to the constitutional requirements associated with the position, the Code of Virginia provides that the lieutenant governor may serve as a member of several state commissions, councils, and boards. Virginia's current Lieutenant Governor Bill Bolling serves on the board of directors of the Virginia Tourism Authority and the Virginia Economic Development Partnership, on the board of trustees of the Jamestown-Yorktown Foundation and the Center for Rural Virginia, and is a member of the Virginia Military Advisory Council, the Commonwealth Preparedness Council, and the Council on Virginia's Future. Lieutenant Governor Bolling also serves as the chairman of the governor's Commission on Economic Development and Job Creation and is Virginia's chief jobs creation officer. See Chapter 11 for more information on Lieutenant Governor Bolling's responsibilities as they relate to economic development and jobs creation.

The Office of Attorney General

Virginia's attorney general and its office can be seen as the Commonwealth's law firm because they represent the governor, executive state agencies, and the state at large. The attorney general is tasked with carrying out the duties prescribed to him or her by law. The attorney general is also responsible for providing legal advice to the governor and General Assembly, is the head of the Virginia Department of Law, and serves as the attorney on behalf of the government of Virginia and all state agencies. In addition, the attorney general is second in line of succession to the governor behind the lieutenant governor.

The Virginia Constitution requires that to be attorney general an individual must be a U.S. citizen and at least thirty years of age. In addition, an individual must possess the qualifications required for a judge of the court of record in Virginia. All Virginia judges and Supreme Court of Virginia justices must have been admitted to the Commonwealth of Virginia Bar Association. The attorney general position does not have term limitations.

Virginia's current Attorney General Kenneth Cuccinelli II was elected to office on January 16, 2010. His current staff consists of 425 employees including a chief deputy attorney general, four deputy attorney generals, assistant attorney generals, legal assistants and secretaries, and lawyers serving as special counsel to particular state agencies.

BOX 6.4   **Duties and Powers of the Attorney General**

Provide legal advice and representation to the governor and executive agencies, state boards, and commissions, and institutions of higher education.

Provide written legal advice in the form of official opinions to government officials.

Defend criminal convictions on appeal and defend the state when prisoners sue concerning their incarceration.

Defend the constitutionality of state laws.

Enforce state laws that protect businesses and consumers when there are violations.

Represent consumers in utility matters before the State Corporation Commission.

Collect debts owed to state agencies, hospitals, and universities.

Conduct or assist criminal investigations and prosecutions.

Represent the Department of Social Services in its efforts to collect child support.

Supervise the appointment and payment of private attorneys hired by other state agencies.

Assist victims of crime who are following criminal cases at the appellate level.

Provide information to the public on identify theft prevention and remediation.

Administer grants to help reduce crimes that involve gangs, drugs, and sexual predators.

Administer the Sexually Violent Predator Civil Commitment Program to protect children from dangerous predators.

Source: http://www.oag.state.va.us/About%20The%20Attorney%20General/index.html.

The Commonwealth was in the national spotlight in late 2011 and early 2012 for its outspoken opposition to the Affordable Care Act, a health care reform bill passed by the U.S. Congress in 2010 along bitterly divided partisan lines. Virginia Attorney General Ken Cuccinelli was elected on his opposition to President Barack Obama's administration, which strongly centered on health care reform. The Virginia legislature passed a law protecting its citizens from government mandates to buy health insurance, an act that was supported by the Virginia General Assembly, in both the Virginia House (90–3) and the Virginia Senate (25–15).

On his website, Ken Cuccinelli publicly expressed his views on the Affordable Care Act and the states' opposition to the federal law: "We in the attorney general's office feel that the new federal individual mandate—the requirement that everyone be forced to buy government-approved health insurance by 2014 or face fines—is unconstitutional" (see http://www.oag.state.va.us/FAQs/FAQ_Why_VA_Suing.html). According to Cuccinelli, its unconstitutionality comes from the federal government's claim that the source of its power to impose the legislation is in the Constitution's commerce clause. The commerce clause gives the federal government the power to regulate commerce among the states. The attorney general's office argues that individuals who refuse to purchase health insurance are not, in fact, participating in commerce, which would therefore make the federal government's law inapplicable to individual states, and it cannot override state legislation that may contradict the law.

Conclusion

The Virginia executive branch has a long history of important political figures. These leaders shaped not only Virginia's system of government but also helped shape the U.S. system of government we all know today. Virginia's chief executive position is unique in that the Virginia Constitution is the only constitution in the United States that prohibits the governor from serving successive terms. Virginia's governor wears many hats while in office. Virginia's two other elected executive branch officials include the positions of lieutenant governor and attorney general. Knowing more about the roles and responsibilities of Virginia's executive branch officials will enable you to have a better understanding of and appreciation for governance of the Commonwealth and enforcement of Virginia's laws and policies.

Key Concepts

Appointment powers
Attorney general
Bureaucracy
Chief executive officer
Executive branch

Executive order
Governor
Line-item veto
Lieutenant governor
Veto

Suggested Resources

- http://www.oag.state.va.us/: Virginia's Attorney General's Office.
- http://www.governor.virginia.gov/: **Virginia's Governor's Office.**
- http://www.ltgov.virginia.gov/: Virginia's Lieutenant Governor's Office.
- http://www.ncsl.org/issues-research/health/state-laws-and-actions-challenging -aca.aspx#2011_bills: **National Conference of State Legislators.**

Notes

1. Warren M. Billings, *The Old Dominion in the Seventeenth Century: A Documentary History of Virginia, 1606–1689* (Chapel Hill, NC: The University of North Carolina Press, 1975).
2. Ibid., 40–41.
3. VirginiaConstitutionof1776,http://www.law.gmu.edu/assets/files/academics/founders/ VA-Constitution.pdf, p. 8.
4. Ibid., p. 8.
5. Virginia Constitution, Article V, Sec. 1.

CHAPTER 7

OUTLINE

Virginia's Court Structure

Magistrates

District Courts

Circuit Courts

Court of Appeals

Virginia Supreme Court

The Administration of Justice

The National Court System

Judicial Policymaking

State Judicial Selection

Who Are Our Judges?

Tenure and Compensation

Conclusion

Law and Order in Virginia

The State Court System

The courts make up Virginia's third branch of state government. Along with the police and corrections, the judiciary is a key component of the state's criminal justice system. In contrast to the legislative and executive branches, members of the judicial branch are not elected by the people. The courts play a special role in ensuring that government and its policies reflect democratic values. Unlike representatives in the elected branches, whose decisions reflect the preferences of the majority, courts are charged with making sure that the will of the many does not infringe upon the rights of the few. They also have the difficult task of balancing individual rights and liberties with the interests and greater good of society. As we will see, its relationship to the national court system also sets the judiciary apart from the other branches. This chapter presents an introduction to the judicial branch in Virginia and provides an overview of the structure and responsibilities of the courts, Virginia's methods for choosing judges, and the state's tenure and compensation policies.

Virginia's Court Structure

The Supreme Court of Virginia is the only court established by the state constitution; all others were created by the legislature. According to Article VI, Section 1, "The judicial power of the Commonwealth shall be vested in a Supreme Court and in such other courts of original or appellate jurisdiction subordinate to the Supreme Court as the General Assembly may from time to time establish. Trial courts of general jurisdiction, appellate courts, and such other courts as shall be so designated by the General Assembly shall be known as courts of record."[1] Virginia's court system includes four different levels of courts: the Supreme Court of Virginia, the Court of Appeals of Virginia, circuit courts, and district courts. The state employs magistrates to perform additional judicial functions (see Figure 7.1, Virginia's Court Structure). Together, the judicial branch employs more than 2,600 people, including judges, clerks, and magistrates.[2] Each of these is discussed in more detail below.

Magistrates

The **magistrate system** provides a first point of contact in the Virginia judicial system. Although magistrates are considered "judicial officers," they are not judges and cannot preside over trials, nor are they law enforcement officers. Before 1974, many of the duties that magistrates performed were carried out by Justices of the Peace (a designation that remains in many states). Magistrates have a wide variety of responsibilities. They act as an impartial party to determine whether there is probable cause to issue arrest warrants, summonses, bonds, search warrants, and subpoenas.

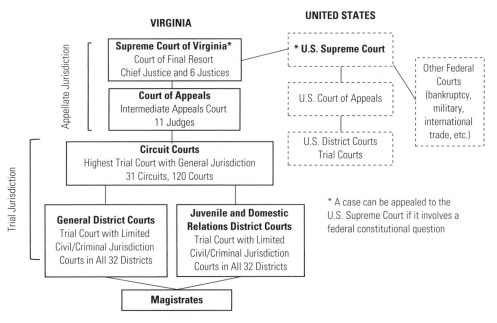

FIGURE 7.1

Virginia's Court Structure

Source: Adapted from Supreme Court of Virginia, Office of the Executive Secretary, "Virginia's Courts in Brief" (web rev. 7/11), http://www.courts.state.va.us/courts/cib.pdf.

Magistrates issue emergency mental and medical custody orders, temporary mental and medical detention orders, emergency protective orders, and other civil processes. They also conduct bond hearings in order to set bail when criminal charges have been filed and are able to accept prepayments for traffic infractions and minor misdemeanors. Importantly, magistrates can provide an independent review of complaints from both citizens and law enforcement officers.[3]

Every city and county has at least one magistrate. Like law enforcement officers, magistrates provide service to the Commonwealth twenty-four hours a day, seven days a week.[4] Virginia has eight magisterial regions, each with three to five magisterial districts. Magistrates are appointed by the chief circuit court in each district and can serve for unlimited four-year terms. The system is supervised by the Office of the Executive Secretary for the Supreme Court of Virginia, which is responsible for training magistrates and providing them with necessary legal and procedural advice.[5] Magistrates are not required to have any formal legal training; however, in 2008, state legislators increased the qualifications for becoming a magistrate. In addition to on-the-job training and continuing legal education, new applicants must now have at least a bachelor's degree (although existing employees without degrees are exempted) and chief magistrates must be members of the Virginia State Bar.[6]

District Courts

Virginia is divided into thirty-two judicial districts, with a two-tiered system that distinguishes adult from juvenile offenders. General district courts and juvenile and domestic relations district courts are located in every city and county. Both are courts of **original jurisdiction;** they are the first courts to hear testimony, review evidence, and render judgments in a dispute (rather than those on appeal from other courts).

General district courts are the lowest level courts in the Virginia judicial system and hear both civil and criminal cases. **Civil cases** involve legal disputes between two or more individuals or organizations. For example, if you are in an accident and your insurance does not cover the full cost of the damages or the medical costs of an injured party, the individual could take you to court to try to make you pay for them. General district courts have jurisdiction (meaning the authority to hear a case) in civil trials when the amount in question is less than $25,000. **Criminal cases**, on the other hand, involve violations of law. General district courts preside over cases involving violations of ordinances, laws, and bylaws of the county or city where it is located when the crime is a **misdemeanor.** This includes events such as reckless driving, driving under the influence, marijuana possession, shoplifting, and assault and battery. Misdemeanors have penalties of up to one year in jail, a fine, or both. In some cases, individuals who are found guilty may get probation and are allowed to stay out of jail as long as they remain on good behavior for a specified period of time. Certain traffic violations are also heard in general district courts.

Trials in general district courts are presided over by a judge without a jury. This is also known as a "bench trial." In addition to jurisdiction over misdemeanors, general district courts also hold preliminary hearings in felony cases (a crime punishable by more than one year in prison) to decide if there is sufficient evidence to bring the defendant before a **grand jury**. Citizens convened for a grand jury hearing have the responsibility of determining if the accused party will be indicted and brought to trial in a circuit court.[7]

While juveniles were once tried alongside adults, all states now have separate courts for juvenile offenders. In Virginia, cases involving minors are heard in **juvenile and domestic relations courts.** These separate venues recognize that children and youth have not reached full cognitive development and have different decision-making capacities than do adults. Juvenile courts (and juvenile detention centers) have much greater emphasis on rehabilitating offenders, rather than just punishing them, so that they may develop into properly socialized adults. According to Virginia state statute, the purpose of the juvenile and domestic relations court system is to ensure "that in all proceedings the welfare of the child and the family, the safety of the community and the protection of the rights of victims are the paramount concerns of the Commonwealth."[8] Juvenile and domestic relations courts try most criminal cases when the perpetrator is younger than eighteen years old. They also preside over delinquency and **status offenses**. These are violations that would be legal if they were committed by adults, such as running away from home, skipping school, smoking cigarettes, or drinking alcohol. Additionally, juvenile courts have jurisdiction over custody disputes and cases involving child abuse and neglect.

Prosecutors (lawyers who try cases for the state) can decide if they want to transfer juveniles as young as aged fourteen to adult courts, even when juvenile judges recommend against it. This discretion can result in wide variation across the state in the rate at which young people are tried as juveniles or as adults, leading to drastically different sentencing for the same crime. However, over the past decade, Virginia has made it more difficult to transfer juvenile cases to adult courts and to house young people in adult facilities. In 2007, the General Assembly unanimously voted to overturn Virginia's "once an adult, always an adult" rule. Previously, if a child was tried in adult court and had charges dismissed, he or she would automatically be charged as an adult in all future proceedings. Additionally, legislation passed in 2010 prohibits holding juveniles in adult pretrial detainment, where they are at high risk of physical and sexual victimization.[9] Attempts to pass legislation allowing juveniles to appeal decisions to transfer them to the adult court system have failed in recent years.[10]

Circuit Courts

The Commonwealth is served by 120 circuit courts (one in each city and county), which are organized into thirty-one different judicial circuits. As in the district system, circuit courts are trial courts that are presided over by a single judge; however, they are the only level in the Virginia court system where there are jury trials. Circuit courts have broad jurisdiction. In civil cases where claims range from $4,500 to $25,000, they share jurisdiction with general district courts. If a lawsuit involves more than $25,000 in damages, it can be tried only at the circuit level. The circuit court also hears divorce and permanent custody cases and disputes over wills, estates, and real estate.

The circuit court has jurisdiction over criminal cases that involve **felonies** (offenses that carry a prison sentence of more than one year). Juveniles who have been charged with felonies and whose cases have been transferred to adult court also stand trial in the circuit court.[11] Defendants charged with felony violation can request a trial by a jury of their peers as long as they do not plead guilty. The vast majority of felony cases in circuit courts (89 percent in 2011) are resolved through guilty pleas. Bench trials occurred in 10 percent of felony cases and just 1.5 percent of involved jury trials. State law does not allow juries to recommend sentences for juveniles and instead gives this responsibility to circuit court judges.[12]

Unlike district courts, circuit courts have both original jurisdiction and **appellate jurisdiction.** If a party does not like the ruling of a district court, they can appeal it to the circuit courts. However, on appeal, a trial is held only to determine if the judge in the trial court applied the law correctly and does not allow lawyers to present new evidence. They also hear appeals from administrative agency rulings. For example, rejected Medicaid claims or denial of special education benefits can be appealed to the circuit court once all other administrative avenues have been exhausted.

Court of Appeals

The Court of Appeals of Virginia is the most recent addition to the Virginia judicial system and was established by the General Assembly in 1985 in order to reduce the number of cases being appealed from trial courts to the state supreme court. The court of appeals has eleven judges who, like Supreme Court of Virginia justices, represent the state and not local areas. Most cases are presided over by a rotating panel of at least three justices, who are assigned by the chief judge. Judges sit *en banc* (all together) in a limited number of circumstances, including when the panel's decision conflicts with an earlier appeals court ruling.

As its name implies, the majority of cases brought before the Court of Appeals of Virginia are on appeal from a circuit court. Appeals are brought to the court in one of two ways: through petition or as a matter of right. In the latter, the Court of Appeals of Virginia must take all appeals that involve circuit court decisions with regard to family issues (annulment, divorce, custody, spousal or child support, adoption, etc.), the final decisions of the Virginia Workers' Compensation Commission regarding workers' compensation claims, or an appealed administrative agency ruling. The court has discretion over whether or not it hears petitions for appeal (also called writs) in a number of other cases. The judges consider petitions on appeal in the case of criminal sanctions that do not involve the death penalty, traffic convictions, denial of concealed weapons permits, involuntary medical or mental health treatment of prisoners, or when a person's free exercise of religion has been violated by state or local government.[13] Other cases are appealed directly from the circuit courts to the state supreme court.

While most of the work of the court of appeals stems from its appellate authority, it also has original jurisdiction to issue *writs of mandamus* (orders compelling a lower court to comply with particular actions) and of *prohibition* (orders directing a lower court to cease actions that are not within its jurisdiction). In cases over which they have jurisdiction, the Court of Appeals of Virginia can also issue a **writ of habeas corpus** in order to force authorities to bring a prisoner before the court to determine whether they have been legally jailed. If prosecutors cannot prove that they have enough evidence to charge the accused, they can be forced by the courts to release them. Appeals court judges can also issue *writs of actual innocence* when a person who pled not guilty but was convicted of a felony wants to bring new, non-biological evidence of their innocence before the court. For example, if a person is convicted of murder and the victim is later found stranded on a desert island, the convicted person would want to ask the court to revisit the case and declare them not guilty.

Virginia Supreme Court

The Supreme Court of Virginia is one of the oldest judicial bodies in the country. It is the only court in the Commonwealth's judicial system to be formally established by the state constitution and serves as the state's court of last resort. It is presided over by a chief justice and six justices. Although the supreme court has both original and appellate jurisdiction, its primary role is to review lower court rulings. Almost all appeals to the supreme court are filed by petition. The only appeals that are heard as a matter of right are those involving the death penalty, attorney discipline, or the State Corporation Commission (a state regulatory agency dealing with utilities,

Members of the Virginia Supreme Court welcome Justice Cleo Elaine Powell, the court's 102nd justice and first female African American judge. Other members of the court are (*from left*) Justice Elizabeth McClanahan, Justice LeRoy Millette Jr., Justice Donald Lemons, Chief Justice Cynthia Kinser, Justice S. Bernard Goodwyn, and Justice William Mims.

insurance, financial institutions, retail franchising, and railroads). Even though only one of the seven justices needs to agree to hear a case, the court accepts just a small percentage of the petitions for appeal.

Like the court of appeals, the state supreme court has original jurisdiction in cases of mandamus and prohibition. This power enables these justices to direct the actions of the court of appeals (whose justices, in turn, can only order action or inaction of circuit and district court officials). They can also issue writs of habeas corpus for cases in their jurisdiction, and writs of actual innocence in cases involving biological (e.g., DNA) evidence. Finally, their original jurisdiction extends to suits filed by the Judicial Inquiry and Review Commission in regard to censure, retirement, and removal of judges.[14]

Verdicts reached by the supreme court are issued in a **majority opinion**, a document outlining the legal reasons for a court decision. A rotation system is used to decide which justice will be responsible for writing up the court's reasoning. Of note, written opinions were not issued by the state supreme court until the late eighteenth century. Nor did justices usually give reasons for their decisions. In 1788, Thomas Jefferson disagreed with those who argued that not issuing opinions gave the appearance of unanimity on the court and strengthened their decisions. Instead, he began recording court decisions himself.[15]

The Administration of Justice

As the state's highest court, the Supreme Court of Virginia also plays a role in overseeing the Virginia judicial system. This responsibility falls primarily on the court's chief justice, a role outlined by the state constitution. The executive secretary of the state supreme court and its eleven judicial departments assists in administration so that "litigation may be expedited and the administration of justice improved."[16] The Office of the Executive Secretary comprises an assistant executive secretary and counsel, the Court Improvement Program, Educational Services, Fiscal Services, the Historical Commission, Human Resources, Judicial Information Technology, Judicial Planning, Judicial Services, Legal Research, and Legislative and Public Relations. The chief justice also presides over four policymaking bodies created by the General Assembly to assist in court operations. These include the Judicial Council, the Committee on District Courts, the Judicial Conference of Virginia, and the Judicial Conference of Virginia for District Courts.

The National Court System

State court systems operate alongside a national court system, making a complex institution even more so. American federalism sets up a governing structure in which federal and state governments are both **sovereign**, meaning that each has the ultimate authority to make decisions within their respective jurisdictions. The national government can use the powers granted to them by the U.S. Constitution to make laws that affect citizens, while states exercise authority in the areas reserved to them. Therefore, each needs a court system that can apply and interpret their own laws. What determines whether a case will be heard in a state or federal court? Jurisdiction depends on whether or not a state or a federal law has been broken. This includes differences in **statutory law**—laws made by Congress and state legislatures—as well as **constitutional law**, which involves constitutional questions. For example, the U.S. and state constitutions differ regarding the right to equal schooling. The U.S. Supreme Court has held that education is *not* a constitutionally protected right under the U.S. Constitution.[17] As will be seen in Chapter 11, however, state constitutions (including Virginia's) are much more explicit about state responsibility for public education. As a result, successful challenges to unequal per pupil expenditures have largely occurred in state, rather than federal, courts. In fact, the vast majority of all cases are tried in state, rather than federal, courts.

In some policy areas, the two levels of government have **concurrent powers**, which can result in laws and regulations that conflict with each other. When conflict occurs, federal law is supreme, as long as the particular power has been explicitly or implicitly granted to the national government. However, as mentioned in the previous chapter, what is considered federal or state prerogative is not always clear. This can be seen by the state's lawsuit, concerning the 2010 Patient Protection and Affordable Care Act in which Virginia argued that national policy should not take legal precedence over the state's Healthcare Freedom Act. Disagreements between a state and the federal government (or between two or more states) fall under federal court jurisdiction. This is also true of cases that concern federal constitutional rights, those that involve violations of national laws, or that take place across multiple states.[18]

Judicial Policymaking

Alexander Hamilton once remarked that the courts were the weakest of the three branches of government, explaining that "the judiciary ... has no influence over either the sword or the purse ... merely judgment."[19] Judges could neither create new laws, like the legislature, nor carry them out, a power reserved for the executive branch. Hamilton was describing the federal judiciary, but this sentiment likely extended to state courts of his day. Over time however, courts have become extremely politicized and now have a more prominent role in the processes of governance. Today's judicial system has been referred to as "politics by other means"—a venue in which to achieve political interests if attempts at legislative or executive action fail. Although court decisions need the support of other branches to carry out their rulings, they have the same weight as laws passed by the legislature.

While lower courts concern themselves with hearing cases and applying law, the Supreme Court of Virginia has the ability to interpret whether a state law is constitutional. The court can use **judicial review** to overturn state laws, executive orders, and administrative actions. The power of the courts to make law is often quite controversial, especially when court rulings contravene the decisions made by elected officials. Across the country, many criticize "activist" judges, who they see as substituting their personal opinions for the will of the people. Such allegations of judges "inventing" rather than implying law come from both the left and the right. Proponents, on the other hand, argue that state and federal constitutions must adapt as society changes. They also emphasize the fact that the judiciary plays a fundamentally different role in democratic societies than do popularly elected branches: to protect the rights of the minority rather than the interests of the majority.

Compared with many other states, judicial activism is limited in Virginia. The Supreme Court of Virginia generally defers to the state legislature and tends to issue opinions that are closely tailored to the state constitution. A recent review of Supreme Court of Virginia decisions on controversial legal issues, such as abortion, assisted suicide, cloning, and embryo research, concludes that the justices "appear to be models of judicial restraint."[20] The constitutional questions before the court are relatively limited; instead, the state court predominantly concerns itself with cases and controversies involving torts and criminal matters on appeal from lower courts. However, the Supreme Court of Virginia does from time to time overturn legislation that they think unconstitutionally expands the authority of state government or violates the separation of power between branches. For example, in 2008, the court heard a challenge to legislation in which the General Assembly had given the Northern Virginia Transportation Authority (NVTA) the ability to collect taxes to fund its transportation projects. Writing for the majority, Justice Goodwyn argued that according to the state constitution, only elected representatives can levy taxes; therefore, allowing the NVTA (whose members are appointed) to impose its own regional taxes and fees is unconstitutional.[21]

State Judicial Selection

Virginia's method of choosing judges is very unique. In fact, Virginia and South Carolina are the only two states in which the legislature decides who will be appointed to the judiciary. In other states, judges are elected by *citizens* in either partisan or nonpartisan elections, or they are appointed by the governor. Many states use a merit system that relies on a bipartisan commission to generate a list of qualified candidates from which the governor can choose. New judges may still be subject to a retention election by popular vote. States often use different methods, depending on whether the judge in question will preside over a trial, appellate, or court of last resort.[22] Judicial selection in Virginia has changed a great deal since the state's founding. Justices were initially elected by the General Assembly for life. In 1850, reforms changed this method to popular election by citizens. Just fourteen years later, this switched to nomination by the governor and selection by the General Assembly. And then in 1870, the governor's nomination of judicial candidates was repealed, leaving this responsibility solely in the hands of state legislators.

Proponents of popular elections assert that citizens should be able to hold judges directly accountable for their decisions on the bench (gubernatorial and legislative elections also have accountability mechanisms, but they are indirect and operate through the election of state representatives). Opponents, however, argue that the courts should be insulated from politics and free to take legal positions that are unpopular with voters. Moreover, because judges need to raise money to be elected, the influence of campaign contributions can raise questions about judicial neutrality. Judicial appointments by governors or legislators are also subject to criticism. Virginia's Lieutenant Governor Bill Bolling is among those who have criticized the state's method of judicial section. Relying on the General Assembly, he argues, tends to result in partisan disagreements, political "horse-trading," and gridlock that can delay filling needed judicial vacancies. Instead, Bolling has supported establishing a bipartisan commission that would select judges based on merit rather than political interests.[23] Since the state constitution outlines the methods for choosing state judges, reform would have to occur through constitutional amendment.

The method for selecting justices in Virginia differs from the typical legislative process. As David Albo explains, "A bill passes by the majority of those *voting* [while] a judge has to be appointed by the majority of those *elected*."[24] This means that regardless of whether or not the House and Senate have all members present, they must secure fifty-one and twenty-one votes respectively. Another key distinction is that the governor has no veto power over judicial appointments. When new judgeships become available (due to retirement, death, or population growth), candidates are invited by their local delegate or senator to appear before the Virginia Senate and House Courts of Justice Committees. The committees certify that the applicant is technically qualified for the position and investigate whether they have committed any crimes or have complaints against them. Applicants are typically asked how they will interpret the law once on the bench. In making a recommendation, committee members often defer to the senators and delegates from the local judicial district with a vacancy to fill. If a vacancy occurs when the General Assembly is not in session, the governor uses his or her appointment power to fill positions on the circuit courts, the Court of Appeals of Virginia, or the Supreme Court of Virginia. Vacancies in district courts are filled by the circuit court judges where the lower court is located. However, in both instances, appointees must stand for election when the legislature reconvenes.[25]

Who Are Our Judges?

To be eligible for a state judicial appointment, a candidate must be a current Virginia resident, and trial court judges are required to live in the jurisdiction they serve. All judges must be a member of the Virginia Bar for five years prior to appointment. Virginia has a mandatory retirement age of seventy. Following recommendations by the Judicial Council of Virginia, in 2012 the Virginia Senate approved a bill that would increase the mandatory retirement age for judges from seventy to seventy-three. However, a similar measure died in the House Courts Committee.

States' methods of judicial selection impact the diversity of state court justices. Studies have shown that minority judges are much more likely to be appointed than to be popularly elected to the state bench.[26] In 2008, 12.6 percent of all Virginia state judges were African American. Interestingly, while 28.6 percent of Supreme Court of Virginia justices (2 of 7) were black, this proportion drops to 27.3 percent for appellate courts (3 of 11), and just 10.8 percent of circuit court judges (17 of 157 seats). No Hispanics, Asians, or other minorities served as state judges.[27] Although Virginia governors have used their recess appointments to diversify the courts, women continue to be underrepresented in the Virginia judicial system.[28] There are currently two women serving on the Supreme Court of Virginia, including the current Chief Justice Cynthia Kinser and one full-time female justice on the Court of Appeals of Virginia.

Though less visible than gender, race, or ethnicity, gays and lesbians have faced significant obstacles to achieving equal rights and securing descriptive representation in state government. In 2013, Judge Tracy Thorne-Begland became the first openly gay justice in Virginia. A year earlier, his appointment to the Richmond General District Court had been rejected by the Virginia House of Delegates amid controversy concerning his sexual orientation and activism for gay rights.[29]

Tenure and Compensation

Virginia judges serve on the bench for limited terms before coming up for reappointment by the legislature. Appointments to the Supreme Court of Virginia are for twelve years. Terms in office are shorter for other judges: eight years for court of appeals and circuit court judges and just four years for district court positions. Chief justices to the supreme court and court of appeals are selected by a vote of

Delegate G. Manoli Loupassi (*left*), Richmond Republican, joins newly appointed Richmond General District Court Judge Tracy Thorne-Begland (*right*) during Thorne-Begland's testimony for a 2013 meeting of the joint House and Senate Courts of Justice Committee.

their peers and hold the position for four years. While federal and some states judges are appointed for life, framers of the Virginia Constitution thought that life tenure reduced judicial accountability. Still, even with legislative reelection, there is very little turnover on the courts, with most judges reappointed by the General Assembly.[30] Some argue that life terms are important to ensure an impartial and independent judiciary. One mechanism that the Commonwealth does use to insulate the judiciary from politics is to forbid lowering judicial compensation during a judge's term in office. The fear is that, otherwise, judges' salaries could be manipulated to reflect legislators' dissatisfaction with court rulings. Similarly, although localities can supplement judicial compensation in order to attract highly qualified candidates, they must do so between terms.[31]

Sitting judges can be removed during their term in office for judicial misconduct or if they develop serious mental or physical impairments that interfere with their duties. The Judicial Inquiry and Review Commission (JIRC) investigates claims of misconduct or incompetency. If they establish that there is basis for the complaints, then the case is adjudicated by the Supreme Court of Virginia. Judges may also be **impeached** (removed from office) by a two-thirds vote of the state Senate.[32]

Conclusion

Virginia's judiciary has developed into a complex court system that is fundamental to governing the Commonwealth. The courts ensure social order by adjudicating disputes between private citizens and organizations and hold citizens accountable for violating state laws. The judiciary also has an important role in the balance of power between Virginia's governing institutions and acts as a check on arbitrary and unlawful government action. The Supreme Court of Virginia, especially, helps to ensure democratic governance by protecting the rights and liberties of Virginia's citizens.

Key Concepts

Appellate jurisdiction
Civil cases
Concurrent powers
Constitutional law
Criminal cases
Felonies
General district courts
Grand jury
Impeached
Judicial review

Juvenile and domestic relations courts
Magistrate system
Majority opinion
Misdemeanor
Original jurisdiction
Sovereign
Status offenses
Statutory law
Writ of habeas corpus

Suggested Resources

- http://www.courts.state.va.us/courts/home.html: Explore the **Virginia judicial system** in more detail.
- http://www.courts.state.va.us/courts/home.html: Browse **Virginia's Supreme Court and Court of Appeals decisions**.
- http://www.ncsc.org/: Compare state courts nationwide at the **National Center for State Courts**.
- http://www.justiceatstake.org: The **Justice at Stake Campaign** is a nonpartisan group working to keep courts fair and impartial.

Notes

1. Virginia Constitution, Article VI, Sec. 1.
2. Supreme Court of Virginia, Office of the Executive Secretary, "Virginia's Courts in Brief" (web rev. 7/11), http://www.courts.state.va.us/courts/cib.pdf.

3. Ibid.; Tom Dempsey and David Coffey, "The Criminal Justice System: Providing Public Safety in Virginia," in *Government and Politics in Virginia: The Old Dominion at the 21st* Century, ed. Quentin Kidd (Needham Heights, MA: Simon & Schuster, 1999), 149–161.

4. Robert L. Dudley, *Governing the Commonwealth* (Fairfax, VA: GMU Press, 2010), 77.

5. Supreme Court of Virginia, Office of the Executive Secretary, "Virginia's Courts in Brief" (web rev. 7/11), http://www.courts.state.va.us/courts/cib.pdf.

6. Alan Cooper, "Magistrate System Is Upgraded, Pay Is Not," *Virginia Lawyers Weekly*, April 7, 2008, http://valawyersweekly.com/2008/04/07/magistrate-system-is-upgraded-pay -is-not; see also "Lawyers Have Key Role in Reorganized Magistrate System," *Virginia Lawyer*, no. 29 (June/July 2009): 25–26. For more on the structure of the magistrate system, see http:// www.courts.state.va.us/courtadmin/aoc/djs/programs/mag/home.html.

7. Supreme Court of Virginia, Office of the Executive Secretary, "Virginia's Courts in Brief" (web rev. 7/11), http://www.courts.state.va.us/courts/cib.pdf.

8. Virginia Code, Ann. § 16.1–227 (2010), http://leg1.state.va.us/cgi-bin/legp504.exe? 000+cod+16.1-227.

9. Neelum Arya, "State Trends: Legislative Changes from 2005 to 2010 Removing Youth from the Adult Criminal Justice System" (Washington, DC: Campaign for Youth Justice, 2010), 26, http://www.campaignforyouthjustice.org/documents/CFYJ_State_Trends_Report.pdf.

10. "Circuit Court Hearing; Termination of Juvenile Court Jurisdiction (HB1198)," *Richmond Sunlight*, January 19, 2012, http://www.richmondsunlight.com/bill/2012/hb1198.

11. Supreme Court of Virginia, Office of the Executive Secretary, "The Circuit Court," n.d., http://www.courts.state.va.us/courts/circuit/circuitinfo.pdf.

12. Virginia Criminal Sentencing Commission, *2011 Annual Report* (Richmond, VA: Author, December 2011), 25–27, http://www.vcsc.virginia.gov/reports.html.

13. Supreme Court of Virginia, Office of the Executive Secretary, "The Court of Appeals of Virginia," September 2010, http://www.courts.state.va.us/courts/scv/scvinfo.pdf.

14. Ibid.

15. Ibid.

16. Ibid., p. 5.

17. See *San Antonio v. Rodriguez*, 411 U.S. 1 (1973), http://laws.findlaw.com/us/411/1 .html.

18. Administrative Office of the U.S. Courts, "Understanding Federal and State Courts," n.d., http://www.uscourts.gov/EducationalResources/FederalCourtBasics/CourtStructure/ UnderstandingFederalAndStateCourts.aspx.

19. Alexander Hamilton, "Federalist 78," in *The Federalist Papers*, ed. Clinton Rossiter (New York: New American Library, 2003 [1961]), http://www.constitution.org/fed/federa78 .htm, 464, para. 7.

20. Lynne Marie Kohm, "Virginia: Judicially Honoring the Rule of Law," *Americans United for Life, State Supreme Court Project* (2008), 10, http://www.aul.org/docs/statecourts/ VA.pdf.

21. *Marshall v. Northern Virginia Transportation Authority*, 071959, 071979 (2008), http://caselaw.findlaw.com/va-supreme-court/1078370.html.

22. Kevin B. Smith, Alan Greenblatt, and Michele Mariani Vaughn, *Governing States and Localities* (Washington, DC: CQ Press, 2011), 338.

23. Vivian J. Paige, "The Wrong Way to Appoint Judges," *Virginian Pilot*, December 14, 2011, http://hamptonroads.com/2011/12/wrong-way-appoint-judges.

24. David Albo, "Selecting Virginia's Judges," in *Governing Virginia*, ed. Anne Marie Morgan and A. R. "Pete" Giesen Jr. (Boston: Pearson, 2012), 160–167.

25. Ibid.

26. Barbara L. Graham, "State Judicial Diversity," in *The Book of the States 2009* (Washington, DC: The Council of State Governments, n.d.), 282–284, http://knowledgecenter .csg.org/drupal/system/files/graham_2.pdf.

27. Ibid., p. 289.

28. John T. Whelan, "Virginia's Judicial Selection Process: Still Unique though Its Partisan Stripes Are Changing," in *Government and Politics in Virginia: The Old Dominion at the 21st Century,* ed. Quentin Kidd (Needham Heights, MA: Simon & Schuster, 1999), 41–52.

29. Julian Walker, "Gay Judge Can Keep His District Court Seat," *Virginian-Pilot,* January 16, 2013, http://hamptonroads.com/2013/01/gay-judge-can-keep-his-district-court-seat.

30. David Albo, "Selecting Virginia's Judges," in *Governing Virginia,* ed. Anne Marie Morgan and A. R. "Pete" Giesen Jr. (Boston: Pearson, 2012), 160–167.

31. Virginia Constitution, Article VI, Sec. 9.

32. American Judicature Society, "Methods of Judicial Selection: Virginia, Removal of Judges" (Des Moines, IA: Author, 2013), http://www.judicialselection.us/judicial_selection/ methods/removal_of_judges.cfm?state=VA; see also, Virginia Constitution, Article VI, Sec. 10.

OUTLINE

Sources of Bureaucratic
and Administrative Power
in Virginia

The Virginia Merit System

Measuring Effectiveness
and Improving Efficiency

Conclusion

CHAPTER

8

Administering Government

Bureaucratic Power and Politics in Virginia

The scope of state government activities in the United States has gradually increased during the last century—from the number of state agencies to the number of individuals working in those agencies. Citizens continue to place more and more demands on the services received from their state government, and as a result, state bureaucracies continue to expand. It would be difficult to list all the services we receive from our state and local governments. We expect our government to protect us from harm and to help maintain and improve our quality of life through an efficient and effective delivery of the services it provides. This is mainly achieved through the many bureaucratic institutions that makeup our state government. These bureaucratic institutions receive their fair amount of criticism from the general public, mainstream media, and proponents of small government. This trend is no different in Virginia. According to Charles Goodsell's *The Case for Bureaucracy: A Public Administration Polemic,* bureaucracy is an effective and important component of our political system that is heavily demonized and shrouded in myths. Robert Daniel Wallace argues that Goodsell's thesis, "that the 'bureaucratic aspect' of the U.S. government is overwhelmingly effective, is well supported by both scholarly and anecdotal evidence."[1] Many associate bureaucracy with red tape. This may be because of frustrations associated with having to fill out long registration forms or because of having to wait in long lines at the Department of Motor Vehicles in order to renew a driver's license. However, we need rules, regulations, and proper procedures in order to make sure all citizens are treated equally and services are not arbitrary.

This chapter presents an overview of Virginia's bureaucracy, including bureaucratic power in Virginia, the structure of the Virginia bureaucracy, Virginia's merit system, and ways the state measures effectiveness and improves efficiency in the day-to-day operations of its many bureaucratic institutions.

Sources of Bureaucratic and Administrative Power in Virginia

The first Virginia Constitution granted most of the administrative power to the state legislature. The legislature was in charge of appointing the governor, members of the judicial branch, and other typical appointments in order to run the day-to-day operations of the Virginia bureaucracy. It was not until the 1851 constitutional revision that the governor of Virginia was elected by popular vote, taking away the appointment power from the legislature. Under the current constitution, the governor is granted a number of administrative responsibilities. The executive branch of government therefore is given the responsibility of overseeing the implementation of all laws passed by the Virginia General Assembly.

As the head of the executive branch, the governor manages all state agencies, known as the **bureaucracy**. Similar to that of the federal government, the Commonwealth's bureaucracy comprises all agencies and institutions responsible for delivering services to the citizens of Virginia. This includes essential governmental organizations, such as the Virginia Department of Emergency Management, and organizations that receive public funds and need oversight such as the Science Museum of Virginia. For a complete listing of the departments and agencies that make up Virginia's bureaucracy, see Figure 8.1.

The organization of Virginia's bureaucracy is hierarchical in nature as seen in Figure 8.2. The governor is at the head of the Virginia administration. Because of the increasing complexity of Virginia's state government, the governor has many layers of advisers and administrators to help manage the state's affairs. While there is no specific mention of a cabinet in the Virginia Constitution or any subsequent legislation, there are currently twelve cabinet departments: Administration, Agriculture and Forestry, Commerce and Trade, Finance, Health and Human Services, Education, Commonwealth, Natural Resources, Veterans Affairs and Homeland Security, Transportation, Public Safety, and Technology. Each of these executive departments is responsible for overseeing the daily operations of its bureaucratic agencies. For instance, the Department of Education oversees all

AGRICULTURE AND FORESTRY

-Department of Agriculture & Consumer Services
-Division of Charitable Gaming
-Department of Forestry

FINANCE

-Department of Accounts
-Department of Planning & Budget
-Department of Taxation
-Department of the Treasury

HEALTH AND HUMAN SERVICES

-Department for the Aging
-Department for the Blind & Vision Impaired
-Office of Comprehensive Services for At-Risk Youth and Families
-Department for the Deaf and Hard-of-Hearing
-State Department of Health
-Department of Health Professions
-Department of Medical Assistance Services
-Department of Mental Health, Mental Retardation & Substance Abuse Services
-Virginia Board for People with Disabilities
-Department of Rehabilitative Services
-Department of Social Services
-Tobacco Settlement Foundation

ADMINISTRATION

-Compensation Board
-State Board of Elections
-Department of Employment Dispute Resolution
-Department of General Services
-Council on Human Rights
-Department of Human Resource Management
-Department of Minority Business Enterprise

TECHNOLOGY

-Virginia Information Technologies Agency
-Innovative Technology Authority

NATURAL RESOURCES

-Department of Conservation & Recreation
-Department of Environmental Quality
-Department of Game & Inland Fisheries
-Department of Historic Resources
-Virginia Recreational Facilities Authority
-Virginia Museum of Natural History
-Marine Resources Commission

COMMERCE AND TRADE

-Board of Accountancy
-Department of Business Assistance
-Virginia Employment Commission
-Department of Housing &Community Development
-Department of Labor & Industry
-Department of Mines, Minerals & Energy
-Department of Professional & Occupational Regulation
-Virginia Resources Authority
-Tobacco Indemnification & Community Revitalization Commission
-Virginia Tourism Authority
-Virginia Baseball Stadium Authority
-Virginia Coalfield Economic Development Authority
-Virginia Economic Development Partnership
-Hampton Roads Sanitation District Commission
-Hampton Roads Sports Facility Authority
-Virginia Racing Commission

VETERANS AFFAIRS & HOMELAND SECURITY

-Department of Veterans Services
-Virginia War Memorial
-Virginia Military Advisory Council
-Secure Commonwealth Panel
-Virginia Commission on Military & National Security Facilities
-State Interoperability Executive Committee
-Board of Veterans Services
-Joint Leadership Council
-Veterans Services Foundation
-Veterans Care Center Advisory Committee

PUBLIC SAFETY

-Department of Alcoholic Beverage Control
-Department of Correctional Education
-Department of Corrections
-Department of Criminal Justice Services
-Department of Emergency Management
-Governor's Office on Substance Abuse Prevention
-Department of Fire Programs
-Department of Juvenile Justice
-Department of Military Affairs
-Virginia Parole Board
-Department of State Police
-Department of Forensic Sciences
-Commonwealth Attorney's Services Council
-Department of Veterans' Services

TRANSPORTATION

-Department of Aviation
-Motor Vehicle Dealer Board
-Department of Motor Vehicles
-Virginia Port Authority
-Department of Rail and Public Transportation
-Department of Transportation

EDUCATION

-Virginia Community College System
-Virginia Commission for the Arts
-Christopher Newport University
-State Council of Higher Education
-Department of Education
-Virginia Museum of Fine Arts
-Frontier Culture Museum of Virginia
-George Mason University
-Gunston Hall
-James Madison University
-Jamestown-Yorktown Foundation
-Library of Virginia
-Longwood University
-Norfolk State University
-Old Dominion University
-Radford University
-Richard Bland College
-Science Museum of Virginia
-University of Mary Washington
-University of Virginia
-Virginia Commonwealth University
-Virginia Military Institute
-Virginia State University
-College of William & Mary
-Virginia Business Education Partnership
-Roanoke Higher Education Authority
-Virginia Polytechnic Institute & State University

FIGURE 8.1

Listing of Virginia's Executive Branch Agencies

Source: http://www.virginia.gov/government/executive.

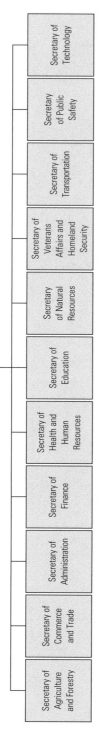

The organizational chart shows:

Governor → **Chief of Staff**

Reporting to the Chief of Staff:
- Secretary of Agriculture and Forestry
- Secretary of Commerce and Trade
- Secretary of Administration
- Secretary of Finance
- Secretary of Health and Human Resources
- Secretary of Education
- Secretary of Natural Resources
- Secretary of Veterans Affairs and Homeland Security
- Secretary of Transportation
- Secretary of Public Safety
- Secretary of Technology

- **Secretary of Agriculture and Forestry:** Oversees the Virginia Department of Agriculture and Consumer Services, the Department of Forestry, the Virginia Agricultural Council, and the Virginia Marine Products Board, as well as provides policy guidance.
- **Secretary of Commerce and Trade:** Oversees the economic, community, and workforce development for Virginia.
- **Secretary of Administration:** Oversees the general government operations for the Commonwealth to ensure efficient and effective management of the people's resources.
- **Secretary of Finance:** Provides guidance to the four agencies within the Finance Secretariat that handle the financial transactions of the Commonwealth, which include anything from paying bills and collecting taxes to distributing aid to localities.
- **Secretary of Health and Human Services:** Oversees twelve state agencies that provide vital services to Virginians with mental retardation, mental illness, substance abuse and physical disability concerns, as well as low-income working families and aging members of the population.
- **Secretary of Education:** Assists the governor in the development and implementation of the state's education policies. Also provides guidance and oversight to the sixteen colleges and universities, the Virginia Community College System, five higher education and research centers, the Department of Education, state-supported museums, and other educational agencies.

- **Secretary of the Commonwealth:** Assists the governor in appointments of over 4,000 individuals to serve on Virginia's boards and commissions.
- **Secretary of Natural Resources:** Advises the governor on natural resource issues and works to advance the governor's environmental priorities.
- **Secretary of Veterans Affairs and Homeland Security:** Leads the governor's initiatives focused on relationship building with the active duty military community, response to Base Realignment and Closure actions, veterans issues and Homeland Security initiatives.
- **Secretary of Transportation:** Ensures that Virginia's transportation system is safe, allows for easy movement of people, and enhances the economy and improves the quality of life.
- **Secretary of Public Safety:** Provides guidance to the state's agencies and 22,000 employees in the public safety sector.
- **Secretary of Technology:** The agencies under the secretary are responsible for the efficient and effective use of information technology to simplify government operations, advance technology applications to improve public service, and drive innovation economy through the Commonwealth's leadership.

FIGURE 8.2

The Organizational Structure of Virginia's Bureaucracy

Source: http://www.commonwealth.virginia.gov/stateqovernment/StateOrqChart/orqChart.cfm.

public institutions of higher learning, the Library of Virginia, the State Council of Higher Education, the Virginia Commission for the Arts, and various other educational authorities and partnerships.

Each **cabinet** department is headed by a cabinet secretary. All cabinet secretaries are appointed by the governor and confirmed by the Virginia General Assembly. The cabinet secretary serves as a channel between the governor and the department the individual oversees. The ultimate role, power, and influence given to a cabinet secretary is largely determined by how connected the individual is to the governor. Despite being led by political officials, most **street-level**, or lower-level, bureaucrats are career employees who go through a formal hiring process, rather than an appointment. In Virginia, this is the difference between a police officer who attends an academy and undergoes extensive testing prior to being hired and the secretary of finance who is appointed by the governor. Both individuals are qualified to do their jobs, but the cabinet position helps the governor in setting and implementing their policy agenda and therefore is usually a member of the governor's party.

Chapter 4 discussed the roles of organized interests and their structure in Virginia. An **iron triangle** is one way of thinking about how organized interests can and do impact the policymaking and implementation process in Virginia. Iron triangles, or patterns of mutually beneficial relationships that involve support, funding, and legislation among actors such as legislators, lobbyists and/or interest groups, and agencies have significant impact on the policymaking process. Iron triangles are typically discussed through the lens of federal policymaking, but iron triangles exist at all levels of government. These relationships can be observed at the local, regional, and state levels—the Commonwealth of Virginia is no exception. It is important to take a closer look at the legislative, lobbying, and bureaucratic actions that take place in Virginia to illustrate how iron triangles emerge in state governance and the policymaking process.

The issue of drunk-driving prevention and road safety in Virginia can better help us understand the relationships described above. These issues are important and benefit from a variety of support from the local, state, and federal levels of government. Mothers Against Drunk Driving (MADD) is a nonprofit organization that works to prevent drunk driving and combat underage drinking. MADD has state and local offices throughout Virginia. The Virginia MADD offices' staffs work together with the Virginia Department of Motor Vehicles and the Virginia General Assembly in order to create policies and programs to achieve their goals (see Figure 8.3). One example of their efforts is Virginia House Bill 279, which is an effort to institute stricter ignition interlock regulations to prevent drunk driving and the harmful effect of driving under the influence.

The relationship that exists between the Virginia General Assembly, the bureaucratic agencies within the Virginia Department of Motor Vehicles, and the state and local offices of Virginia's Mothers Against Drunk Driving is just one example of many of a state-level iron triangle at play in Virginia.

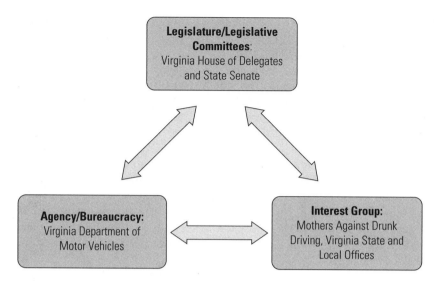

FIGURE 8.3

Iron Triangle: Virginia General Assembly, Virginia Department of Motor Vehicles, and Mothers Against Drunk Driving (MADD)

The Virginia Merit System

Because many senior bureaucratic officials operate under the discretional authority of the governor, it is necessary to have a strong system in place to ensure transparency in the hiring and compensation process of Virginia employees. For this reason, the Commonwealth has a strong **Virginia Personnel Act** and operates under a **merit system**. The first merit system in the United States was established in New York in 1883. Since that time, all states have adopted some form of their own merit system.[2] See Box 8.1 to see how it is done in New York today. Merit systems are sometimes referred to as a civil service system. In contrast to the **spoils system,** which rewards political supporters with government jobs, merit systems recruit from a pool of qualified individuals, providing them fair compensation based on their qualifications and on market values.[3] The Virginia Department of Human Resources Management clearly defines each step in the hiring process, beginning with recruitment (see Figure 8.4).[4]

When an agency wishes to hire a new employee, it must first write a detailed job description. The description must include information regarding the salary range, position duties, and education and/or experience requirements. The next step is to determine whether or not the position will be open to the general public or only to current employees. The agency may begin to receive applications only after a review date is set and the position has been advertised.

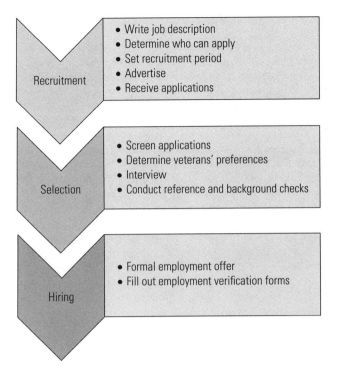

FIGURE 8.4

Steps to Virginia's Hiring Process

Source: http://www.dhrm.state.va.us/hrpolicy/policy/hiring2_10.pdf.

The selection process involves screening applications to ensure all candidates meet the minimum requirements necessary to perform the job. As organizations of the state, all bureaucratic agencies are required by Virginia Code §§ 2.2–2903 to give preference to veterans during the selection process. According to the state's human resources policy guide, no classified positions may be filled without interviewing qualified candidates. Throughout the selection process, the agency may also conduct reference and background checks as needed. To comply with the merit system and ensure transparency throughout the hiring process, Virginia agencies involve a panel of current employees in the decision-making process related to hiring.

Once the agency has selected a candidate, the agency must make a formal employment offer. Upon acceptance, the new hire must fill out employment verification forms to determine eligibility based on an individual's citizenship or immigrant status. The U.S. government requires all employees (citizens and noncitizens) who are hired after November 6, 1986, to complete a Form I-9 Employment Eligibility

BOX 8.1 How Is It Done in New York?

The executive branch of New York State government is headed by twenty departments—the maximum allowed under the state's current constitution. This limitation came about as a result of various constitutional reforms during the 1920s that were designed to make the state government more manageable, by eliminating many of the independently elected executive officers and curbing the creation of new departments. The New York Civil Service Commission is made up of three members: The president of the commission and two commissioners. Each officer serves six-year terms, which are filled by gubernatorial appointment with the advice and consent of the state Senate. No more than two officers can be from the same political party. The Civil Service Commission adopts and modifies rules governing a wide range of state civil service matters. Rules are subject to approval from the governor and have the full force of law. The New York Civil Service Commission is also tasked with hearing and ruling on appeals in regard to examination qualifications, examination ratings, position classifications, pay grade determinations, disciplinary actions, and requests to continue employment for individuals who are retired. The commission also oversees the operations of all municipal civil service commissions and city and county personnel.

The New York State Civil Service Commission (CSC) exercises authority over all classified civil servants of the state. The CSC retains broad merit system oversight responsibilities. The functions of the CSC can be divided into three categories:

1. Quasi-Legislative Authority: The CSC promulgates rules and regulations for all classified services.

2. Appellate Authority: The CSC hears appeals in disciplinary cases for employees not covered by contract, appeals regarding involuntary leaves of absence, and appeals from actions of the president of the CSC.

3. Investigative Authority: The CSC investigates any matter concerning the enforcement and effect of any of the state's Civil Service Commission laws or rules.

Source: http://www.cs.ny.gov/commission/observersguide/guide.cfm.

Verification. This form requires the agency to document that each new employee is authorized to work in the United States. The Commonwealth of Virginia requires agencies to complete this form for all new hires but does not require individuals to be a citizen of Virginia.

Certain departments, however, continue to utilize a system that rewards employees on the basis of the time spent with the organization rather than just relying on performance completed throughout the year. The Virginia Department of Education, for example, conducts reviews of all of its teachers to ensure satisfactory performance. While most pay increases are on the basis of seniority, Governor McDonnell authorized a pilot performance pay system for twenty-five schools in the Commonwealth for the 2011–2012 and 2012–2013 school years. This new system evaluates and rewards teacher performance based on a formula accounting for student academic growth and teacher's knowledge, planning, delivery, assessments, learning evironment, and professionalism. The pilot program seeks both to establish accountability in education and to recruit more teachers in hard-to-staff urban and rural areas in Virginia.[5]

Measuring Effectiveness and Improving Efficiency

To ensure the accountability and transparency of the bureaucracy's day-to-day operations, the Commonwealth has established various **performance measures** for each department and agency. By using these measures, the state can evaluate the effectiveness and efficiency of each dollar spent. Agencies in the Virginia bureaucracy measure their performance based on their missions, costs, administrative procedures, and service levels. Listed in each department's Strategic and Service Area Plan, these criteria link activities to the agency's and the state's long-term goals.

Each agency in the Commonwealth uses a three-step process in establishing performance measures. First, it identifies its **mission statement** or goal statement. This is usually a general statement concerning the general welfare of the public through fiscal responsibility and service delivery. For example, the Virginia Department of Accounts' mission statement is "to provide a uniform system of accounting for the Commonwealth's financial resources, while supporting and enhancing the recognition of Virginia as the best managed state in the union."[6] Based on its mission statement, the agency then formulates objectives, or ways, through which to achieve its stated goals. The agency then lists its goals, objectives, and measures by which it will assess its effectiveness and success. The measures are all grounded in research that establishes specific benchmarks necessary to securing the welfare of the public. See Table 8.1 for a comparison of bureaucratic agency productivity in Virginia from 2009 to 2012. Productivity was measured by things like number of customers served, budgets, and/or other performance outcomes as established by each agency. Overall, most agencies (twenty-six) improved their productivity between 2009 and 2012 while eighteen agencies maintained the same level of productivity during the period under review. Eleven agencies saw a decline in their overall productivity. See Box 8.2 for a more detailed overview of one particular agency—the Virginia Department of Motor Vehicles.

On June 29, 2010, Governor Bob McDonnell issued Executive Order No. 15. This executive order highlighted the importance of efficiency in government and the wise use of taxpayer dollars. Governor McDonnell emphasized this by demanding vigilance to prevent fraud, waste, and abuse in the operation of the state's government. The executive order, by the power granted to the governor under Article V of the Virginia Constitution and laws of the Commonwealth, ordered the state's internal auditor to continue the anonymous State Employee Fraud, Waste, and Abuse Hotline to encourage state employees to report cases in which fraud, waste, and abuse were present in the operation of state government. The Executive Order

TABLE 8.1 Bureaucratic Agency Productivity in Virginia from 2009–2012

Agency Name	Productivity
Board of Accountancy	Improving
Business Assistance	Improving
Blind and Vision Impaired	Improving
Correctional Education	Improving
Conservation and Recreation	Improving
Environmental Quality	Improving
Fire Programs	Improving
Game and Inland Fisheries	Improving
Health Professions	Improving
Historic Resources	Improving
Juvenile Justice	Improving
Minority Business Enterprise	Improving
Mines, Minerals and Energy	Improving
Accounts	Improving
Labor and Industry	Improving
Eastern Virginia Medical School	Improving
Jefferson Science Associates	Improving
Jamestown-Yorktown Foundation	Improving
Marine Resources Commission	Improving
Taxation	Improving
Treasury	Improving
Deaf and Hard-of-Hearing	Improving
Health	Improving
Transportation	Improving
Employment Commission	Improving
Museum of Natural History	Improving
Commonwealth's Attorneys' Services Council	Maintaining
Behavioral Health and Development Services	Maintaining

Agency Name	Productivity
Forensic Sciences	Maintaining
Human Resources Management	Maintaining
Medical Assistance Services	Maintaining
Motor Vehicles	Maintaining
Corrections	Maintaining
Education	Maintaining
Professional and Occupational Regulation	Maintaining
Social Services	Maintaining
Frontier Culture Museum of Virginia	Maintaining
Motor Vehicle Dealer Board	Maintaining
Science Museum of Virginia	Maintaining
Aging	Maintaining
Agriculture and Consumer Services	Maintaining
Port Authority	Maintaining
State Police	Maintaining
Tourism Authority	Maintaining
Comprehensive Services for At-Risk Youth and Families	Worsening
Criminal Justice Services	Worsening
Housing and Community Development	Worsening
Forestry	Worsening
Rehabilitative Services	Worsening
Employment Dispute Resolution	Worsening
Gunston Hall	Worsening,
Virginia Board for People with Disabilities	Worsening
Economic Development Partnership	Worsening
Museum of Fine Arts	Worsening
Racing Commission	Worsening

Source: Virginia Performs, "The Virginia Report 2012," accessed January 14, 2013, http://vaperforms.virginia.gov.

BOX 8.2   Virginia's Department of Motor Vehicles

- **Overview:** The DMV is responsible for vehicle titling and registration, driver licensing, and maintenance of driver and vehicle records. The DMV is responsible for collecting the state's fuel tax and car rental tax, monitors the state's trucking industry, and serves as the state's Highway Safety Office. The agency is also charged with effectively enforcing motoring and transportation-related tax laws and efficiently collecting and distributing transportation-related revenues. In fiscal year 2010, the DMV collected $2.1 billion in revenue for Virginia's transportation programs, with a current operating budget of $198.5 million.
- **Mission Statement:** The department is to promote security, safety, and service through the administration of motor vehicle and tax-related laws.
- **Vision:** The department is to operate at peak performance—everyone, every time.
- **Organizational Goals:**
  - Accomplish our mission by ensuring that credentials are issued in an accurate, secure, and efficient manner.
  - Provide customers with the information they need to access DMV services and comply with state laws and regulations.
  - Improve the safety of Virginia's highway system.
  - Accurately collect and manage transportation data.

- **Budget Summary:**
  - 2006–2008 Biennium Budget:
    Year 1: $261,287,528
    Year 2: $285,901,428
  - 2008–2010 Biennium Budget:
    Year 1: $214,479,009
    Year 2: $217,244,208
  - 2010–2012 Biennium Budget:
    Year 1: $217,244,208
    Year 2: $217,541,260

Source: http://dpb.virginia.gov/budget/buddoc11/agency.cfm?agency=154.

No. 15 protects employees from reporting abuses of fraud, waste, or abuse. The executive order seems to be highly effective thus far. For instance, Attorney General Kenneth Cuccinelli stated in 2012 that he is "committed to stopping fraud against taxpayers" and has made "fighting Medicare fraud a priority in Virginia by increasing the size of our fraud team by 50 percent over the last two years."[7] According to a report released in 2012, "The Medicaid Fraud Control Unit was extremely successful in fiscal year 2011–2012, particularly through its participation in multi-state agency investigations." As a result of this unit, substantial amounts of fraudulent activities have been detected just in the area of Medicaid alone. This has resulted in over $40 million recovered and twenty-one convictions.[8]

Conclusion

The term *bureaucracy* is oftentimes associated with a negative connotation despite the many services we expect and demand from the many bureaucratic agencies responsible for the day-to-day delivery of services and operations of state government. This chapter provided an overview of Virginia's bureaucracy. Having a better understanding of Virginia's bureaucracy will help you understand not only the many services provided by Virginia government, but also it will hopefully provide you a greater appreciation for this oftentimes underappreciated and misunderstood important part of our government and day-to-day lives.

Key Concepts

Bureaucracy

Cabinet

Iron triangle

Merit system

Mission statement

Performance measures

Personnel Act, Virginia

Spoils system

Street-level bureaucrat

Suggested Resources

- http://vaperforms.virginia.gov: Virginia Performs
- http://www.governor.virginia.gov/Cabinet: The Governor's Cabinet.
- http://www.madd.org/local-offices/va: Mother's Against Drunk Driving in Virginia.
- http://www.dhrm.state.va.us: Virginia Department of Human Resource Management.
- http://www.dmv.state.va.us: Virginia Department of Motor Vehicles.

Notes

1. Robert D. Wallace, "Review of *The Case for Bureaucracy: A Public Administration Polemic,*" *Journal of Political Science Education* 6, no. 2 (2010): 212–213.

2. Joan E. Pynes, *Human Resources Management for Public and Nonprofit Organizations* (San Francisco: Jossey-Bass, 2009).

3. United States Merit Systems Protection Board, "Merit System Principles (5 USC § 2301)," n.d., http://www.mspb.gov/meritsystemsprinciples.htm.

4. Department of Human Resources Management Policies & Procedures, "Policy 1.40—Performance Planning and Evaluation," August 1, 2001, http://www.dhrm.virginia.gov/hrpolicy/web/pol1_40.html.

5. Virginia Department of Education, "Teaching in Virginia: Performance and Evaluation," 2012, http://www.doe.virginia.gov/teaching/performance_evaluation.

6. United States Merit Systems Protection Board, "Merit System Principles (5 USC § 2301)," n.d., http://www.mspb.gov/meritsystemsprinciples.htm.

7. Office of the Attorney General of Virginia, *2011–2012 Annual Report* (Richmond, VA: Author, 2012), 14, accessed January 17, 2013, http://www.oag.state.va.us/Programs%20and%20Resources/Medicaid_Fraud/MFCU_2012/MFCU_Publications.html.

8. Ibid., 28.

OUTLINE

The Biennial Budget

The Virginia Budget
Process

  Timeline

  Where the Money
  Comes From

  Where the Money Goes

Virginia's Fiscal Health
and Solvency

How Is Virginia Doing?

Conclusion

CHAPTER 9

Paying the Bill

Budgeting and Finance in Virginia

A state's **budget** serves as an agenda-setting tool. It is a policy document outlining what a government intends to do or not do for a specific time period. The budget process is a battle between conflicting priorities and objectives from among the state's elected officials, interest groups, and leaders of the state's agencies and organizations. The budget also reflects the demands placed on government by its citizens. Without budgetary appropriations, state and local governments would cease to exist. This chapter presents an overview of Virginia's biennial budget, including the budget process, the state's revenues and expenditures, and a look into how the state is performing compared to other states, the nation, and itself.

The Biennial Budget

Virginia is one of only nineteen states that uses a **biennial budget** process (see Table 9.1 for a listing of states using an annual vs. biennial budget). This is down from forty-four in the 1940s. There are no real commonalities among the states using the biennial budget versus an annual budget in terms of population, political culture, demographics, location, and so on. A biennial budget differs from an **annual budget** in that when state legislatures convene, they adopt a budget that spans two years instead of one. In Virginia, the budget is adopted in even-numbered years and amended in odd-numbered years. This means that Virginia's current budget for the 2012–2014 biennium was adopted by the General Assembly in 2012. Why do some states (including Virginia) still use a biennial budget? First, biennial budgeting came about at a time when state legislatures did not meet every year and was therefore a necessary fiscal tool. Second, a biennial budget provides more oversight on the direction and fiscal health of the state. Finally, advocates of biennial budgeting highlight the theory that adopting two budgets in the same legislative session can save time and resources, thus, allowing legislators to focus more attention to evaluating programs and other matters. Creating two budgets in the same year can also minimize the amount of time the governor and the heads of state agencies spend on the development of their budget proposals. Volatility in the market, however, has made using biennial budgeting more difficult. Some **revenues** and **expenditures** are highly dependent on market conditions. These revenues and expenditures tend to fluctuate greatly and are therefore difficult to project for more than a single year. An additional weakness of using biennial budgeting is that it can be a very costly and time-consuming process—especially if the state revisits the budget in the second year to make revisions. Particular reasons a state may need to revisit their budget during the second year vary, but mainly, they revolve around overestimating revenue sources and/ or unbudgeted expenses that are incurred such as the response to natural (hurricane, snow, drought, etc.) and human-made disasters (terrorist attacks, school shootings, etc.).

The Virginia Budget Process

Pursuant to §2.2–103 of the Code of Virginia, the governor "shall be the chief planning and budget officer of the Commonwealth." In essence, the governor is in charge of budgeting for the state, though the General Assembly has the reserved duty to approve the state's budget.

TABLE 9.1   Annual versus Biennial Budgets in the States

ANNUAL Budget (31 states)	BIENNIAL Budget (19 states)
Arizona, Alabama, Alaska, Arkansas, California, Colorado, Delaware, Florida, Georgia, Idaho, Illinois, Iowa, Kansas, Louisiana, Maryland, Massachusetts, Michigan, Mississippi, Missouri, New Jersey, New Mexico, New York, Oklahoma, Pennsylvania, Rhode Island, South Carolina, South Dakota, Tennessee, Utah, Vermont, West Virginia	***Annual Legislative Session Biennial Budget (15 states):*** Connecticut, Hawaii, Indiana, Kentucky, Maine, Minnesota, Nebraska, New Hampshire, North Carolina, Ohio, Oregon, **Virginia**, Washington, Wisconsin, Wyoming ***Biennial Legislative Session (4 states)*** Montana, Nevada, North Dakota, Texas

Timeline

The Virginia budget development process (see Figure 9.1) takes many months and involves many actors, including the governor, the governor's cabinet, state agencies, the General Assembly, and Virginia citizens. The budget process begins in an even-numbered year as the governor reviews current revenues and expenditures and evaluates requests for funding from various agencies. Assisted by the Departments of Planning and Budget and of Taxation, the governor drafts a **balanced budget**. Unlike the U.S. government, all but one of the fifty states has some form of a balanced budget amendment in their state constitutions or state statutes—meaning, the state budget's anticipated expenditures must equal the state budget's anticipated revenues. Vermont is the only state that does not require a balanced budget. Once the Virginia budget is drafted, the government then delivers it to the House Appropriations, House Finance, and Senate Finance Committees in late December. As the House Appropriations and Finance and Senate Finance Committees hold public hearings on the executive budget, representatives may make amendment requests to the Appropriations Committee. These requests are evaluated in subcommittees, and further action is then recommended to the Appropriations Committee. After the budget document has been amended, the budget bill is introduced to both the Virginia House and the Virginia Senate. Each house has four days to pass or veto the budget bill.

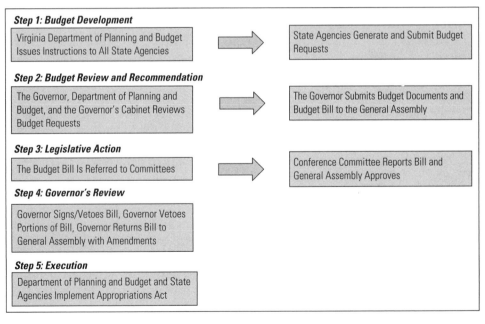

FIGURE 9.1

Virginia's Budget Development Process

Source: Virginia Department of Planning and Budget, http://dpb.virginia.gov.

Once both versions of the bill have been adopted, a conference committee of delegates and senators meet to reconcile differences between versions. The finalized bill is then sent back to both houses for a final vote. If the bill passes, it is sent to the governor for review. The governor may pass, veto, or make amendments to the bill. The governor also has the power to use a line-item veto. Once the budget bill has been signed into law, the executive branch is then in charge of implementing the Commonwealth's budget by way of the state's many agencies, including offices in the Department of Motor Vehicles, Department of Education, and many others. For more information on the state's bureaucracy, see Chapter 8.

Virginia's **fiscal year** begins on July 1 of each year. A fiscal year is the twelve-month period used for collecting and spending money. This date parallels that to all states except four. Alabama and Michigan follow the federal government's fiscal year, which begins on October 1. New York's fiscal year begins on April 1, and Texas's fiscal year begins on September 1.

Where the Money Comes From

The Commonwealth of Virginia has many services it needs to provide to its citizens. In order to provide these services, money must be collected. These monies are typically referred to as revenues. Revenues for the state come from a variety of sources. These sources include taxes, grants, fees, sales, earnings, transfers, and balances. Revenues are typically grouped into two categories: (1) general fund and (2) non-general fund. For the current budget period (2012–2014), total state revenues are projected to equal a little more than $82.2 billion.

General fund revenues are largely monies collected from general taxes paid by citizens and businesses, such as the sales or income tax. Taxes are the Commonwealth's largest revenue source, accounting for 45 percent, or approximately $22.4 billion, of revenue in fiscal year 2011. Of these amounts, individual income tax is the largest revenue source, followed by general sales and use taxes and then corporate income taxes. See Figure 9.2 for a breakdown of general fund monies collected in 2011. Table 9.2 reveals these revenue sources. The revenue sources are shown as a percentage of all general fund revenue monies collected between fiscal years 2005 and 2011. These sources have remained fairly steady, with slight variations from one year to the next. Figure 9.3 provides a breakdown of the anticipated general fund revenues for the 2012–2014 biennium.

Individual Income Tax: 65%

Corporate Income Tax: 3%

Insurance Premiums: 2%

Sales and Use Tax: 20%

Wills and Deeds Recordation: 3%

Other Revenues: 8%

FIGURE 9.2

General Fund Money Collected in 2011

Source: Virginia Auditor of Public Accounts, "Statewide Revenues by Class," *Commonwealth Data Point: Transparency at Work in Virginia,* n.d., http://datapoint.apa.virginia.gov/rev/rev_srccls.cfm.

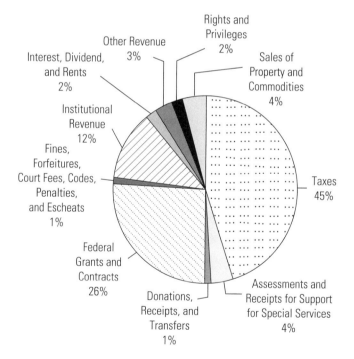

FIGURE 9.3

Virginia's Fiscal Year 2011 Revenues

Source: Virginia Auditor of Public Accounts, "Statewide Revenues by Class," *Commonwealth Data Point: Transparency at Work in Virginia,* n.d., http://datapoint.apa.virginia.gov/rev/rev_srccls.cfm.

Citizens often assume that the Commonwealth's only revenue source is from taxes. The majority of revenue found in most state budgets is from **non-general fund revenues**. While taxes makeup the largest proportion of Virginia's revenues, there are multiple revenue sources. Virginia receives approximately $11 billion each year in grants from the federal government. Money from these grants may be used to administer programs at the state level, such as funding for highway maintenance, or may be passed down to local governments or citizens such as the Federal Pell Grant Program for college students. See Table 9.2 for a review of the state's revenue sources other than taxes[1] and Figure 9.3 for a breakdown of all revenues collected in fiscal year 2011. Figure 9.4 provides a breakdown of anticipated non-general fund revenue sources for the 2012–2014 biennium.

TABLE 9.2 Virginia Revenue Sources

Revenue Source	Explanation
Fees for Services	These charges are levied on services the Commonwealth provides, therefore, only the recipients of these services pay the associated fees. Examples of Fees for Service in Virginia include mortgage lender licensure fees, health care premiums, and assessments on localities.
Donations, Receipts, and Transfers	These may be donations from private citizens or businesses, receipts from local and special purpose governments for state services, and intergovernmental transfers.
Grants and Contracts	Many of the grants awarded to the Commonwealth are from the federal government in the form of categorical or block grants. Others are awards from businesses or institutions for use in a specific programmatic area.
Fines and Forfeitures	Revenues from this category include state court fees, fines associated with breaking the law, and fines for failing to pay taxes or charges.
Interest, Dividends, and Rents	Much of this revenue source is related to investments the Commonwealth has made. The invested bonds and loans accrue interest each year. Private entities may rent state-owned property.
Sale of Property and Commodities	Revenues from this source include proceeds from lottery tickets, the sale of buildings, surplus and equipment, and revenue from alcoholic beverage sales.
Institutional Revenue	This revenue source is collected by state institutions, such as colleges, hospitals, and correctional institutions.

Source: Governor Robert F. McDonnell, "Executive Amendments to the 2011–2012 Biennial Budget," Virginia Department of Planning and Budget, December 17, 2010, pp. 15–20, http://dpb.virginia.gov/budget/buddoc11/pdf/budgetdocument2011.pdf.

BOX 9.2   The Fifty-first State—NOVA vs. "Real Virginia"

Southern Virginia is a distinct region of the state and known as a place of idyllic beauty filled with national parks, walking trails, small towns, and Southern hospitality; it is known to many, including former Republican presidential nominee John McCain's campaign manager, as "real Virginia" when compared to the state's Northern counterparts.[2] Southern Virginians typically view Northern Virginia, or NOVA, as the fifty-first state, a distinct region filled with rich couples with no respect for the Southern heritage and simple way of life. There are, however, two sides to every story. Northern Virginia residents may describe their Southern counterparts as clinging to a discriminatory history. Cultural arguments aside, just three counties in Northern Virginia—Fairfax, Loudon, and Prince William—accounted for 40 percent—yes, 40 percent—of the state's total population growth since the 2000 Census.[3] This area is the financial powerhouse of the state, generating a large percentage of the state's revenues each year. Southern Virginia must rely on the revenue from the Northern region to maintain the level of services it currently receives without having to suffer significant increases in taxes. In return, the region of Southern Virginia offers intrinsic values and getaways for residents of the Northern region.

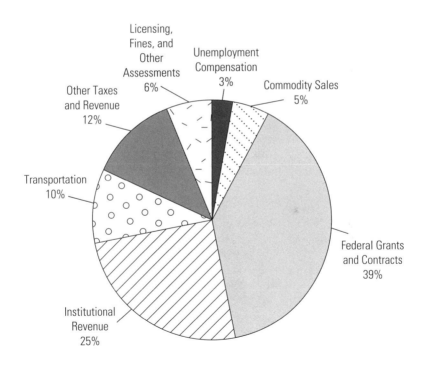

FIGURE 9.4

Non-General Fund Revenues, 2012–2014

Source: Virginia Auditor of Public Accounts, "Statewide Revenues by Class," *Commonwealth Data Point: Transparency at Work in Virginia*, n.d., http://datapoint.apa.virginia.gov/rev/rev_srccls.cfm.

Where the Money Goes

The governor of Virginia and the General Assembly have significant discretion when it comes to expenditures associated with general fund revenues since these revenues support a variety of government programs in Virginia. Non-general funds are funds collected and earmarked for specific purposes. For example, in Virginia, all student tuition and fees collected from college students must support higher education. Statewide expenditures in 2011 were over $43 billion. This is compared to $41.7 billion in 2010, $40.7 billion in 2009, and $38.4 billion in 2009. An expenditure breakdown by category is provided for fiscal year 2011 in Figure 9.5. The Commonwealth's largest expenditure category was individual and family services, including programming for Medicaid and workforce assistance. Closely following were expenses related to education, approximately $12.5 billion in fiscal year 2011. This amount includes expenditures related to primary, secondary, and postsecondary education in the Commonwealth.

According to the Virginia Department of Planning and Budget, the Code of Virginia requires that the governor's executive budget show the "amount of each

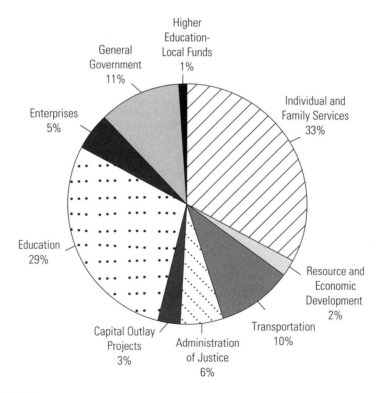

FIGURE 9.5

Virginia's Fiscal Year Expenditures, 2011

Source: Virginia Auditor of Public Accounts, "Statewide Expenditures by Program," *Commonwealth Data Point: Transparency at Work in Virginia*, n.d., accessed September 5, 2011, http://datapoint.apa.virginia.gov/exp/exp_fcn.cfm.

A July 17, 2011, *Washington Times* article highlighted the information that as Congress struggled with the national debt, twelve states ended fiscal year 2011 with a budget surplus. The state of Indiana reported one of the largest surpluses in 2011: $1.2 billion. What did it do with all the extra money? Governor Mitch Daniels authorized up to a $1,000 bonus for all state employees. Of course, not everyone received the bonus. Bonuses were awarded based on whether or not an employee met expectations ($500 bonus), exceeded expectations ($750 bonus), or were outstanding workers ($1,000 bonus). Other states had different priorities. Some states decided to put funds away as rainy-day funds or reserve accounts. One-half of Maine's $50 million surplus went to the state's reserve funds. A majority of Idaho's $85 million surplus went to the state's public schools and colleges.

Source: Ben Wolfgang, "Many States Celebrate Surpluses as Congress Struggles with Debt," *Washington Times*, July 17, 2011, Politics section, http://www.washingtontimes.com/news/2011/jul/17/many-states-celebrate-surpluses-as-congress-strugg.

primary agency's budget that represents direct aid to" local governments (counties, cities, and towns) in Virginia.[4] Aid to localities is defined as "any payment made directly to a local government or school division; any payment made on behalf of a local government or school division; or any payment made to an organization or group that provides a direct benefit to a local government or its residents, such as a public library, planning district commission, or Community Services Board."[5] Virginia residents receive a direct benefit through the services provided by the operations of their local public schools, police departments, and the construction and maintenance of the state's secondary roads. The estimated distribution of aid to local governments in Governor McDonnell's 2013 budget is a little more than $5.7 billion.

Virginia's Fiscal Health and Solvency

Virginia was one of twelve states to post a budget surplus in fiscal year 2011. Virginia's fiscal year 2011 surplus was $541 million. In response to fears of major credit rating agencies (Moody's Fitch, Stand & Poor's) that the Virginia economy is too closely linked to that of the federal government, Governor Bob McDonnell proposed a portion of the surplus be used to create a contingency fund in the event of drastically decreased federal funding. See Box 9.3 to read about what other states are doing with their surplus money.

A snapshot of Virginia's fiscal health does not paint the entire picture. In fiscal year 2010, the Commonwealth deferred payment into pensions for public employees enrolled in the Virginia Retirement System. This raised the total amount of unfunded liabilities to $17.6 billion. The state is not required to report this amount on its audited annual financial statements, making it look like there is more of a surplus when there would not have been otherwise. Lawmakers in Richmond continue to debate the degree to which the state and its public employees should contribute to the state's pension system. Despite this, Virginia is performing much better than its neighbor to the south—North Carolina. See Table 9.3 for a comparison of Virginia to North Carolina and the national average.

How Is Virginia Doing?

Virginia Performs seeks to link state agency missions and goals with those of the state at large. Through this program, Virginia and her citizens can monitor progress toward its goals and regularly monitor the effectiveness of agency expenditures. See Figure 9.6 for Virginia's Scorecard at a Glance, showing how Virginia is performing in the seven programmatic areas identified in Table 9.4. Of the forty-four indicators, in 2011 Virginia improved in twenty-six areas, maintained in eleven areas, and worsened in seven areas. Virginia performed the best in the area of public safety; the state performed the worst in the area of the economy, especially in the areas of personal income, poverty, and unemployment. The goal under public safety is "to protect the public's safety and security, ensure a fair and effective system of justice, and provide a prepared response to emergencies and disasters of all kinds" (Public Safety section, para. 1, http://vaperforms .virginia.gov/indicators/publicSafety/summary.php). Virginia improved in all public safety indicators, including crime, emergency preparedness, juvenile intakes, recidivism, and traffic fatalities.

TABLE 9.3   How Is Virginia Doing?

	Virginia	North Carolina	National Average
Average 2011 unemployment rate	6.24%	9.99%	8.95%
Fiscal year 2011 budget shortfall as a percentage of General Fund	8.5%	30.6%	19.9%
Gross domestic product per capita	$53,463	$42,884	$47,482
Bond ratings (S&P/Moody's/Fitch)	AAA/Aaa/AAA	AAA/Aaa/AAA	AA+/AAA/AAA

Source: Bureau of Labor Statistics, 2011, http://www.bls.gov/data/#unemployment; Kaiser Family Foundation, 2011, http://kff.org/statedata; Virginia Performs, "Bond Rating," September 14, 2011, http://vaperforms.virginia.gov/indicators/ govtcitizens/bondRating.php.

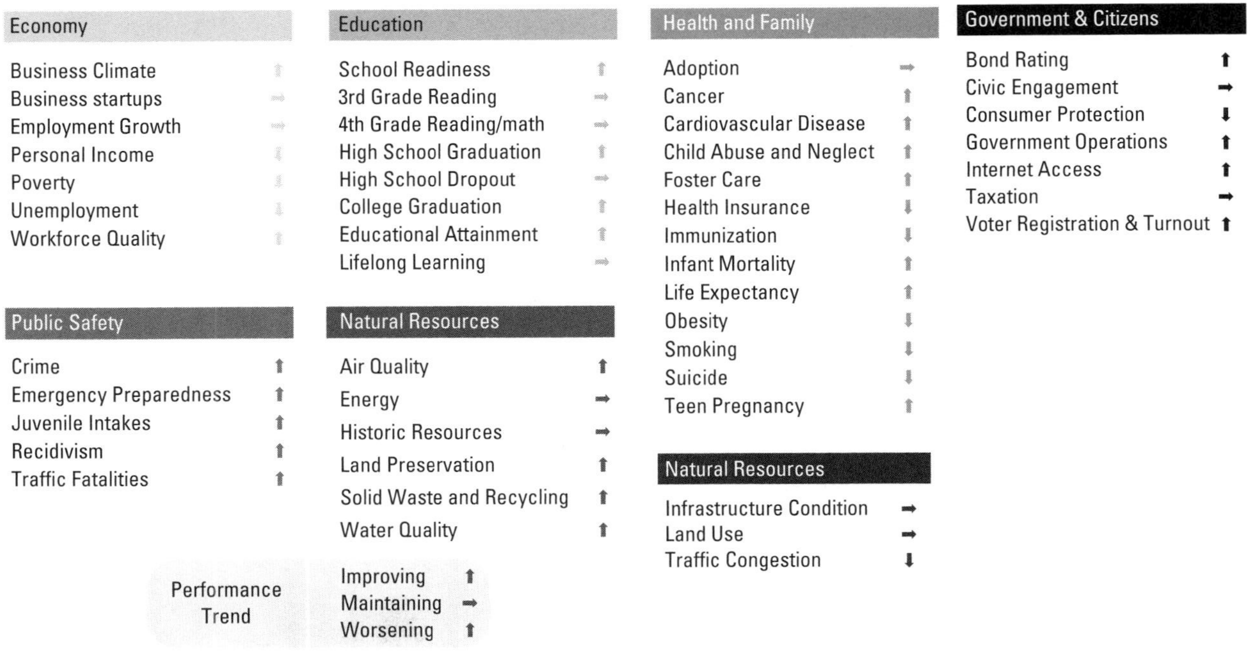

Economy

Business Climate ↓
Business startups ↑
Employment Growth ↑
Personal Income →
Poverty →
Unemployment →
Workforce Quality →

Education

School Readiness ↓
3rd Grade Reading ↑
4th Grade Reading/math ↑
High School Graduation →
High School Dropout ↑
College Graduation ↓
Educational Attainment ↓
Lifelong Learning ↑

Health and Family

Adoption ↑
Cancer →
Cardiovascular Disease →
Child Abuse and Neglect →
Foster Care →
Health Insurance →
Immunization →
Infant Mortality →
Life Expectancy →
Obesity →
Smoking →
Suicide →
Teen Pregnancy →

Government & Citizens

Bond Rating ←
Civic Engagement ↑
Consumer Protection →
Government Operations ←
Internet Access ←
Taxation ↑
Voter Registration & Turnout ←

Public Safety

Crime ↑
Emergency Preparedness ↑
Juvenile Intakes ↑
Recidivism ↑
Traffic Fatalities ↑

Natural Resources

Air Quality ↑
Energy ↑
Historic Resources ↑
Land Preservation ↑
Solid Waste and Recycling ↑
Water Quality ↑

Natural Resources

Infrastructure Condition ↑
Land Use ↑
Traffic Congestion →

Performance
Trend

Improving ↑
Maintaining ↑
Worsening ↑

FIGURE 9.6

Virginia Performs Scorecard at a Glance

Source: http://vaperforms.virginia.gov/extras/about.php.

TABLE 9.4 Virginia Performs Program

Goal 1 *Economy*	Be a national leader in the preservation and enhancement of our economy.
Goal 2 *Education*	Elevate the levels of educational preparedness and attainment of our citizens.
Goal 3 *Health and Family*	Inspire and support Virginians toward healthy lives and strong and resilient families.
Goal 4 *Natural, Historic, and Cultural Resources*	Protect, conserve, and wisely develop our natural, cultural, and historic resources.
Goal 5 *Public Safety*	Protect the public's safety and security, ensure a fair and effective system of justice, and provide a prepared response to emergencies and disasters of all kinds.
Goal 6 *Transportation*	Ensure Virginia has a transportation system that is safe, allows the easy movement of people and goods, enhances the economy, and improves quality of life.
Goal 7 *Government and Citizens*	Be recognized as the best-managed state in the nation.

Source: http://vaperforms.virginia.gov/extras/about.php.

Conclusion

Budgeting represents one of the most important decision-making processes involved with public institutions. Virginia's budget reflects the state's policy priorities as well as the program objectives of all of the state's agencies and institutions. Knowing more about Virginia's budget process, where the revenues come from and where the expenditures go, not only helps you know how the state is spending your tax dollars, but it also helps you to better evaluate the state's fiscal health—an important part in increasing the state's accountability to its citizens.

Key Concepts

Annual budget
Balanced budget
Biennial budget
Budget
Expenditures

Fiscal year
General fund revenues
Non-general fund revenues
Revenues

Suggested Resources

- http://future.virginia.gov/: **Council on Virginia's Future.**
- http://www.nasbo.org/: National Association of State Budget Officers.
- http://dpb.virginia.gov/: Virginia Department of Planning & Budget.
- http://www.apa.state.va.us/: Virginia Auditor of Public Accounts.
- http://vaperforms.virginia.gov/: **Virginia Performs.**

Notes

1. Virginia Auditor of Public Accounts, "Statewide Revenues," *Commonwealth Data Point: Transparency at Work,* n.d., http://datapoint.apa.virginia.gov/rev/rev_statewide.cfm.

2. Julia Hoppock, "McCain Adviser Says Northern Virginia Not 'Real' Virginia," October 18, 2008, http://abcnews.go.com/blogs/politics/2008/10/mccain-adviser-2.

3. Hayar El Nasser, "Northern Virginia Counties Are 'the Engines' of State's Growth," *USA Today,* February 7, 2011, http://usatoday30.usatoday.com/news/nation/census/2011 -02-03-census-virginia_N.htm.

4. Virginia Department of Planning and Budget, "Executive Amendments to the 2012–2014 Biennial Budget," December 17, 2012, p. C-53, http://dpb.virginia.gov/budget/ buddoc13/pdf/budgetdocument2013.pdf.

5. Ibid., C-53.

CHAPTER 10

OUTLINE

Municipal Governments

Incorporation and
the Growth of Local
Governments in Virginia

County Governments

Local Government
Revenue

Annexation and
Governmental Consolidation
in Virginia

Regionalism in Virginia

Conclusion

Municipalities and Metropolitanism

Local and Regional Governance in Virginia

While we typically think of federal and state governments as the major players in our governing system, a significant portion of public life takes place at the local level. Counties, cities, towns, and special districts share responsibility for the provision of public services to Virginia residents. These political subdivisions of the Commonwealth work to improve the quality of life of the residents within their jurisdictional boundaries or together within a regional framework. Local governments provide multiple services—from hiring schoolteachers who educate our youth to regulating the built environment through building code regulations to providing local law enforcement who police our streets. According to the most recent data from the Census of Governments, Virginia had 498 local governments in 2012. This places Virginia forty-forth among the fifty states in total number of local governments. The state with the fewest was Hawaii with twenty-two local governments in 2012. The state with the largest number of local governments in 2012 was Illinois with 6,968 local governments. In that same year, the Bureau of the Census identified a total of 89,004 local governments in the United States.[1] Local government in Virginia may be established as a town, city, county, or regional government, such as a special district. This chapter will discuss each of these political subdivisions in greater detail.

Municipal Governments

Article VII of the Constitution of Virginia outlines the basic framework for the function and structure of local governments in the Commonwealth. Municipal governments are the town and independent city governments in Virginia. The main distinction between a city and a town deals with minimum population requirements. Cities must have five thousand or more residents while towns must have at least one thousand residents. Another distinction is that towns are municipalities *within* a county, whereas an independent city is by definition and statute independent of county government. Services within a county are shared and divided between the county and a town(s).

Perhaps the single most distinctive feature of local government in the Commonwealth is the principle of city and county separation.[2] There are forty-one independent cities in the United States. Thirty-eight of these are located in Virginia![3] In fact, Virginia is the only state in the United States that has city-county separation statewide. An **independent city** is a city that is not a part of another general-purpose government. Each Virginia city, referred to as an independent incorporated community in the state constitution, is politically independent of the county within which it is located. Independent cities interact only with the Commonwealth—not a county government. Cities elsewhere in the United States are a geographical and political subdivision of their county government (except Baltimore, Maryland; Carson City, Nevada; and St. Louis, Missouri).

Since Virginia cities are independent of their county (even though geographically they may be completely surrounded by one), city residents do not pay county taxes,

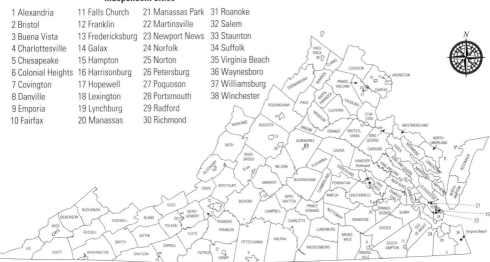

Independent Cities

1 Alexandria	11 Falls Church	21 Manassas Park	31 Roanoke
2 Bristol	12 Franklin	22 Martinsville	32 Salem
3 Buena Vista	13 Fredericksburg	23 Newport News	33 Staunton
4 Charlottesville	14 Galax	24 Norfolk	34 Suffolk
5 Chesapeake	15 Hampton	25 Norton	35 Virginia Beach
6 Colonial Heights	16 Harrisonburg	26 Petersburg	36 Waynesboro
7 Covington	17 Hopewell	27 Poquoson	37 Williamsburg
8 Danville	18 Lexington	28 Portsmouth	38 Winchester
9 Emporia	19 Lynchburg	29 Radford	
10 Fairfax	20 Manassas	30 Richmond	

FIGURE 10.1

Map of Virginia Counties and Independent Cities

Source: Virginia Association of Counties, http://www.vaco.org/vamap.html.

receive services from county government, nor vote for countywide offices. This is similar to the distinction between two counties: They are both separate political and geographic entities. For example, the City of Harrisonburg is geographically located in Rockingham County. However, property owners in Harrisonburg pay property taxes only to the city—not to the county government. Therefore, they receive services only from the City of Harrisonburg. While county governments in Virginia were created to serve the needs of rural residents and less densely populated areas, city governments reflect the need for additional services specific to urban areas. As a result, property taxes are usually higher in a city based on the additional demand placed on and expected by city residents.[4] All Commonwealth cities have been independent cities since 1871 when a revised state constitution took effect following the Civil War. Independent cities may serve as a county seat of an adjacent county even though the city is not, by definition, a part of the county. A county seat is typically referred to as the center of government for the county. Government services, such as a courthouse, jail, sheriff's office, social services, hospital, and so on, are typically concentrated within a county seat. An example is Fairfax, Virginia, which is an independent city as well as the county seat for Fairfax County.

All but one of Virginia's independent cities have a council-manager **form of government**. The City of Richmond has operated under a strong **mayor-council form of government** since 2004. According to the International City/County Management Association, 43 percent of U.S. cities use the mayor-council system— especially in cities with more than 500,000 residents. A distinguishing characteristic of this system is the separation of executive and legislative powers. The extent of authority granted to the executive (mayor) varies considerably. On the other hand, a **council-manager form of government** centralizes legislative authority and responsibility to a city council. Administrative responsibility and authority rests with a city manager who is appointed by and serves at the pleasure of the city council. The city manager is hired to oversee the implementation of the policies enacted by his or her city council and oversees the delivery of public services. The mayor within a council-manager form of government usually helps set the council agenda, oversees

BOX 10.2 Typical Powers Associated with Weak Mayor vs. Strong Mayor Town/City Councils

Weak Mayor	Strong Mayor
• The town/city council (including the mayor) exercise all power as a body	• The town/city council serves as the legislature while the mayor serves as the executive
• No formal authority outside the council	
• Exercise influence by powers of persuasion, rather than the authority vested in their office	• Mayor has full appointive powers and veto powers over legislative actions of council
• Lacks veto power over council votes	• Given authority to appoint and/or remove officials
• Given relatively little executive power	
• Ceremonial duties, such as ribbon cutting ceremonies	• Runs the day-to-day operations of municipal government
	• Prepares the budget

Source: Kevin B. Smith, Alan Greenblatt, and John Buntin, *Governing States and Localities* (Washington, DC: CQ Press, 2005); David Miller, *The Regional Governing of Metropolitan America* (Boulder, CO: Westview Press, 2002), 30–32; David H. Rosenbloom, Robert S. Kravchuk, and Richard M. Clerkin, *Public Administration, Understanding Management, Politics, and Law in the Public Sector,* 7th ed. (New York: McGraw-Hill, 2009).

city council meetings, and serves a ceremonial role representing the city at various functions, such as groundbreaking ceremonies. On the other hand, the mayor of Richmond serves a full-time, four-year term. His or her responsibility is to oversee the executive management of the city's departments and agencies. The mayor, serving as chief executive officer of the city, appoints a chief administrative officer who is directly responsible for the city's day-to-day operations. This individual must be approved by the Richmond City Council. For more information on the differences between a **weak-mayor**/council-manager form of governments and a strong-mayor form of government see Box 10.2.

Local governments, be it a town or a city, are **creatures of the state** (explained further in Chapter 2, "A Framework for Governing: Exploring the Virginia State Constitution"). Virginia law requires each local government to have a municipal charter. The charter outlines the government's powers and responsibilities. Cities and towns provide essential public services, such as police, fire, water and sewer, public health, parks and recreation, zoning, libraries, schools, planning, and economic development. The degree of power a local government possesses rests with the state government.

Dillon's Rule and Home Rule are models of governance that define the scope of authority given to local governments. In **Home Rule** states, the state constitution provides local governments (such as towns, townships, cities, counties, boroughs, perishes, or other municipalities) with the ability to govern themselves as they see fit,

BOX 10.3   **Dillon's Rule vs. Home Rule States**

Dillon's Rule	Home Rule
• Local governments are "creatures of the state"* and are granted power via the state constitution of the home state.	• Local governments are "creatures of the state," however, they are granted greater flexibility in decision making.
• Local governments have limited autonomy.	• Local governments have greater autonomy.
• Local government have limited, specific authority.	• Local government has relative authority over its own affairs, sometimes referred to as "local legal autonomy."**

*From John G. Grumm and Russell D. Murphy, "Dillon's Rule Reconsidered," *Annals of the American Academy of Political Science* 416, no. 1(1974): 120–132, accessed September 17, 2012, http://www.jstor.org/stable/1041787.

**From David J. Barron, "Reclaiming Home Rule," *Harvard Law Review* 116, no. 8(2003): 2255–2386, accessed September 17, 2012, http://www.jstor.org/stable/1342767.

as long as they are not in violation of the U.S. or state constitution. In other states, only limited authority has been granted to local governments by passage of statutes in the state legislature. In **Dillon's Rule** states, a local government must acquire permission from its state legislature to pass a specific law, ordinance, statute, and so forth that is not explicitly outlined in existing legislation and/or the constitution. Individuals in Home Rule states, such as North Carolina, may see local governments as the building blocks of democracy. However, in Virginia, as a Dillon's Rule state, political power starts at the state level and trickles down to the counties, cities, towns, and regional commissions and/or districts. Municipalities in the Commonwealth do not possess any power outside of their charter and must seek approval from the Virginia General Assembly for additional power. See Box 10.3 for more information about the differences between a Home Rule and a Dillon's Rule state.

Incorporation and the Growth of Local Governments in Virginia

The number of cities and towns in Virginia is not static; localities can become political jurisdictions through the process of incorporation. Towns in the Commonwealth are incorporated by judicial proceeding by the circuit court of the county in which the community is located or by a special act of the Commonwealth of Virginia General Assembly. **Incorporation** by special act is more complicated since several criteria enumerated in the Virginia Code must be satisfied. Residents of any community may initiate action for incorporation by petition to the circuit court if several conditions are present. First, the community must have a minimum population of one thousand residents. Second, the population density of the affected county must not exceed two hundred persons per square mile. Third, the petition is signed by at least one hundred qualified voters residing in the area to be incorporated. Fourth, the Commission on Local Government must determine that "the services required by the area seeking to be incorporated cannot be provided by the establishment of a sanitary district or the extension of existing services currently provided by the county."[5] Fifth, the petition must include a plan prepared by a registered surveyor, showing the boundaries of the potential town. Finally, the petition must show that the general good of the community will be promoted by the incorporation. Community in this sense refers not only to the area desiring incorporation but also to the county in which the incorporation is to occur.[6] The goal of the general good of the community is looked at in terms of government responsiveness, government accountability, and enforcement powers. This includes an analysis of the governance capability, if any, of a property owners' association and the county versus what improvements could be attained by a newly created town council. A group of citizens may want to incorporate into a town out of fear of being annexed by a neighboring town, to control land use and zoning regulations, or to receive additional funding from the state and federal governments through intergovernmental aid. The court may request a hearing conducted by the State Commission on Local Government to determine if the community in fact complies with the criteria.

Virginia has not experienced many new incorporations since 1952. Figure 10.2 reveals the creation of six new municipal governments and 144 new special districts in Virginia between 1952 and 2007. This equates to a 2.69 percent increase in municipal governments and a staggering 342.86 percent increase in the number of special districts. During the same time horizon, in the United States as a whole, municipal governments grew by 15.9 percent and special purpose governments by 202.9 percent (see Figure 10.3). Virginia's growth in special districts can be attributed to rapid population growth in the Washington, D.C., suburban areas of northern Virginia. Special districts in Virginia are explained in more detail later in this chapter.

County Governments

All territory not within independent cities in Virginia is part of one of Virginia's ninety-five counties. Counties, like cities and towns, are an arm of the state of

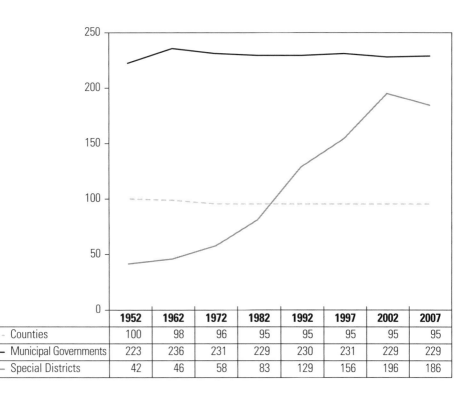

	1952	1962	1972	1982	1992	1997	2002	2007
---- Counties	100	98	96	95	95	95	95	95
—— Municipal Governments	223	236	231	229	230	231	229	229
—— Special Districts	42	46	58	83	129	156	196	186

FIGURE 10.2

Growth in the Number of Virginia Governments

Source: U.S. Census Bureau, Census of Governments, http://www.census.gov/govs/cog2012.

Virginia and therefore exist at the will of the state government. In terms of population, most counties are very rural; however, county populations vary significantly across the state. Fairfax County, a suburban area of Washington, D.C., is the state's largest county in terms of population. In 2011, Fairfax County had a population estimate of 1.1 million people. The area known as Tysons Corner is located in Fairfax

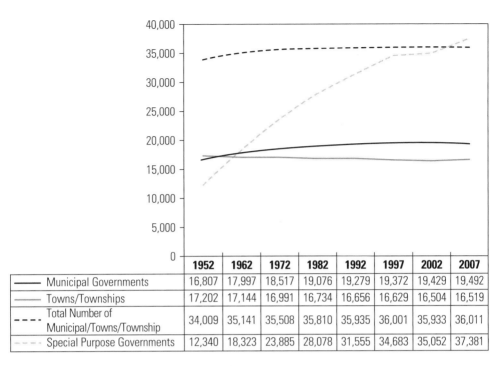

	1952	1962	1972	1982	1992	1997	2002	2007
—— Municipal Governments	16,807	17,997	18,517	19,076	19,279	19,372	19,429	19,492
—— Towns/Townships	17,202	17,144	16,991	16,734	16,656	16,629	16,504	16,519
- - - - Total Number of Municipal/Towns/Township	34,009	35,141	35,508	35,810	35,935	36,001	35,933	36,011
- - - - Special Purpose Governments	12,340	18,323	23,885	28,078	31,555	34,683	35,052	37,381

FIGURE 10.3

Growth in the Number of Governments in the United States

Source: U.S. Census Bureau, Census of Governments, http://www.census.gov/govs/cog2012.

Note: Data for 2012 from the U.S. Census are only estimates. The number of local governments in Virginia has not changed since 2007.

County. Tysons Corner is the nation's twelfth largest employment center—yet is an unincorporated area (meaning, it is not a city or a town). Virginia's smallest county in 2011, in terms of population, was Highland County with a population estimate of 2,319 people. Highland County is located in southwestern Virginia.

Article VII, Section 4 of the state constitution requires the following positions be elected by qualified voters within each county and in each independent city:

- Treasurer (four-year term)
- Sheriff (four-year term)
- Attorney for the Commonwealth (four-year term)
- Clerk of Court (eight-year term)
- Commissioner of Revenue (four-year term)

The county governing body is typically called the County Board of Supervisors, County Board, or Urban County Board of Supervisors. The elected officials set the agenda for public administrators and career bureaucrats to implement. They work to maintain and improve the quality of life of their county by providing various services to residents. Typical government services provided by Virginia counties include planning; parks and recreation; public utilities, such as water and sewer; education; fire protection; welfare; police and sheriff protection; refuse or garbage collection; health and sanitation; economic development; zoning; and code enforcement. Provision of services is dependent upon the population and density (population and buildings) of the county. Counties levy taxes (most often sales taxes and property taxes), charge user fees (such as water or trash pickup fees), and receive intergovernmental aid from the state and federal governments in order to provide and maintain services to their residents (see Figure 10.4 for a breakdown of local government revenue by category and jurisdictional class for counties).

Local Government Revenue

Cities and counties rely heavily on taxes and fees to finance their operations. Local governments across the country use property taxes as major vehicles of funding support for services. Virginia is no exception. Figure 10.5 shows a breakdown of local government revenue by category for all jurisdictions (city and county) in Virginia

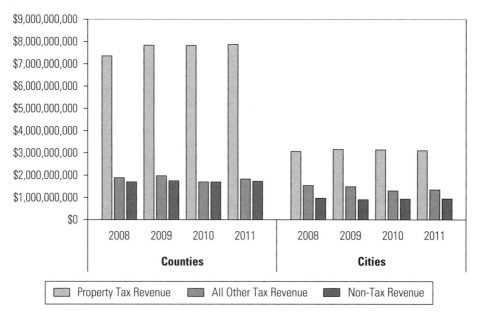

FIGURE 10.4

Local Government Revenue by Category and Jurisdictional Class for Counties and Cities in Virginia

Source: Auditor of Public Accounts, *Comparative Report of Local Government Revenues and Expenditures* (four reports, years ending June 30, 2008, 2009, 2010, 2011), http://www.apa.virginia.gov.

between 2008 and 2011. According to the Virginia Auditor of Public Accounts, property tax revenue represents the largest revenue source for all jurisdictions—accounting for 63 percent of local revenue in 2008 and 65 percent in 2011. This is significantly higher than the national average. The American Council on Intergovernmental Relations reports that the contribution of tax proceeds to the general receipts of local revenue for all U.S. local governments was 27.9 percent in fiscal year 2008. This is remarkably lower than the 47.8 percent contribution in 1960.[7] Other local government revenues include "other tax revenue," such as local sales and use taxes, motor vehicle taxes, restaurant food taxes, and "non-tax revenue" such as user fees, rental of property, and so on (see Box 10.6 for a breakdown of the revenue categories portrayed in Figure 10.4). Figure 10.5 represents a breakdown between counties and cities in terms of revenue collected. Counties relied more on property taxes when compared to cities during the years examined (2008–2011). In 2008, 67 percent of county revenue was from property taxes while 42 percent of city revenue was from property taxes. This increased to 68.9 percent for counties in 2012 while property taxes accounted for 57 percent for cities in 2012 (this was a 15 percent increase between 2008 and 2011).

Figure 10.6 represents operating expenditures by category for all counties and cities in Virginia between 2008 and 2011. Education represents the largest expenditure item over the four year period examined (55.1 percent of total expenditures in 2008 and 53.1 percent in 2011). This is representative of all states across the country.

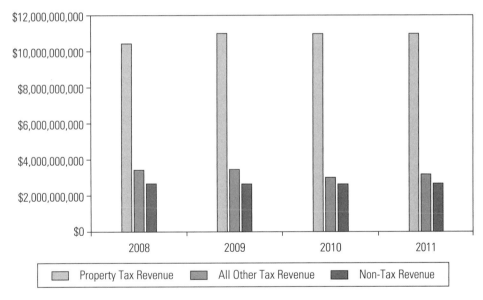

FIGURE 10.5

Local Government Revenue for All Jurisdictions in Virginia

Source: Auditor of Public Accounts, *Comparative Report of Local Government Revenues and Expenditures* (four reports, years ending June 30, 2008, 2009, 2010, 2011), http://www.apa.virginia.gov/.

BOX 10.6   Elaboration of Governmental Revenue Categories

Property Tax Revenue

Real Property

Public Service Corporation

General Personal Property

Mobile Home Property

Machinery and Tools

Merchants' Capital

Property Tax Penalties

Property Tax Interest

All Other Tax Revenue

Local Sales and Use Taxes

Consumers' Utility

Business License

Franchise License

Motor Vehicle License

Bank Stock

Taxes on Recordation and Wills

Tobacco Taxes

Admission and Amusement Taxes

Transient Occupancy Tax

Restaurant Food Tax

Coal-Oil-Gas Taxes

E-911 Service Tax

Other Non-Property Taxes

Non-Tax Revenue

Permits-Fees-Licenses

Fines and Forfeitures

Charges for Services

Investment of Funds

Rental of Property

Payments in Lieu of Taxes from Enterprise Activities

Inter-local Revenue-Sharing Payments

Miscellaneous Non-Tax Sources

Source: Local Government Revenue of Virginia's Counties & Cities, FY 2008, http://www.dhcd.virginia.gov/Commission onLocalGovernment/PDFs/locrev08.pdf, p. 4.

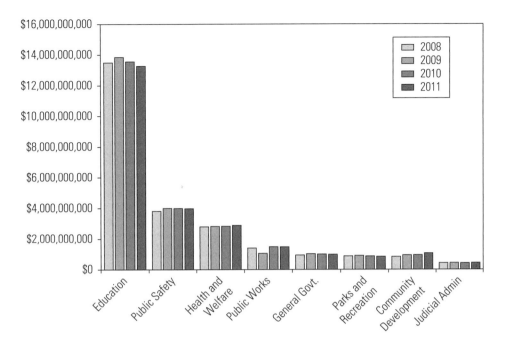

FIGURE 10.6

Operating Expenditures by Category for All Counties and Cities in Virginia

Source: Auditor of Public Accounts, *Comparative Report of Local Government Revenues and Expenditures* (four reports, years ending June 30, 2008, 2009, 2010, 2011), http://www.apa.virginia.gov.

The expenditure categories of general government, parks and recreation, community development, and judicial administration received the least amount of operating expenditures for all cities and counties in Virginia.

Municipalities in Virginia are not allowed to have outstanding debt greater than 10 percent of the value of the taxable real estate within their jurisdiction. There are a few exceptions to this law such as bonds—particularly those that are used for future revenue generating sources (the construction of a new stadium, for example). Local governments in Virginia must seek voter approval through referendum should they decide to levy a local income tax. This limitation is distinct from local taxation in the neighboring state of Maryland where all twenty-three counties and Baltimore City levy a local income tax that is collected on the state income tax return as a convenience for local governments. There are only four counties and seven independent cities in Virginia with the authority to levy a local income tax.

Annexation and Governmental Consolidation in Virginia

Thus far, this chapter has provided an overview of local government in Virginia by focusing on the various provisions of service, growth in the number of governments,

BOX 10.7   Elaboration of Governmental Expenditure Categories

General Government Administration

   Legislative, General and Financial Administration

   Board of Elections

Judicial Administration

   Courts and Commonwealth's Attorney

Public Safety

   Law Enforcement and Traffic Control

   Fire and Rescue Services

   Correction and Detention

   Inspections

   Other Protection

Public Works

   Maintenance of Highways-Streets-Bridges-Sidewalks

   Sanitation and Waste Removal

   Maintenance of General Buildings and Grounds

Health and Welfare

   Health, Mental Health and Mental Retardation

   Welfare/Social Services

Education

   Instruction

   Administration-Attendance-Health

   Pupil Transportation Services

   School Food Services and Other Non-Instructional Operations

   Contributions to Community Colleges

Parks, Recreation, and Cultural Services

   Parks and Recreation

   Cultural Enrichment

   Public Libraries

Community Development

   Planning and Community Development

   Environmental Management

   Cooperative Extension Program

Source: Operating Expenditures of Virginia's Counties & Cities, FY 2008, http://www.dhcd.virginia.gov/Commissionon LocalGovernment/PDFs/oe2008.pdf, p. 4.

and major expenditure and revenue sources. This section focuses on how local governments in Virginia can grow in terms of expanding their geographic borders through governmental annexation or consolidation.

Annexation refers to the legal process through which a city expands its jurisdictional boundary by absorbing adjacent land. Some states such as North Carolina or Illinois have a very liberal annexation policy—meaning it is relatively easy for cities within those states to expand their jurisdictional boundaries through capturing any bordering unincorporated lands. Annexation in Virginia is quite a complicated process as a result of a long history of disputes between cities and unannexed lands. Expanding borders through annexation suits against neighboring counties and towns have long been a way for independent cities and towns to grow in Virginia. An advantage of geographic and population expansion is the inclusion of additional properties to tax and sales taxes to collect for the annexing local government. Annexations are oftentimes quite controversial and in some cases have resulted in lengthy and costly legal proceedings.

The revised state constitution of 1902 allowed for a panel of judges to rule on annexation proposals and their resulting boundaries. These judges were appointed by the Virginia General Assembly and were thus very aware of the political impact of their decisions. Annexation disputes in Virginia became far more common after World War I in the 1920s. Counties became quite urbanized and were unsure how to handle the many externalities and pressures associated with rapid population expansion. Cities, which were immune from annexation by neighboring jurisdictions, had a history of simply capturing these lands. This common practice became politically unacceptable because many residents in unincorporated areas did not feel an identity with the city and thus did not want to become a part of the city. This became a significant problem in the Tidewater region of Virginia—especially after World War II. As a result, cities and counties within the region engaged in merger (or governmental consolidation) and annexation disputes. Many formerly unincorporated areas became incorporated and consolidated areas in order to block the City of Norfolk from expanding. **Governmental consolidation** is defined as the merger of the towns or cities governments and county government within a county to create one unified jurisdiction. There were many governmental consolidations in Virginia between 1952 and 1975—more than in any other part of the country. The General Assembly helped facilitate this process in 1960 by granting any city and adjacent county the power to consolidate by mutual agreement. Five independent cities in the Hampton Roads area of Virginia were formed by consolidating a city with a county. These were Virginia Beach, Newport News, Hampton, Chesapeake, and Suffolk. Eight of the ten independent cities in the Hampton Roads region adjoin each other—the only two that do not are Franklin and Williamsburg, which are surrounded by a traditional county.[8] The Code of Virginia uses the term *consolidated-city* to refer to these consolidated governments due to the complete dissolvement of the county government that the city merged with. This is different from consolidated governments in the rest of the county. There is still one unified government, but the resulting mergers in all other states are considered a municipal incorporation and an administrative division of the state government. The resulting consolidated entity possesses powers of both a city and a county, which is not the case in Virginia.

The Virginia General Assembly adopted legislation in 1979 where counties meeting certain population and density requirements can become permanently immune from annexation by any city with over one hundred thousand residents. The county can do this by petitioning the local circuit court within its jurisdiction. Several counties within the Richmond metropolitan area sought such immunity in 1981. The General Assembly placed a moratorium on future annexations of any county by any city in 1987. This legislation was set to expire in 2010. A bill was introduced in 2007 to extend the existing moratorium from 2010 to 2020. The bill passed both houses, but it was vetoed by then governor Tim Kaine. The moratorium was last extended in 2009 and is now set to expire in 2018—unless the General Assembly decides to place an end on the moratorium.[9]

Regionalism in Virginia

In recent years, lawmakers have taken several steps to encourage cooperation rather than conflict between neighboring jurisdictions. An example of this occurred in 1982 between the city of Charlottesville and its surrounding county, Albemarle. The two entities entered into a revenue-sharing agreement where the city received a portion of the county's tax revenues in lieu of not attempting to annex any of the county's land. This is not uncommon when comparing similar agreements across the country.

Another interesting feature of local government in Virginia is the reliance on special districts. A **special district** provides services that are typically not provided by a **general purpose government** (town, city, or county). Figure 10.2 revealed forty-two special districts in Virginia in 1952 and 186 in 2007. This 342.86 percent increase is more likely a result of a rapid population growth and high service demand that could not be handled by local governments within the sprawling suburban area of northern Virginia. Even though there was a 342.86 percent increase in the number of special districts, they are less important in Virginia than in other states. This could be due to the heavy reliance on planning district commissions (described below) across the state. Some of the more common special districts in Virginia are airport authorities and commissions, area agencies on aging, tourism authorities, parks commissions and authorities, community development authorities, jail authorities, hospital commissions and authorities, transportation authorities and districts, industrial authorities, regional libraries, metropolitan authorities, sanitation districts, soil and water conservation districts, water authorities, waste authorities, economic development authorities, and redevelopment and housing authorities. This list is not exhaustive, but it is representative of special districts found across the United States.

Transportation-related issues (i.e., pollution, congestion, etc.) cut across jurisdictional boundaries and as a result require regional planning and coordination. Transportation planning in Virginia is planned at the local, regional, and statewide levels. Planning typically involves the following actors: the Virginia Department of Transportation, Planning District Commissions (explained in more detail below), various transportation mode agencies including the Department of Rail and Public Transportation, local planning staff, and **Metropolitan Planning Organizations (MPOs)**. Virginia has eight MPOs that serve as regional transportation policymaking organizations devoted to metropolitan and regionwide transportation-related issues and planning. The state with the most MPOs is Florida with twenty-six while the states with the least are Hawaii and Alaska—both with one MPO each. The most recently created MPO in Virginia is the Harrisonburg-Rockingham MPO. It was created in 2002 and has two commissions. The first commission is a policy board made up of elected officials and representatives from various state and federal transportation agencies. There are eleven voting members responsible for making all official decisions. The second commission is the Technical Advisory Committee. This committee is made up of planners, highway engineers, and other transportation experts in the area. There are sixteen voting members that review and make recommendations to the policy board, conduct studies, and provide expert transportation advice. The structure of the state's most recent MPO is representative of MPOs across the country and the ten other MPOs in the state. For a listing of MPOs in Virginia, see Figure 10.7 below.

One unique aspect of regionalism in Virginia is the state's twenty-one **Planning District Commissions** (PDCs). The purpose of a PDC is to encourage and facilitate

BOX 10.9 What Are PDCs Required to Do?

1. Conduct studies on issues and problems of regional significance.

2. Identify and study potential opportunities for state and local cost savings and staffing efficiencies through coordinated governmental efforts.

3. Identify mechanisms for the coordination of state and local interests on a regional basis.

4. Implement services upon request of member localities.

5. Provide technical assistance to state government and member localities.

6. Serve as a liaison between localities and state agencies as requested.

7. Review local government aid applications as required by § 15.2–4213 and other state or federal law or regulation.

8. Conduct strategic planning for the region as required by §§ 15.2–4209 through 15.2–4212.

9. Develop regional functional area plans as deemed necessary by the commission or as requested by member localities.

10. Assist state agencies, as requested, in the development of substate plans.

11. Participate in a statewide geographic information system, the Virginia Geographic Information Network, as directed by the Department of Planning and Budget.

12. Collect and maintain demographic, economic, and other data concerning the region and member localities; and act as a state data center affiliate in cooperation with the Virginia Employment Commission.

Source: Code of Virginia, § 15.2-4200 (PDCs were created by the Regional Cooperation Act).

Metropolitan Planning Organizations

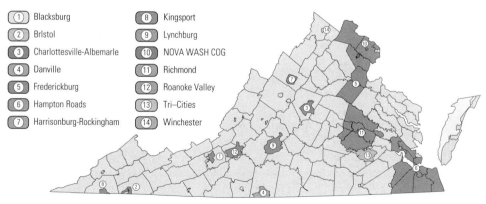

(1) Blacksburg	(8) Kingsport
(2) Brlstol	(9) Lynchburg
(3) Charlottesville-Albemarle	(10) NOVA WASH COG
(4) Danville	(11) Richmond
(5) Frederickburg	(12) Roanoke Valley
(6) Hampton Roads	(13) Tri–Cities
(7) Harrisonburg-Rockingham	(14) Winchester

FIGURE 10.7

Metropolitan Planning Organizations in Virginia

Source: Virginia Department of Transportation, http://www.virginiadot.org/projects/resources/HJR756finalreport-VDOTwebsite.pdf.

local government cooperation in order to address problems that are regional in nature and are greater than local significance. These voluntary associations of local governments bring together citizens and appointed and elected officials to discuss solutions to regional needs and problems. PDCs were created in 1968 through the passage of the Virginia Area Development Act by the Virginia General Assembly. The Virginia Area Development Act was modified by the General Assembly through the adoption of the Regional Cooperation Act in 1995.[10] Each PDC must complete a regional strategic plan. Local governing bodies, citizen organizations, the business community, and other interested parties participate in the creation of the plan. The plan is required to include goals and objectives on a regional scale and strategies to meet those goals. The intent of each plan is to promote the efficient and orderly development of the economic, social, and physical elements of the planning district. See Box 10.9 for additional requirements under the Regional Cooperation Act.

Finally, the state of Virginia has eleven **Metropolitan Statistical Areas** (MSAs). An MSA is designated by the U.S. Office of Management and Budget for the use by federal agencies in collecting, tabulating, and publishing statistics (such as poverty rates, household income, educational attainment, commute time to work, etc.) for metropolitan areas within the United States. There are 374 MSAs in the United States. A metro area must contain an urban core of at least 50,000 residents. Jurisdictions within the MSA must have a high degree of social and economic integration with the urban core. This is measured by commuting time to

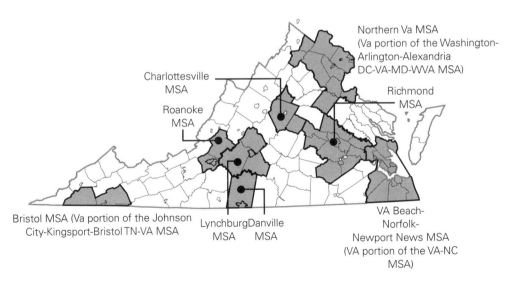

FIGURE 10.8

Virginia's Metropolitan Statistical Areas Established in 1993

Source: University of Virginia Weldon Cooper Center for Public Service, http://www.coopercenter.org.

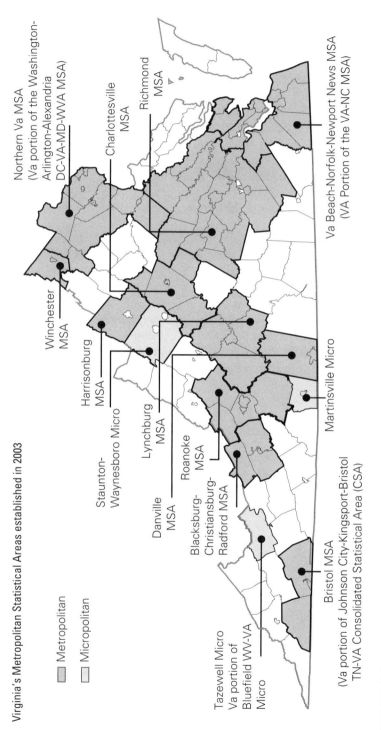

Virginia's Metropolitan Statistical Areas established in 2003

Metropolitan

Micropolitan

Northern Va MSA
(Va portion of the Washington-
Arlington-Alexandria
DC-VA-MD-WVA MSA)

Charlottesville
MSA

Richmond
MSA

Va Beach-Norfolk-Newport News MSA
(VA Portion of the VA-NC MSA)

Winchester
MSA

Harrisonburg
MSA

Staunton-
Waynesboro Micro

Lynchburg
MSA

Danville
MSA

Roanoke
MSA

Blacksburg-
Christiansburg-
Radford MSA

Martinsville Micro

Tazewell Micro
Va portion of
Bluefield WV-VA
Micro

Bristol MSA
(Va portion of Johnson City-Kingsport-Bristol
TN-VA Consolidated Statistical Area (CSA)

FIGURE 10.9

Virginia's Metro and Micropolitan Statistical Areas as of 2003

Source: University of Virginia Weldon Cooper Center for Public Service, http://www.coopercenter.org.

work. On the other hand, Micropolitan Statistical Areas must have an urban core of at least ten thousand residents, but no more than fifty thousand. Virginia's eleven MSAs are Blacksburg-Christiansburg, Radford; Charlottesville; Danville; Harrisonburg; Kingsport-Bristol-Bristol; Lynchburg; Richmond; Roanoke; Virginia Beach-Norfolk-Newport News; Washington, D.C.-Arlington-Alexandria; and Winchester.

Comparing Figures 10.8 and 10.9 reveals significant urban growth within specific parts of Virginia. This can be seen when comparing the 1993 MSAs of Richmond, Roanoke, Charlottesville, Washington, D.C., and Lynchburg to their 2003 MSAs. Each MSA expanded geographically—meaning residential commuting length increased within those MSAs over that ten-year period (referring to the high degree of social and economic integration required as measured through commuting patterns). We also find the introduction of three new MSAs when comparing 1993 to 2003: Harrisonburg, Winchester, and Blacksburg, Virginia—all a part of the Allegheny and Blue Ridge Mountain valley areas along Interstate 81.

Virginia has one MSA, the Washington-Arlington-Alexandria MSA, ranked in the top ten in terms of overall population of MSAs in the United States. The 2011 population estimate for the Washington-Arlington-Alexandria MSA was 5.7 million people. The most populated MSA in the United States is the New York-Northern New Jersey-Long Island MSA with a 2011 population estimate of almost 18.9 million people. Virginia's smallest MSA is Danville with a 2010 population of 106,561. Danville experienced a minus 3.62 percent decrease in population between 2000 and 2010. The Danville MSA was the only Virginia MSA to lose population between 2000 and 2010.

Conclusion

Government in Virginia should be viewed as a complex organism made up of various towns, independent cities, consolidated cities, counties, and special districts. This complex organism receives all of its power from the state government and is constrained by Dillon's Rule. Local governments have the great responsibility and duty to provide citizens with a wide array of services we have grown to expect and appreciate: from protecting us from harm through the provision of fire, rescue, and police services; to maintaining and improving our quality of life through educational opportunities; to local economic development. Though local government in Virginia is unique in many ways, such as city-county separation and less reliance on special districts to tackle regionwide issues, the provision of service and demands of citizens placed on local governments are representative of most local governments across the United States. Virginia has continued to experience rapid population growth in many areas across the state—in particular in the northern suburban areas of Washington, D.C. This population growth continues to place additional burdens on local governments—especially county governments. County governments are being charged with more and more responsibility. It remains to be seen if local officials will put pressure on lawmakers to lift the annexation moratorium that currently prohibits independent cities from annexing these populated areas. Special districts may serve as the alternative. Areas may begin to rely more heavily on special districts to handle growth pressures associated with continued suburbanization and sprawl. Regardless, it will be interesting to see the evolving landscape of local government in Virginia over the next couple of years.

Key Concepts

Annexation

Council-manager form of government

Creatures of the state

Dillon's Rule

General purpose government

Governmental consolidation

Home Rule

Form of government

Incorporation

Independent city

Mayor-council form of government

Metropolitan planning organizations (MPOs)

Metropolitan Statistical Areas (MSAs)

Planning district commissions

Special district

Weak mayor

Suggested Resources

- http://www.census.gov/govs/: Census of Governments.
- http://www.bts.gov/external_links/government/metropolitan_planning_organizations.html: Metropolitan Planning Organizations.
- http://www.apa.virginia.gov/: Virginia Auditor of Public Accounts.
- http://govinfo.library.unt.edu/amcouncil/index.html: American Council on Intergovernmental Relations.
- http://icma.org/: International City/County Management Association.

Notes

1. U.S. Census Bureau, 2012 Census of Governments, "Government Units by State: Census Years 1942 to 2012," http://www.census.gov/govs/cog2012/#; Ibid., "Local Governments by Type and State: 2012," http://www.census.gov/govs/cog2012/#.

2. Chester W. Bain, *A Body Incorporate: The Evolution of City-County Separation in Virginia* (Charlottesville: University Press of Virginia, 1967, for Institute of Government, University of Virginia).

3. U.S. Census Bureau, "2010 Census: Virginia Profile," http://www.census.gov/geo/reference/guidestloc/st51_va.html.

4. David Temple, *Merger Politics: Local Government Consolidation in Tidewater Virginia* (Charlottesville: University Press of Virginia, 1972).

5. Code of Virginia, 2008, Section 15.2–3602.

6. *Bennett v. Garret*, 132, VA. 397, 112 S.E. 772, 1992.

7. American Council on Intergovernmental Relations, *Significant Features of Fiscal Federalism,* vol. 2 (Washington, DC: American Council on Intergovernmental Relations, 1998), 74; and U.S. Department of Commerce, Census Bureau, "State and Local Government Finances by Level of Government and by State: 2005–06," http://www.census.gov/govs.

8. Commonwealth of Virginia, Department of Housing and Community Development, "About the Commission on Local Government," http://www.dhcd.virginia.gov/Commissionon LocalGovernment/.

9. Andrew Sorrell and Bruce Vlk, "Virginia's Never-Ending Moratorium on City-County Annexations," *Virginia News Letter* 88, no. 1(January 2012).

10. Code of Virginia, Chapter 42, Title 15.2. See http://lis.virginia.gov/000/src.htm.

CHAPTER 11

OUTLINE

The Policy Process

K–12 Education Policy

  Funding for K–12
  Education

  Academic Achievement in
  Virginia

  School Choice

Health and Human Services

  Poverty in Virginia

  Major Social Welfare
  Programs

  Accessing Health Care in
  the Commonwealth

  Major Health Policies

Energy and Environmental
Policy

  How Virginia Uses Energy

  Virginia's Energy Policy

  How Does Virginia Stack
  Up?

Emergency Management
and Homeland Security

  Federal Government
  Location and Impact on
  Homeland Security

Economic Development
Policy

  Agencies Aiding Virginia
  Businesses and Workforce
  Development

Conclusion

Inside the Laboratory

Public Policymaking in Virginia

Whether we know it or not, **public policies** impact Virginians every day. Public policy is created at all levels of government; however, the states play particularly important roles not only by initiating a wide variety of state-level policies but also because they implement federal laws and determine how much discretion cities and counties have in crafting policies at the local level (see Chapter 10 for more on the power of local government in Virginia). Simply put, a policy is what the government decides to do or not to do about a public problem. These include laws, rules, and regulations that govern our lives. How often our roads get paved, whether schools are allowed to teach sex education, when and where you can buy alcohol, or whether businesses should get tax incentives to locate in Virginia are all questions addressed through public decision-making processes made by elected and appointed officials, often with citizen input. The rest of this book provides a brief overview of the public policymaking process in Virginia and takes a closer look at a number of important policy areas, including education, health and welfare, emergency management and homeland security, energy and the environment, and economic development. While these are certainly not inclusive of all of the policies made at the state level, they provide a good overview of the unique policy landscape in Virginia.

The Policy Process

In Chapter 5, "The Virginia General Assembly," we looked at the legislative process in Virginia. While state legislatures are charged with primary lawmaking responsibilities, they represent just one part of the policymaking process. Once policies are passed by both the Virginia House of Delegates and the Virginia Senate, the governor can sign or veto the legislation. Administrative agencies in the state bureaucracy then carry out policies signed by the governor. Laws passed by the legislature are often purposefully left vague. This may be for political reasons; sometimes, the fewer the details, the more likelihood that both parties will agree. Also, since lawmakers are generalists rather than specialists, an issue may be too complicated for them to adequately address. This is especially the case in states like Virginia that have citizen legislatures. Whatever the reason, state employees in administrative agencies, who have been hired because of their substantive expertise, play an important role in formulating the details of policies sent to them for implementation. Last, the courts make sure that laws do not conflict with the Virginia Constitution.

While the formal lawmaking process highlighted above is often the most visible type of policymaking, public policies include not only the laws passed by legislatures but also the actions of a variety of other officials in state government. These may be (1) executive orders issued by the governor (for example, between taking office in January 2010 and early 2013, Governor McDonnell issued fifty-seven executive orders, ranging from equal opportunity guidelines for state agencies to the continuation of the Virginia Coastal Zone Management Program); (2) decisions made by the courts (e.g., whether felons who have had voting rights restored can legally possess firearms); and (3) a vast variety of rules and regulations issued by administrative agencies. Some examples include processes for disposing of hazardous waste, the establishment of support systems for disabled citizens, and licensure requirements for medical facilities. All of these have the force of law and impact the lives and well-being of Virginia's citizens. Importantly, while public policies are created by *formal* actors and institutions in the legislative, executive, and judicial branches, the creation and adoption of policies are also influenced by *informal* policy actors, including political parties, interest groups, citizens, and the media.

While there are a number of different theories regarding policy processes and outcomes, the **policy process model** is useful for understanding the factors that influence public policies and the relationships between policy actors. The model is broad enough to capture policy processes regardless of whether they are occurring within the legislative or executive branch or at the national, state, or local level. The policy process model shown in Figure 11.1 depicts five stages of policymaking.

The first step in the policy process is the agenda setting stage, where an issue is identified as a problem in need of fixing. While there are many problems in society, governments have limited agenda space and can address only a select number

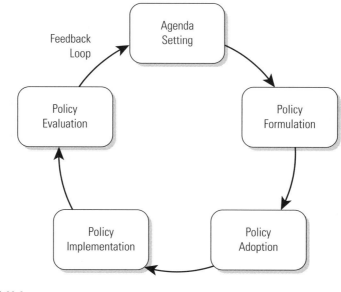

FIGURE 11.1

The Policy Process

of problems at any one time. **Focusing events**—highly visible occurrences such as natural disasters, recessions, or sudden changes in social conditions—can help shift issues from the **systemic agenda** (which includes all the problems to which the general public is paying attention) to the **institutional agenda** (comprising those issues being discussed and considered by government officials). Issues that have a high level of salience or importance to voters and low levels of conflict over how they should be solved have the highest likelihood of being addressed by policymakers.[1] Once a problem is on the institutional agenda, policy solutions must be formulated and support from relevant political actors secured before the policy can be formally adopted. After they are passed, policies are then **implemented** by administrative agencies in states and localities. Ideally, once implemented, policies are evaluated, or studied, to determine whether they are working well and meeting their policy goals. **Policy evaluation** can occur inside government or be conducted by external evaluators in think tanks and universities. Some policies explicitly call for regular assessment, while others are evaluated less systematically. Findings about whether a problem has been solved or is in need of new policy solutions can create a feedback loop to inform future agenda setting and policy formulation. Rather than a step-by-step process whereby a problem is identified, a policy is created, adopted, and then implemented, others have suggested that in order for significant policy change to occur, viable policy alternatives and adequate political support must already exist when a problem gets on the agenda. Otherwise, solutions might take too long to develop and coalitions too long to build before the "window of opportunity" for policy change closes.[2]

States exhibit a lot of variation in the way they respond to the needs and interests of their citizens. Not only are policies shaped by a state's political culture (the prevailing ideas about the appropriate size and scope of government) but also by its economic, demographic, and political contexts. Whether or not a state has a robust budget with which to solve public problems, the shifts in prevailing public opinion, political makeup of state political institutions, and presence and activity of interest groups all impact policy outcomes. Since most policies create winners and losers, the politics of "who gets what, when, and how"[3] is also influenced by the type of policy itself.

Political scientists often put public policies into one of three general categories based on how widespread or concentrated the policy's costs or benefits. **Redistributive policies**, such as progressive taxation and many social welfare programs, are often controversial since they redistribute benefits (money) from one group to another. The zero-sum nature of redistribution often makes these kinds of policies difficult to pass. With **distributive policies**, on the other hand, resources are allocated to individuals and groups in society, but the costs are diffuse, making the "losers" harder to identify and the policies easier to pass and to implement. Often referred to as *pork barrel* spending, examples of such distributive policy include agricultural subsidies, infrastructure and public works projects, museum exhibits, and research funding. Last, **regulatory policies** place constraints on individuals and business to control (i.e., regulate) their behavior. Examples include who businesses can hire and fire and how much corporations can legally pollute without being fined. Virginia's traditional political culture and conservative ethos has historically limited the development of extensive state policy, particularly when it comes to regulating the economy and redistributing resources from the rich to the poor.

Although Virginia has dominion over a wide variety of policy decisions, this authority is not absolute. The principle of **federalism**, whereby states share power with the national government, limits the ability of Virginia to act autonomously in all areas of public policymaking. The U.S. Constitution lays out those matters in which the federal government is supreme, should state and national policies conflict. Officials in Washington can also use their ability to tax and spend to convince states to adopt their preferred policies. Such financial incentives (as well as U.S. Supreme Court interpretations of federal power) have expanded the ability of the national government to have some control over policy areas that were once solely the prerogative of state and local governments. As will be seen in the policy examples that follow, this complicated relationship with the national government provides both opportunities and constraints for Virginia policymakers and creates a framework for state-level policies.

K–12 Education Policy

Unlike the U.S. Constitution, which makes no mention of public education, most state constitutions provide detailed provisions that hold them accountable for educating future citizens. In Virginia, the constitution mandates that the state "provide for a system of free public elementary and secondary schools for all children."[4] Much of the responsibility for education in Virginia and across the country has been decentralized even further, with localities playing a key role in education policy and administration. Although state and local governments continue to be the primary actors, over the last decade, federal policies have shaped the context in which they operate.

Improving public education in the Commonwealth has been an important priority for citizens and policymakers. It is an issue that cuts across party lines, figuring prominently in governors' State of the Commonwealth addresses. Both Republican and Democratic administrations have emphasized the importance of schools in the development of **human capital,** which can be defined as the skills and experiences valued by employers that increase an individual's worth in the labor market. Viewed from this perspective, education plays a fundamental role in ensuring that Virginia has a skilled workforce and will be competitive in a global economy. High quality public schools are also seen as a primary vehicle for advancing the principle of equality of opportunity. Higher levels of education are linked to lower unemployment, poverty reduction, higher earnings, less reliance on other social welfare programs, and lower crime rates.

Public education in Virginia dates back to the early 1600s; however, schooling in the colonies was a local affair. It was not until the end of the eighteenth century that Thomas Jefferson introduced plans for a statewide system of public education—a

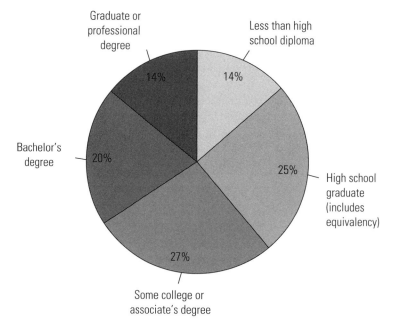

FIGURE 11.2

Educational Attainment in Virginia

Source: U.S. Census Bureau, "2010 American Community Survey 1-Year Estimates," see http://www.census.gov/hhes/socdemo/education/data/acs/index.html.

three-year program that would identify and cultivate the next generation of political leaders. Today, more than 1.2 million students attend Virginia's 2,186 public schools.[5] Education policies are administered by the Virginia Department of Education (VDOE), headed by a Superintendent of Public Instruction. A nine-member Board of Education serves as the governing and policymaking body for the elementary and secondary public school system. Members, who serve four-year terms, are appointed by the governor and confirmed by the General Assembly. The Board of Education is responsible for setting statewide curriculum standards, state testing and assessment programs, and high school graduation requirements; determining qualifications for teachers and principals; establishing standards for school accreditation and teacher preparation; implementing and administering federal programs; and developing rules and regulations for the administration of state education programs.[6]

Education policy is decentralized, with a lot of authority delegated to Virginia's 132 school divisions. Each is governed locally by a publicly elected city or county school board that acts as a liaison with the community and develops policies for the schools in its district. School board elections are nonpartisan in order to insulate them from partisan politics. One of their most important roles is to select a professional district superintendent to administer education policies at the local level. As a "right to work" state, Virginia is among nearly half of all states, predominantly in the South and Midwest, which have enacted right-to-work legislation. This means that non-members do not have to pay union fees if they do not join the union and strikes are prohibited by law. As a result, Virginia has relatively weak teachers unions.

Funding for K–12 Education

Education is primarily a state and local responsibility; therefore, they pay for the vast majority of public school costs. Federal aid to states is meant to be redistributive, and more money is directed to states with higher need. Since Virginia has a relatively strong economy with high per capita income, the state receives less federal funding than many other states.

State education funding is mainly composed of revenue from state income and sales taxes and money made from the Virginia state lottery. Most local funding is from local property taxes. Since localities vary tremendously in their property wealth, without state aid, school districts would have large disparities in per pupil spending. In Virginia, the amount paid varies by school division and is determined by the locality's ability to pay for educational costs in order to meet Virginia's Standards of Quality (the educational requirements that must be met by all school divisions). State funding for K–12 education in Virginia was $5.5 billion in 2012. This represents one third of the state general fund budget and is its largest portion.

Academic Achievement in Virginia

Contemporary education policy is driven by the dual goals of excellence and equity. While Virginia has been a leader in high quality education, it has had a weaker track record in providing equitable educational opportunities for all students. According to Commonwealth Education Poll 2010–2011, "Virginians remain positive about schools but fewer think schools do well in preparing students for jobs." The poll indicates that Virginia's public school system is held in high regard: 63 percent think public schools provide an excellent or good education. Almost three fourths (73 percent) report that the schools "do a good job teaching the basics such as reading, writing and mathematics."[7] Fewer (53 percent), however, say that they "do a good job providing skills useful in obtaining a job."[8]

Virginia students continue to score above the national average on the **National Assessment of Educational Progress (NAEP)** math and reading assessments (a test administered to a sample of students nationwide in fourth and eighth grades) and on all three sections of the SAT college admissions test (math, writing, and reading). The state is third in the country for student achievement rates on Advance Placement tests for college credit.[9] Many trace Virginia's strong scores to its rigorous standards and high expectations. The state's **Standards of Learning (SOL),** which were developed in 1995, lay out learning and achievement expectations for students in grades K–12 in English, mathematics, science, history and social science, technology, the fine arts, foreign language, health and physical education, and driver education.[10] The VDOE recently revised the SOL to include more rigorous content standards in order to better prepare students for college and careers. An important goal has been to create standards that will make Virginia students nationally and internationally competitive.[11] The SOL is accompanied by statewide standardized tests to assess students' content knowledge and hold teachers and schools accountable for student learning.

Since the Standards of Learning precede the passage of the federal **No Child Left Behind** Act, Virginia was one of several states that was opposed to NCLB. In January of 2004, a nearly unanimous Virginia House of Delegates passed a resolution calling on Congress to exempt Virginia from NCLB provisions. Lawmakers argued that Virginia already had a proven successful school accountability program and were resistant to what they saw as unwarranted federal intrusion into education policy.[12] NCLB required all states receiving federal funding to develop a system of standards and testing and publicly report student test scores (including separate reporting categories for low income, minority, disabled, and limited English proficient students). Schools and school districts would be held accountable for students making "adequate yearly progress" (AYP) toward state-set benchmarks, with the goal of 100 percent proficiency by 2014. Failure to make AYP would result in a series of sanctions, such as allowing students to transfer out of "failing schools," providing additional tutoring and afterschool programs, and eventually, school restructuring by district or state officials.

Like most states across the country, federal AYP targets proved unattainable for many schools and school districts in Virginia. In the 2010–2011 school year, 38 percent of schools failed to make adequate progress from the previous year. Although a majority of school (61 percent) did make AYP, the geographic distribution of failing schools meant that 91 percent of Virginia school divisions did not.[13] In 2012, state officials were granted a federal waiver to exempt school divisions from the looming NCLB deadline. Waivers require states to be able to demonstrate that they have a system of high standards and testing and a viable plan to close educational achievement gaps. AYP rates have been replaced by Annual Measurable Objectives (AMOs), which are based on actual student performance the previous year.

While Virginia has a very well-regarded public school system, it is not without challenges. Particularly troubling is a persistent achievement gap. The **achievement gap** refers to the difference in standardized test scores between different groups of students. In both reading and math, there are significant gaps between white students and racial and ethnic minorities (Figures 11.3 and 11.4). Low-income students, students with disabilities, and those with limited English

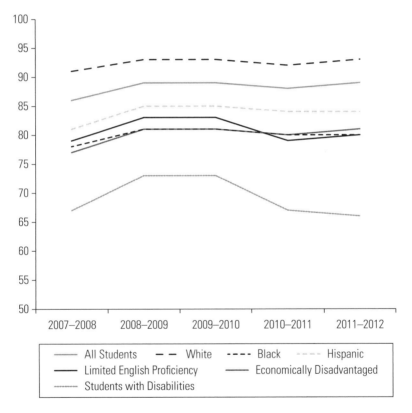

FIGURE 11.3

Gap in Percentage of Virginia Students Passing Reading/Language Arts Assessment

Source: 2007–2008, 2008–2009 data are from Deborah L. Jonas, "Achievement Gaps in Virginia Public Schools" (paper presented at the Virginia Board of Education, April 2012), http://www.doe.virginia.gov/boe/meetings/2012/04_apr/agenda_items/item_c.pdf; 2009–2010, 2010–2011, 2011–2012 data are from Virginia Department of Education, State Report Card, https://p1pe.doe.virginia.gov/reportcard/report.do?division=All&schoolName=All.

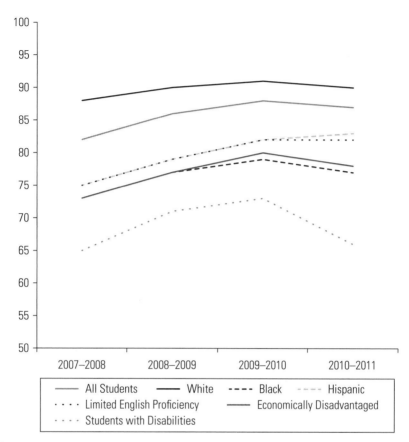

FIGURE 11.4

Gap in Percentage of Virginia Students Passing Mathematics Assessment

Sources: 2007–2008, 2008–2009 data are from Deborah L. Jonas, "Achievement Gaps in Virginia Public Schools" (paper presented at the Virginia Board of Education, April 2012), http://www.doe.virginia.gov/boe/meetings/2012/04_apr/ agenda_items/item_c.pdf; 2009–2010, 2010–2011, 2011–2012 data are from Virginia Department of Education, State Report Card, https://p1pe.doe.virginia.gov/reportcard/report.do?division=All&schoolName=All.

Note: The Virginia Department of Education changed math assessments to be much more rigorous. They were first implemented in 2011–2012, resulting in a decrease in test scores. According to Dr. Patricia Wright, VDOE superintendent of public instruction, lower mathematics pass rates indicate Virginia is "expecting more of students—not that students are learning less" (Patricia Wright, "State of the Commonwealth's Public Schools—January 2012," para. 24, http://www.doe .virginia.gov/about/superintendent/state_of_the_commonwealth_public_schools.shtml). However, it also means that the recent data aren't comparable to the previous years and have been omitted from the above figure.

proficiency also continue to get disproportionately low scores. The new AMO benchmarks created by the VDOE vary by student subgroup with a goal of cutting each group's achievement gap in half over the next six years.[14]

There are also disparities in on-time graduation and dropout rates by subgroup. On-time graduation rates improved for all groups between 2008 and 2011, with black, Hispanic, homeless, and economically disadvantaged students showing the greatest improvement (6.3 percent, 8 percent, 8 percent, and 9.3 percent respectively). However, there continue to be significant differences in four-year school completion rates.

These trends will continue to provide challenges for Virginia public schools, especially as the number of students with limited English proficiency and economically disadvantaged students have been increasing in the state.[15] The percent of students who qualify for free and reduced-price lunch is used as an indicator for the proportion of low-income students. Forty percent of students in Virginia are eligible for free and reduced price lunch. However, since poverty rates vary drastically across the Commonwealth, some schools feel these effects more than others. For example, in a number of schools in Arlington and Fairfax Counties, just 1–2 percent of students qualify for free or reduced lunch. At Thurgood Marshall Elementary in Chesapeake City, on the other hand, the rate is 95 percent.[16]

School Choice

One idea that has gained traction at the state and national levels in recent years is to try to improve school performance through increased competition. Virginia has a number of alternatives to traditional public schools, such as magnet and charter schools, career and technical education, Governor's Schools, private education, and home schooling. In particular, magnet schools have flourished over the last few decades. **Magnet schools** are public schools that have specialized curricula to attract students who would typically attend another school. For example, a school might focus on the arts, environmental science, or technology. There were 158 magnet schools in Virginia in 2008–2009 with a school enrollment of 151,313 students. Only five states had more magnet schools—and all have much larger populations (California, Florida, Illinois, Michigan, and New York).[17] By 2013, Virginia's number of magnet schools had increased to 166.

Although Virginia has allowed **charter schools** since 1998 they have been slow to develop. Forty-one states have charter school legislation. The Center for Educational Reform, a strong advocate for charter schools, ranked Virginia as the second weakest, giving the state an F in facilitating charter schools.[18] There are currently just four charter schools in operation in Virginia, serving 360 students. While charter schools allow for more innovation in curricula and have flexibility in administrative decisions, students must still take standardized assessments for state and NCLB accountability. School charters are subject to approval and renewal every five years by the state Department of Education. They can be operated by a variety of organizational entities (universities, nonprofits, or other organizations) but are supervised by local school boards. Charter schools are not allowed to charge tuition or have selective admissions criteria. They must be nonsectarian and open to all and use a lottery if applicants exceed capacity. The Public School Charter Fund, established by the General Assembly in 2007, provides supplemental support for charter schools in order to provide alternative education opportunities for students who are not finding success in traditional schools.[19] For example, Murray High School in Albemarle County provides "experiential learning opportunities in order to provide academic and personal success for students who are at-risk to leave school or to graduate below potential."[20]

Most high schools (and many middle schools) offer career and technical education (CTE) programs. These programs are "designed to prepare young people for productive futures while meeting the commonwealth's need for well-trained and industry-certified technical workers."[21] Traditionally referred to as vocational education, CTE has expanded from a narrow program designed to serve noncollege-bound students to encompass a wide variety of career exploration and preparation options. Examples of CTE programs across the state include agricultural education, business and information technology, family and consumer sciences, health and medical sciences, marketing, trade and industrial training, and an increasing number of science, technology, engineering and mathematics (STEM)-focused programs.[22]

Virginia also has a network of **Governor's Schools**, designed to provide gifted students with more advanced educational opportunities than are available in their home districts. First established as a summer program in 1973 by then governor Linwood Holton, the Governor Schools Program serves more than 7,500 students at over forty sites throughout the Commonwealth. Programming includes traditional academics as well as visual and performing arts education. There are currently nineteen academic year Governor's Schools with only three serving as full-time programs that fulfill all graduation requirements for students. The other sixteen programs are part-time, where students spend a portion of the school day at the Governor's School and the other portion at their home school in order to meet the requirements for graduation. Each academic year, Governors Schools are financed through the Virginia General Assembly and local school division's fund allocation. Programs are administered by the Virginia Department of Education and the Office of Secondary Instructional Services in conjunction with local school districts and colleges.[23]

Virginia recently took steps to further expand the variety of educational programs in the Commonwealth. In 2010, the General Assembly passed legislation that allows public institutions of higher education in the state with approved teacher-preparation program to establish a College Partnership Laboratory School. These are public schools established by contract between the governing board of a college or university and the Board of Education.[24] Lawmakers also approved online providers for virtual school programs. The state has approved nineteen online providers to contract with local school districts and provide online classes for their students. These include full-time virtual schools, programs that offer supplemental instruction to students, and blended programs in which students have both an on-site mentor and an online teacher.[25]

School-aged children also have education options outside of Virginia's public school system. In the 2009–2010 school year, 103,076 students attended 915 private schools in the state. Private schools are accredited by the Virginia Council for Private Education.[26] Virginia does not have any publicly funded **school voucher** programs that allow parents to send their children to private schools. However, in 2012, a new state law granted tax credits for corporate donations to nonprofits in order to provide low-income students scholarships for private school tuition.[27]

Finally, homeschooling also provides an alternative to traditional public schools. State regulations specify the parents' education and qualification requirements and curriculum guidelines for home school instruction. Nearly 25,000 students were homeschooled in the 2011–2012 school year. An additional 7,300 children received religious exemptions from compulsory public school attendance.[28] Virginia is the only state that has a separate provision for public school exemptions for a "bona fide religious training or belief." Once approved, families with a religious exemption do not have to provide a curriculum description or annual testing or evaluation results to their local school division.[29]

Health and Human Services

While educational policymaking has traditionally occurred at the state and local level, national legislation has had a much larger role in shaping health and welfare policies in Virginia. For the most part, major health and welfare policies are characteristic of American federalism, where policies created at the national level are implemented by states. Virginia's traditional political culture has also impacted state-level decisions regarding health and human service programs. Compared with many other states, Virginia has rather strict participation rules and limited spending on programs for the poor. Although there are many governmental programs that try to improve the welfare of citizens at all income levels, the following section examines poverty across the Commonwealth and highlights a handful of key programs that provide a safety net for low-income Virginians.

Poverty in Virginia

Virginia has long been known for its healthy economy, low unemployment rate, and high standard of living. However, these statistics often mask the large number of Virginians who are struggling to make ends meet. The recent economic recession resulted in an increase in the state's poverty rate, and in 2011, the figure for Virginians living below the poverty line reached 11.5 percent. This represents more than one in ten Virginians.

By comparison, New Hampshire had the lowest poverty rate in 2010 at 8.8 percent while the national average was 15.9 percent (see Figure 11.5, Poverty Rates by State, for a comparison with poverty in other states). Although Virginia has the seventh lowest poverty rate in the United States, particular areas of the state have drastically higher poverty levels. There are enormous economic disparities across the Commonwealth, particularly between northern Virginia, which is home to the three wealthiest counties in the country, and some of the poorest, which are located in southwestern Virginia in rural and mountain areas. Poverty rates also vary greatly within localities. For example, in the state capital, some neighborhoods have poverty rates as low as 1–2 percent, but just one or two miles away are areas with poverty levels reaching above 50 percent. In one Richmond neighborhood, 73 percent of residents live in poverty, more than seven times the state average.

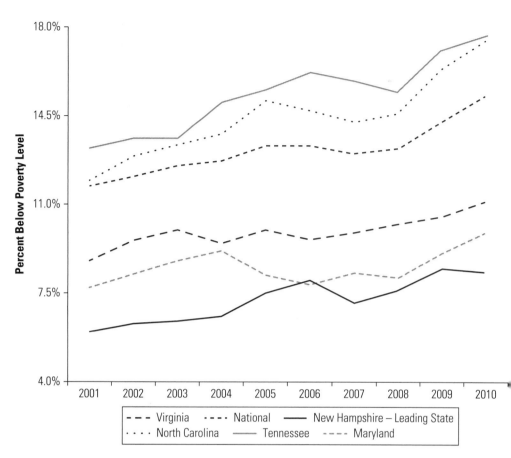

FIGURE 11.5

Poverty Rates by State

Source: http://vaperforms.virginia.gov/indicators/economy/poverty.php.

Poverty rates are disproportionately high for children, female-headed households, and racial and ethnic minorities (see Figure 11.6, Virginia Poverty Rates by Selected Characteristics, 2010).

Major Social Welfare Programs

Poverty has negative consequences for individuals and their families, including a greater likelihood of health problems, early childbearing, risky behavior, crime and delinquency, poor educational outcomes, and lower employment and earnings. These in turn put strain on communities and reduce the overall social and economic health of the Commonwealth. There are a number of **means-tested** social welfare programs to aid Virginians living in or near poverty. Means-tested programs use income or asset tests to determine program eligibility; applicants must demonstrate

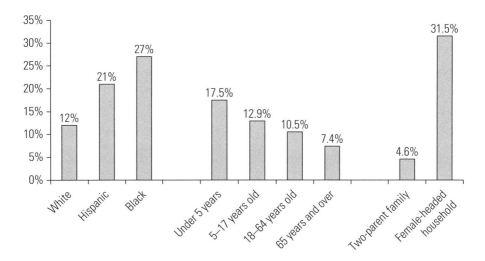

FIGURE 11.6

Virginia Poverty Rates by Selected Characteristics, 2010

Source: Kaiser Family Foundation State Health Facts, "Virginia: Poverty Rate by Race/Ethnicity, States (2010–2011), U.S. (2011)," http://www.statehealthfacts.org/profileind.jsp?ind=14&cat=1&rgn=48&cmprgn=1; and U.S. Census, "Selected Population Profile in the United States, 2010 American Community Survey 1-Year Estimates," http://factfinder2.census .gov/faces/tableservices/jsf/pages/productview.xhtml?pid=ACS_10_1YR_S0201&prodType=table.

that they do not have the means to acquire such goods or services on their own. It should be noted, however, that means-tested programs are generally designed to *alleviate* rather than to *prevent* poverty. Moreover, many people who qualify for these programs are not receiving benefits, either because they do not know they are eligible or because of the stigma attached to redistributive social policies.

Temporary Assistance to Needy Families (TANF) is the program that most people associate with "welfare," and it provides cash assistance to the very poor. TANF is a federal block grant program that was created by the 1935 Social Security Act (it was initially called Aid to Dependent Children, and later, Aid to Families with Dependent Children, or AFDC). Criticized for creating welfare dependency, AFDC was replaced with TANF in the 1996 Personal Responsibility and Work Opportunity Reconciliation Act (PRWORA). PRWORA has broad objectives, including reducing dependency, increasing work, promoting marriage, and reducing out-of-wedlock pregnancies. Unlike its predecessor, TANF is not an entitlement program, meaning that states can deny benefits to qualifying individuals. There is a five-year lifetime limit on assistance (and families can receive aid only for two years at any one time). Most program recipients are also required to work for thirty-five hours a week. While the federal government continues to fund half of the program costs, states have significant discretion over setting eligibility levels, benefit rates, and other program requirements, resulting in wide variation across states. Virginia provides a maximum monthly benefit of $389 a month for a family of one adult with

BOX 11.1   The Complexity of Assessing Poverty

The government uses two different measures to determine poverty in the United States: the **poverty threshold** and **poverty guidelines.** The poverty threshold is set by the U.S. Census Bureau, based on before-tax income, and does not include noncash benefits (public housing, Medicaid, food stamps, etc.). Poverty thresholds vary by household size and whether an individual is elderly or nonelderly. They are also updated to reflect changes in the Consumer Price Index (which measures changes in the cost of goods and services from year to year). This is what is referred to as the "official" poverty measure and is used by the Census Bureau to determine how many people are in poverty. If an individual or family's income falls below the set threshold, they are counted as "poor." Many have criticized this measure. According to Virginia's Poverty Reduction Taskforce, "The official poverty threshold understates basic living costs, and the poverty rate does not measure the impact of government assistance in reducing poverty."[30]

Poverty guidelines, on the other hand, are simplified versions of the poverty threshold that are issued by the U.S. Department of Health and Human Services (HHS) to determine eligibility for means-tested programs. For example, FAMIS (Virginia's children's health insurance program) serves children in families who have incomes up to 200 percent of poverty. Using the guidelines below, a family of three could make up to twice the poverty level, or $38,180, to qualify for the FAMIS. Unlike the poverty threshold, which is uniform across the fifty states, HHS issues separate guidelines for Alaska and Hawaii, but they do not make a distinction based on age.

2012 Poverty Guidelines for the Forty-eight Contiguous States and the District of Columbia

Persons in Family/Household	Poverty Guideline
1	$11,170
2	15,130
3	19,090
4	23,050
5	27,010
6	30,970
7	34,930
8	38,890
Add $3,960 for each additional person.	

Source: Office of the Assistant Secretary for Planning and Evaluation, "Frequently Asked Questions Relate to the Poverty Guidelines and Poverty," U.S. Department of Health and Human Services, http://aspe.hhs.gov/poverty/faq.shtml#official.

two children; some areas of the state have an even lower ceiling. Low benefit rates are common in conservative, southern and southwestern states.[31] The **Virginia Initiative for Employment Not Welfare (VIEW)** provides temporary employment, training, and education opportunities to TANF participants. The state has taken a "work first" approach that emphasizes immediate employment rather than an augmentation of education and training prior to entering the labor market.

While TANF provides poor families with cash assistance, the food stamp program—officially called the **Supplemental Nutrition Assistance Program (SNAP)**—provides Virginians with in-kind benefits that can be used only to purchase food. SNAP is federally funded, with states sharing the administrative costs. Eligibility is based on both an income test (about 130 percent of poverty) and an asset test, typically limited to no more than $2,000 ($3,000 for elderly and disabled residents). In January 2012, the program, which provides an average per person benefit of $128 a month, served 11.4 percent of Virginians. Virginia also implements federal nutrition programs for school-aged children through the National School Lunch and Breakfast Programs and Summer Food Service Program, providing free meals to children under 130 percent of poverty and reduced-priced meals to kids in families living under 185 percent of poverty. The Special Supplemental Nutrition Program for Women, Infants, and Children (WIC) targets extra nutritional support for low-income pregnant and breastfeeding women, infants, and children under five at "nutritional risk." The program also provides nutritional education, health screenings, and program referrals to improve maternal and child health.

Accessing Health Care in the Commonwealth

Access to health care is a growing problem in Virginia and around the country. Although those with limited incomes are most likely to lack health insurance and be at risk for poor health outcomes, reforming state health policy is an important issue that impacts a broad range of stakeholders. Two interrelated problems are the high cost of health care and the number of people who are uninsured (see Figures 11.7 and 11.8). Increases in health care costs and insurance premiums are outpacing increases in incomes, and, in Virginia, have also risen faster than health care costs in the rest of the country (though overall health care spending in Virginia is still lower than the national average). Between 1999 and 2009, health care costs per capita increased by 6 percent, compared with a 5.5 percent national growth rate. Some states experienced even higher rates of growth. For example, in Alaska, health costs increased by 8.4 percent and in Nevada by 9.2 percent. If we control for population growth, the increase is not so dramatic (5.5 percent in Virginia). However, incomes in Virginia grew by just 4.1 percent over the same period. Moreover, the average family premium (the amount paid annually by employees) increased by 9.6 percent and deductibles by 9.7 percent.[32] This reflects a national trend in which the cost burden has been shifting from employers to employees.

Growing health care costs have made purchasing health insurance unattainable for many Virginians. In 2009 (the most recent year such data is available), 13.2 percent of Virginians under aged 65 (nearly 900,000) did not have health insurance. Although health insurance is more widespread in Virginia than the rest of the country (17.1 percent of Americans lack coverage), those with limited education levels and racial and ethnic minorities are much more likely to be uninsured. Among nonelderly Virginians, 33.2 percent of Hispanics were uninsured, compared to 16.6 percent of blacks, 15.9 percent of Asian-Pacific Islanders, and 9.7 percent of white residents. Although most citizens get health insurance through their employers, access to health care is not just a problem of the unemployed. The percentage of small businesses providing health insurance to their employees has decreased over the past decade, from 48 percent to 37 percent, and almost half of the uninsured are in families in which at least one parent works full time.[33]

Not surprisingly, lack of health insurance reduces access to health care and is linked to poorer health outcomes. In 2009, 11 percent of adults in the Commonwealth reported needing to see a doctor but could not because of cost. Even when citizens have health insurance, good health care may be difficult to obtain. Many rural areas (especially in southern and southwestern Virginia) and some cities are "medically underserved," with limited numbers of physicians and health centers. Postponing care can lead to high medical bills and out-of pocket expenses and even medical bankruptcy. Poor health increases time off work and decreases workers

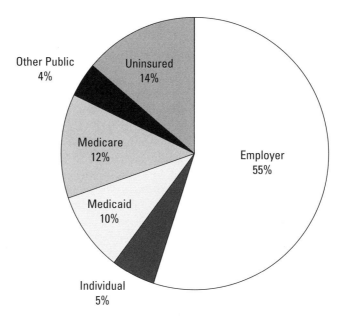

FIGURE 11.7

Sources of Health Insurance Coverage in Virginia, 2010–2011

Source: Kaiser Family Foundation State Health Facts, "Virginia: Health Insurance Coverage of the Total Population, States (2010–2011), U.S. (2011)," http://www.statehealthfacts.org/profileind.jsp?ind=125&cat=3&rgn=48.

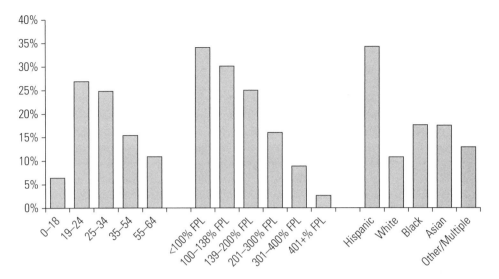

FIGURE 11.8

Virginians without Health Insurance, 2010

Source: Juliana Macri, Victoria Lynch, and Genevieve Kenney, *Profile of the Uninsured* (Washington, DC: The Urban Institute, 2012), Table 1: Health Insurance Coverage of the Nonelderly in Virginia and the United States, ACS 2010, http://www.vhcf.org/wp-content/uploads/2010/10/VHCF-Profile-of-the-Uninsured-Chartbook.pdf.

productivity. Moreover, without access to primary care, many rely on expensive emergency care, increasing costs for taxpayers. In order to improve the health of its citizenry, Virginia offers government-funded health insurance programs to some people who cannot afford coverage. Like other social welfare programs, these are largely federal programs that are implemented by the states and with costs shared between state and national governments.

Major Health Policies

The **Medicaid** program provides health insurance to poor and very low-income elderly, children, pregnant women, persons with disabilities, and some parents or caregivers of dependent children. Only U.S. citizens or qualified legal immigrants can receive Medicaid. While **Medicare** (a program that is funded by the federal government) provides insurance to the elderly regardless of income, *poor* seniors and the disabled rely on Medicaid for acute and long-term health care services. As a result, aging baby boomers and increased life expectancy have put tremendous pressure on the states, with the Medicaid program representing the fastest growing portion of state budgets. Consider, although 70 percent Medicaid beneficiaries are children and their parents or caregivers, this group receives only 33 percent of direct Medicaid spending. The remaining 67 percent of spending goes to individuals with disabilities and the elderly. Even though the federal government pays for about half the program costs, Medicaid is still the second largest program in Virginia's general fund budget.[34] States have flexibility in setting income and eligibility guidelines, resulting in variation among states. According to Virginia's Department of Medical Assistance Services, eligibility requirements in the Commonwealth are among the strictest in the country. The state ranks twenty-fourth in the nation for the lowest level of spending per recipient.

In 1997, the U.S. Congress created the State Children Health Insurance Program (SCHIP) to provide health insurance to uninsured children whose families make too much money to qualify for Medicaid but still find themselves unable to afford coverage. Virginia's SCHIP program is called **Family Access to Medical Insurance Security (FAMIS).** Insurance is given to children up to age eighteen from families with incomes less than twice the poverty level. The majority of states have gone above this threshold, expanding coverage to families with incomes up to 300 percent (twelve states) and, in the case of New Jersey and New York, to 350 and 400 percent of poverty.[35] In order to streamline the state's health insurance programs for children, Virginia refers to children's Medicaid as FAMIS Plus; low-income pregnant women can qualify for FAMIS MOMS to increase access to prenatal care. Medicaid and FAMIS programs are both administered by the Virginia Department of Medical Assistance Services (DMAS), one of twelve state agencies under the Secretary of Health and Human Resources.

The **Patient Protection and Affordable Care Act (PPACA),** widely known as the Affordable Care Act, was signed into law by President Obama in 2010. The Affordable Care Act will have a significant impact on Virginians' access to care and on state-funded health programs. The law has many provisions, including allowing young people to stay on their parents' insurance until aged twenty-six, prohibiting insurance companies from denying coverage to individuals with preexisting conditions, requiring large businesses to provide health insurance to their employees, and expanding Medicaid and subsidies for low-income citizens. However, none has received as much criticism as the "individual mandate," which requires all Americans to have health insurance or pay a tax. In order to try to block implementation of PPACA, Virginia lawmakers preempted the federal legislation with a law of their own, the **Virginia Health Care Freedom Act**. The Health Care Freedom Act prohibits either the federal or state government from requiring Virginians to buy health insurance. Soon after PPACA passed, Attorney General Ken Cuccineli sued the federal government on behalf of Virginia, claiming that the Affordable Care Act's individual mandate was unconstitutional. A number of other states filed a separate class action lawsuit and more than twenty state legislatures passed bills designed to challenge or to try to opt out of the law's provisions.[36]

Some of the resistance to the Affordable Care Act is ideological—expanding the role of the national government fits uneasily with Virginia's political culture. Other opposition stems from the law's projected fiscal impact on the state budget. The PPACA initially required states to expand Medicaid coverage to all individuals with incomes below 133 percent of the poverty level or risk losing federal Medicaid funding. Because Virginia has traditionally had limited coverage, compliance with the

Governor Bob McDonnell signs the 2010 Virginia Health Care Freedom Act as the media, members of the General Assembly, and health care professionals look on. McDonnell and other supporters of the bill hoped that it would exempt Virginians from the "individual mandate," a key feature of the federal Affordable Care Act that requires all Americans to purchase health insurance or pay a fine.

federal law would cost the state relatively more than states that already had more liberal benefits. In June 2012, a closely divided U.S. Supreme Court declared that the Affordable Care Act's individual mandate is constitutional under Congress's taxing power but that the federal government could not force states to expand the Medicaid program. Since it will take a few years for the law to be fully implemented, it remains to be seen whether these recent health care changes will improve the cost and coverage of health insurance in Virginia.

Energy and Environmental Policy

The U.S. government is extensively involved in environmental and energy policy as are state and local governments across the country. These two policy areas are inherently intertwined—you really cannot talk about one without talking about the other as each significantly impacts the other. In recent years, state and local governments have taken on greater responsibility for operating and financing statewide environmental protection programs. The protection and improvement of Virginia's environmental quality is a top priority for the Commonwealth in order to protect its abundance of natural resources, facilitate energy conservation, and support its economy.

How Virginia Uses Energy

Virginia is the fifteenth largest primary energy producer of all states. Virginians use energy to light, heat, cool, and control their homes and buildings. They also use energy to transport goods and services through vehicles, airplanes, trains, and ships. This energy is provided through a number of sources, including coal, petroleum, natural gas, electricity, nuclear power, and new alternative forms of renewable energy. In 2010, Virginia transportation accounted for 29.8 percent of all energy used in Virginia, with the residential sector accounting for 27.3 percent of energy consumption, the commercial sector using 25.3 percent of the state's energy, and the industrial sector consuming 17.6 percent.[37] Virginia's energy policy covers the following broad areas: the provision of reliable energy supplies at reasonable costs, sufficient infrastructure to support energy systems, efficient use of resources through conservation, increased development of low-cost energy resources (such as clean coal and natural gas), greater use of low-pollution energy resources, research and development, and environmental protection.

Energy consumption depends on a number of factors, including population growth, personal income, economic activity, transportation usage, implementation of new products, and the use of energy efficiency and conservation practices by producers and consumers. Energy consumption tends to follow the ebb and flow of general economic activity in the region. Virginia energy consumption is projected to grow at an annual rate of 1.5 percent, and Virginia will need to expand its internal energy supply by 14.6 percent to meet this growing demand through 2020.[38]

As part of the policy goal to make Virginia less energy dependent, Virginia aims to increase its own energy production and experiment with **renewable energy sources.** For every 1 percent of reduced energy imports, Virginia's economy would keep an additional $150 million, which could increase Virginia gross domestic product (GDP) by $20 million while increasing Virginia jobs within the energy industry.[39] By decreasing the amount of energy imported to Virginia, the state could witness considerable expansion in its economy, and this theme plays a central role in the energy policy in Virginia.

Virginia's Energy Policy

The Virginia Department of Mines, Minerals and Energy developed a 2010 Virginia Energy Plan to outline the state's energy policy. This plan, which will be updated every four years, provides a thorough analysis of the primary energy sources used in Virginia. The plan outlined three energy-related goals for Virginia for the four-year period from 2010 to 2014. They include making Virginia the energy capital of the East Coast; expanding education about energy production, consumption, and efficiency; and improving clean energy research and development. A systematic evaluation of Virginia's current energy conditions helped to develop Virginia's policy initiatives, and the 2010 Virginia Energy Plan outlines recommendations to help Virginia meet these energy-related goals. The Virginia Energy Plan provides a sturdy foundation for Virginia's energy policy.

According to the U.S. Energy Information Administration, Virginia's 2009 Power Sources were 44 percent from coal, 38 percent from nuclear, 13 percent from natural gas, 3 percent from renewable sources, and 2 percent from petroleum?

Virginia's mining companies produce nearly 10 percent of U.S. coal east of the Mississippi from underground and surface mines in southwest Virginia?

Electricity use in Virginia is roughly 40 percent from homes, 30 percent from offices and businesses, and 20 percent from the largest energy users, like factories? The other 10 percent primarily is used from schools and government facilities.

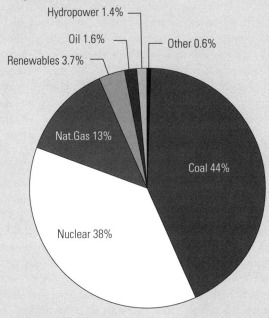

Virginia's Power Sources

Hydropower 1.4%
Oil 1.6%
Other 0.6%
Renewables 3.7%
Nat. Gas 13%
Coal 44%
Nuclear 38%

Source: U.S. Energy Information Administration. "Virginia: State Profile and Energy Estimates," 2010, http://www.eia.gov/beta/state/?sid=VA.

Source: Department of Mines, Minerals and Energy, "The Virginia Energy Plan" (July 1, 2010), 1–7, http://www.dmme .virginia.gov/DE/VEP_TitlePage.html.

To meet its first goal of making Virginia the energy capital of the East Coast, Virginia will increase in-state energy production, jobs, and investment in both traditional and alternative energy resources by 20 percent over the next ten years.[40] To accomplish this, plans have been instituted to begin offshore natural gas and oil drilling while increasing onshore energy development. The recommendations focus on safety, environmental friendliness, and easing market entry to other energy businesses. Before offshore drilling can begin, Virginia needs to build the necessary infrastructure to support this expansion. This infrastructure provides plants with the ability to generate, refine, and store energy sources, allowing energy to be reliable and affordable to Virginians. Furthermore, Virginia plans to improve its renewable energy capabilities to increase the in-state energy output, primarily through biomass, waste, and wind resources. Particular emphasis is placed on energy processes that produce secondary benefits, such as water quality improvements. To provide economic incentives for energy businesses to develop these alternative fuel sources, Virginia will lend financial support to these businesses, including green job tax credits and a revision in the solar photovoltaic manufacturing incentive grant fund to encompass renewable energy.

The Virginia Energy Plan advocates for the construction of a third nuclear reactor at the North Anna Power Station to meet the state's increased electrical demand and supports the development of state-of-the-art nuclear power plants. In addition, Virginia plans to complete its study on the impacts of uranium mining to determine if this is a viable and safe alternative energy source. As a means to improve energy efficiency, the Virginia Energy Plan proposes that efficiency should be marketed as a way to help low-income, fixed-income, and elderly populations tackle their energy needs. The Virginia Energy Plan also intends to create additional systems to help deliver stable energy services during emergency conditions. In effect, the sum of these initiatives should help Virginia to realize its first goal: to make Virginia the energy capital of the East Coast.

Virginia's second goal from the 2010 Virginia Energy Plan is to expand public education about energy in the following areas: energy production and consumption, energy's impact on Virginia's economy, and how Virginia citizens can use energy more efficiently.[41] To do this, the state will implement the State Corporation Commission's Virginia Energy Sense program to educate consumers about energy efficiency. In an effort to send clear messages to consumers, the Department of Mines, Minerals and Energy (DMME) plans to market information regarding efficiency to its constituents, with help from federal, state, local, and utility sources. Also, for continued education efforts, the state will support both community college and university programs contributing to energy-related jobs. These initiatives will help Virginia to educate consumers about efficient energy uses, helping the state achieve the second goal of the Virginia Energy Plan.

The third goal from the 2010 Virginia Energy Plan is to maximize investment in clean energy research and development by using the Universities Clean Energy Development and Economic Stimulus Foundation. To do this, leaders will facilitate research and development initiatives between universities and private companies to maximize Virginia's energy-related resources. By bringing together business and political leaders, as well as research from many institutions, this plan can help to increase energy jobs, promote offshore development, and research alternative fuel technologies. Together, this proposition will work to establish Southside and Southwest regions of Virginia as the national hub for both traditional and alternative energy research and development. The Virginia Department of Environmental

Quality (DEQ) works as the primary center for state and federal laws and regulations pertaining to environmental issues. The DEQ focuses on several aspects of environmental quality including air and water quality, water, and waste management. The organization also partners with local communities, businesses, educators, and government agencies to protect the environment through technical and financial assistance. Collaboration with these partners has produced several programs that work toward educating the Commonwealth's communities, businesses, governments, and students on ways each individual and business can help protect the environment and Virginia's natural resources.

How Does Virginia Stack Up?

In 2005, the U.S. Environmental Protection Agency (EPA) ranked Virginia as twentieth among all states for reported toxic chemicals and, in 2007, was ranked second for the amount of important municipal solid waste. The Northern Virginia–Washington D.C.–Maryland region was ranked the fourteenth worst region nationally for ozone contaminants.[42] However, considerable improvements have been made since then as a result of Virginia's environmental policy initiatives.

The DEQ has taken a variety of measures to promote the air quality in Virginia. As of 2009, Virginia has met compliance standards with most federal air quality regulations, which has led to cleaner environments, greater economic development opportunities, and a healthier quality of life for its citizens. Collected data show that federal air quality standards have not been met in the following areas: Northern Virginia, Richmond, Hampton Roads, Fredericksburg, Roanoke, and Winchester. To come into compliance with these federal standards, the DEQ has taken a number of steps. The DEQ voluntarily partnered with the State Air Pollution Control Board to create Early Action Compact agreements to improve the air quality in the Winchester and Roanoke regions. Also, they have implemented better methods to collect air quality data and implemented a system to create air quality reports. New air monitoring stations have been established in additional areas and air quality forecasts are produced to allow better monitoring of air quality in specific regions, namely, the Richmond, Roanoke, and Hampton Roads areas. The future plans of the DEQ involve establishing additional monitoring stations, focusing on the problematic regions.

To ensure a safe and sufficient water supply, the DEQ emphasizes **water supply planning**. This is increasingly important as the demand for usable water is increasing due to increases in population. As a response, the DEQ has implemented minimum standard requirements for local water supplies to ensure Virginians have an adequate water supply, even in the face of a drought. In addition to ensuring adequate water supplies, the DEQ works to mitigate water pollution by implementing controls for wastewater. For example, the DEQ has focused on limiting the amount of pollution in the Chesapeake Bay, Virginia rivers, streams, and lakes to improve the health of the state's waterways. To accomplish this, the DEQ has issued standards to limit the levels of nutrient discharges from wastewater treatment plants, which will consequently decrease costs for the Bay restoration project. In the two years following the implementation of this initiative, they have worked to decrease nitrogen discharges in the Chesapeake Bay by more than 2 million pounds.[43] Future plans involve focusing on state waters that are either unsafe for swimming, do not support aquatic life, or fall below water quality standards, which will require decreases in waste from many sources.

The Virginia Environmental Excellence Program (VEEP) is an example of one of the successful programs developed by the Department of Environmental Quality. VEEP works to encourage businesses to adopt environmental management systems. Through these environmental management systems, businesses throughout the Commonwealth are able to improve their practices and become more environmentally conscious and energy efficient. The department also encourages communities and businesses to help clean up **brownfields** (such as abandoned factories or manufacturing plants). In addition to the VEEP, the Virginia Department of Environmental Quality also works with an environmental education initiative to meet the Virginia Standards of Learning. Through collaboration with other government agencies, the department promotes pollution reduction and recycling. With the diverse geography found in Virginia, the department's responsibilities extend to protection and restoration of water quality in the Chesapeake Bay as well as the rivers that run through the state. Investigating fuel and chemical spills and other environmental incidents is another function of the DEQ.

In 2009, the department shifted its priorities to encompass several renewable energy goals after the Virginia General Assembly enacted legislation calling for the department to regulate construction and operation of renewable energy projects. In an effort to make Virginia the energy capital of the East Coast, in 2011, Governor Bob McDonnell signed into law eight pieces of new legislation aimed at promoting clean and renewable energy. By emphasizing the need for clean renewable energy, the Commonwealth hopes to "maximize availability, reliability, and price opportunities to the benefit of all user classes and the Commonwealth's economy" (Virginia Energy Plan, p. i).

Other efforts in protecting Virginia's environment and natural resources are a part of the mission of Virginia Energy Sense and the Division of Energy under Virginia's Department of Mines, Minerals and Energy. **Virginia Energy Sense** is an environmental education program that seeks to educate Virginia residents on how to save energy easily and cost effectively. The Department of Mines, Minerals and Energy created a separate division within the department to focus specifically on fostering growth of **sustainable energy**. According to the department, "Virginia has a voluntary goal to reduce electricity use by 2022 through methods of conservation efficiency, by an amount equal to 10 percent of 2005 electricity use" (Virginia Energy Plan).[44]

In 2007, the Virginia legislature took action toward achieving goals outlined in the Commonwealth's energy plan by creating the Virginia Coastal Energy Research Consortium (VCERC). The consortium is located in Norfolk, Virginia at Old Dominion University and is governed by a fourteen-member board. The mission of the consortium is geared toward meeting the objectives of the Virginia Energy Plan by providing research and development in regard to sustainable energy and environmental improvement. VCERC's wind energy research group examines specifically offshore wind power in the southern mid-Atlantic region. According to VCERC's final report in 2010 about "the large offshore wind resource that exists in shallow waters beyond the visual horizon off Virginia and the center of shipbuilding and military-trained workforce candidates that exist in Hampton Roads, the Commonwealth has every reason to become a national leader in the development" (VCERC.org, *Virginia Offshore Wind Studies, July 2007 to March 2010: Final Report*, p. 29). Researchers at VCERC partner with several organizations around the Commonwealth including the Virginia Wind Energy Collaborative to educate Virginians on the benefits of wind power. While these organizations support generating wind power in the Commonwealth, the initiative remains a controversial topic. Opponents claim that wind turbines, as seen in this photo of a wind farm, pose harmful threats to wildlife and forest habitat, suggesting that researchers need to take a better look of the costs and benefits of this newly emerging industry. However, an increasingly high number of incentives for onshore and offshore wind power continue to help facilitate the demand for new projects.

Another highly controversial topic related to environmental and energy policy in Virginia is the process of **hydraulic fracturing**, commonly referred to as **hydrofracking**. The United States Environmental Protection Agency (EPA) defines the hydrofracking process as "fractures in the rock formation that stimulate the flow of natural gas or oil, increasing the volumes that can be recovered." The EPA terms hydrofracking as "an unconventional natural gas production" in that it can "produce

A key objective of Virginia's 2010 energy plan is to make the Commonwealth the "energy capital of the East Coast" by utilizing both traditional and alternative sources. Harnessing energy from offshore wind farms (such as the one pictured here) could be a way to expand energy production while reducing the environmental impact of traditional resources like coal and petroleum.

cost-effectively gas only by using a special stimulation technique" (http://www2
.epa.gov/hydraulicfracturing/process-hydraulic-fracturing). However, the negative
impacts of this unconventional production of natural gas may outweigh its benefits.
In 2010, Carrizo Energy, a Houston, Texas-based energy company sought to begin
the process of hydrofracking on private lands in Rockingham County. Rockingham
County is located in Virginia's Shenandoah Valley. Several concerned Rockingham
County residents petitioned against the idea, claiming that the process is dangerous
and could result in chemical spills causing harmful toxic waste. Carrizo Energy put
the project on hold. Meanwhile, Rockingham County residents continue to urge
the county's Board of Supervisors to reconsider the proposed use of hydrofracking
and to wait until the Environmental Protection Agency has completed an extensive
evaluation of the costs and benefits associated with this process.

Emergency Management and Homeland Security

Natural disasters (such as earthquakes, droughts, tornadoes, floods) can have an
impact on thousands if not millions of individuals. Human-made disasters (industrial accidents, oil and gas leaks, fires, terrorism) can also place a burden on the
lives impacted by such disasters. Attention to and preparation for these natural
and human-made disasters, especially in a post–September 11 environment, have
placed additional burdens on local, state, and federal governments. States and their
local governments are growing in importance in preparing for and responding to
these disasters.

There are two main mechanisms to address emergency management and
homeland security at the state level in Virginia. The first, Virginia Department
of Criminal Justice Services' Homeland Security Program manages the state's
responses to homeland security threats and oversees preparedness measures. The
agency provides training in areas related to suicide bombings, improvised explosive
devices (or IEDs), emergency communications, and preventative efforts (Virginia
Department of Criminal Justice Services, 2011). The Homeland Security Program
also includes Law Enforcement Information Exchange, known as LInX. According
to the Virginia Department of Criminal Justice, LInX is a "state of the art information sharing system that links the crime information of more than 300 local, state,
and federal law enforcement agencies."[45] Being able to breakdown jurisdictional
boundaries enhances communication and increases the level of preparedness across
the Commonwealth.

The Homeland Security Program awards grants specifically geared toward homeland security. Funds from these programs can be used to enhance overall preparedness and response capabilities for a full range of hazards. The Homeland Security
Grant Program and the Law Enforcement Terrorism Prevention Program (LETPP)
funds are two ways in which security initiatives are implemented throughout the
Commonwealth. Another reference tool utilized by the Virginia Department of
Criminal Justice is known as the *Virginia Law Enforcement Anti-Terrorism Pocket*

BOX 11.3 Declaration of a State of Emergency

Similar in timing to Governor McDonnell's Executive Order No. 38 in response to the August 23, 2011, 5.8 magnitude earthquake, Executive Order No. 40 was also a result of a naturally occurring event. On August 25, 2011, Governor McDonnell issued a state of emergency for the Commonwealth of Virginia based on the National Hurricane Center and the National Weather Service forecasts that projected lasting impacts from Hurricane Irene as it made its way on shore along the East Coast of the United States. Forecasts called for damaging high winds, periods of heavy rainfall, and coastal and lowland flooding primarily in the eastern portions of Virginia.

In order to marshal all public resources and appropriately prepare for the upcoming event, response, and recovery measures, McDonnell issued a **state of emergency**. In addition to countless other moves, the act granted permission for local governments to issue evacuation orders as deemed necessary and set orders for the deployment of the Virginia National Guard and Virginia Defense Force.

Guide. The pocket guide serves as a source of information for "preparing for, preventing and responding to a terrorist or other man-made or natural critical incident" (http://www.dcjs.virginia.gov/cple/ohs).

The Statewide Mutual Aid (SMA) Program is another way in which the Commonwealth's cities and counties are able to provide assistance to each other in the case of a major disaster.

In accordance with the Homeland Security Presidential Directive Number 5, the Commonwealth adopted the **National Incident Management System**—otherwise known as NIMS.[46] NIMS is a federally mandated system requiring all states and their localities to have comprehensive homeland security plans and a uniform method for communicating threats and emergency management activities. Local governments are tasked with carrying out the state's plans and coordinating services directly with citizens.

The Virginia Department of Emergency Management (VDEM) oversees emergency responses within the state as they relate to natural disasters.[47] Examples of recent natural disasters in Virginia include flooding, fires, tornadoes, drought, hurricanes, and even an earthquake. Its four main programmatic areas include preparedness, response, recovery, and mitigation. As the liaison between localities and the federal government, VDEM works to ensure all citizens' needs are met. Most of the local governments in Virginia have an Office of Emergency Management.

Virginia Governor Bob McDonnell has also taken action to increase the level of preparedness for homeland security and emergency management preparedness in the Commonwealth. In 2011, McDonnell created Executive Order No. 41 on "Continuing Preparedness Initiatives in State Government and Affirmation of the Commonwealth of Virginia Emergency Operations Plan."

This executive order focuses on state agency preparedness that include institutions of higher education. The Executive Order states, "It is the responsibility of state government to provide for the well-being of the citizens of the Commonwealth and to ensure the continuity of state government operations, including the delivery of essential state government services." Priority is placed in the following areas: preparedness as an agency mission, preparedness planning, and preparedness as an individual responsibility. The executive order also created an emergency coordination officer position within each state agency and institution. According to the executive order, each emergency coordination officer is responsible for a wide range of preparedness activities, such as maintaining a current roster of agency personnel designated to assist in disaster operations and to ensure that all personnel on the roster are accessible and available for training, exercises, and activities of the plan. In addition, these individuals are responsible for developing and adopting a written Emergency Action Plan for their office.

Federal Government Location and Impact on Homeland Security

Bordering the nation's capital has heightened awareness of homeland security issues in Virginia. Virginia's many assets put it at a high risk for external attacks. Some of the state's unique characteristics are its principle industries. While Virginia began as an agricultural state, it has diversified into other industries such as shipbuilding and textile manufacturing. Most predominately, however, Virginia's largest employer is the federal government, which operates more than two thousand offices in the state.[48] The Department of Defense has been the primary employer in the state since the year 2000.[49]

In addition to the state's unique mix of industries, Virginia's infrastructure heightens the homeland security risk as it provides easy access to the nation's capital. The state's network of highways offers many access points to the nation's capital. Interstates 81, 66, and 95 all travel through northern Virginia and near the Metropolitan D.C. area. Though not as prominently used as they once were, multiple railroad lines, including Norfolk-Southern and CSX, run throughout Virginia and into Washington, D.C.[50] Potential threats may enter into the region through any of Virginia's major airports, located in Roanoke, Richmond, Hampton Roads, Arlington, and Dulles. On the coast, the Commonwealth is home to one of the busiest harbors in the world, the Port of Virginia. Surpassing all of these **infrastructure**-related risks, however, is the heavy concentration of military stationed in the state. Virginia is home to twenty-seven military bases, representing each branch of the country's armed forces.[51] Most of these bases are located in the Tidewater and Northern Virginia regions.

The Department of Homeland Security, under the Urban Areas Security Initiative (UASI), identified thirty-one high-risk areas in terms of population density and threat risk, categorizing these areas as either Tier I or Tier II urban areas. Virginia is home to three regions on the list (see list in Table 11.1 below): the Washington, D.C., metropolitan area, Norfolk, and Richmond. As a Tier I urban area, the nation's capital received $59.4 million in 2010 for homeland security initiatives. Norfolk and Richmond received $7.3 million and $2.6 million respectively. These funds are intended to enhance regional preparedness efforts. The Department of Homeland Security labels the state of Virginia as a Tier II Urban Area, meaning that it is eligible for $126,926,000 in funds through the Urban Areas Security Initiative Program. The funding is intended to address the unique planning, organization, equipment,

TABLE 11.1   All Thirty-one High-Risk Areas for Urban Areas Security Initiative (UASI)

Tier I	
State	**Urban Area**
California	LA/Long Beach Area/Bay Area/San Diego Area
District of Columbia	National Capital Region
Illinois	Chicago Area
Massachusetts	Boston Area
New Jersey	Jersey City/Newark Area
New York	New York City Area
Pennsylvania	Philadelphia Area
Texas	Houston Area/Fort Worth/Arlington Area
Tier II	
State	**Urban Area**
Arizona	Phoenix Area
California	Anaheim/Santa Ana Area/Riverside Area
Colorado	Denver Area
Florida	Miami/Fort Lauderdale/Tampa Area/Orlando Area
Georgia	Atlanta Area
Maryland	Baltimore Area
Michigan	Detroit Area
Minnesota	Twin Cities Area
Missouri	St. Louis Area
Nevada	Las Vegas Area
North Carolina	Charlotte Area
Ohio	Cleveland Area/Cincinnati Area
Oregon	Portland Area
Pennsylvania	Pittsburgh Area
Virginia	Norfolk Area
Washington	Seattle Area

Source: Federal Emergency Management Agency (FEMA).

training, and exercise needs of high-threat, high-density urban areas, and it assists them in building an enhanced and sustainable capacity to prevent, protect against, respond to, and recover from acts of terrorism. Under the Homeland Security Act, states are required to ensure that at least 25 percent of USAI appropriated funds are dedicated toward law enforcement terrorism prevention activities.

Economic Development Policy

The Commonwealth of Virginia has been recognized as one of the best states for business because of its wide range of services and manufactured goods. Economic development in the Commonwealth is defined as "the process that influences the growth and restructuring of the local economy."[52] Economic development goals at the local and state levels are constantly revisited in order to protect Virginia's striving economy.

The aggregate network that generates economic development within the Commonwealth is best understood as an increasing collaboration between the public and private sectors, innovative practices emerging in the field, and changes in the economy that force markets to advocate through a regional forum. The forces that drive economic development in the Commonwealth are quite diverse.

At the state level, Virginia's bureaucratic institutions (described in more detail below) provide assistance and, in some instances, direct funding for nongovernmental organizations to in turn enhance particular markets within the state (such as agriculture, biotechnology, etc.). Prospective companies from throughout the United States and world "shop" for the best relocation option—typically on a regional scale as opposed to evaluating individual local markets by themselves. This practice lends itself to the need for regional collaboration. The General Assembly shares responsibility with the executive branch for economic development initiatives within Virginia. Together these representatives oversee a large majority of Virginia's business opportunities through formal and informal functions. The General Assembly allocates money each year to ensure the state remains a competitive force in today's global economy. The governor and lieutenant governor work alongside members of the General Assembly to oversee the economic development agenda. The governor's principle adviser is the Virginia Workforce Council (VWC), a constituency of business leaders who provide leadership to workforce development within the state. The VWC is also charged with creating statutory guidelines for **workforce development centers** located throughout the state.

Governor Bob McDonnell's first executive order established Virginia's chief job creation officer and the Governor's Economic Development and Job Creation Commission. In his executive order, Governor McDonnell stated that "Virginia is home to abundant resources, fiscal responsibility, and boundless human potential, and the entrepreneurial spirit is evident throughout this great Commonwealth" (Executive Order No. 1, 2010). Maintaining Virginia's status as a top state for business is one of Governor McDonnell's main priorities.

Commonly referred to as a "jobs governor," McDonnell has issued several executive orders calling for economic competitiveness and versatility. Governor McDonnell created the position of job creation officer to "help coordinate all economic and workforce development and job creation initiatives, assist with recruiting new industries and job creation opportunities, oversee and ensure that all agencies are working together, expand existing businesses, and create new jobs across the Commonwealth" (Executive Order No. 1, 2010). See Box 11.4 for more information on the Virginia's chief jobs creation officer. In addition, the executive order also called for a Job Creation Commission to evaluate current programs, identify impediments, and make recommendations on how to expand economic opportunities throughout the Commonwealth. The commission's final report in 2010 provided an extensive analysis of their research and recommendations. The report identified subcommittees that examined specific areas of economic development throughout the Commonwealth and provided comprehensive recommendations intended to address the challenges that were seen as roadblocks to potential economic growth. The commission's 2010 report suggested that one of the most widely recognized deficiencies in Virginia's economic development policy is the "lack of appropriate coordination with higher education institutions and infrastructure needed to capitalize and commercialize on future emerging technologies and industries" (*Governor's Commission on Economic Development & Job Creation,* Final Report, October 16, 2010, p. 2, http://www.ltgov.virginia.gov/initiatives/jcc/JCC_final_report.pdf).

Other efforts to maintain Virginia's status as one of the top states for economic growth and development include Governor McDonnell's 2011 overseas trade mission. Governor McDonnell ventured on his fourth international trade mission

BOX 11.5   Economic Development at the Local Level

While the Commonwealth remains a top state for doing business, cities like Martinsville, Virginia, were unable to escape the consequences of a deteriorating economy. As observed by the Martinsville-Henry County Taxpayer Association, throughout the past seventeen years, Martinsville has experienced a tremendous net loss of local jobs. The city that once employed thousands of people in the textile and furniture industries was left with an unemployment rate close to 20 percent, with a quarter of the population living below the poverty line. The job crisis in Martinsville worsened when the city's largest private employer, StarTek, closed and eliminated 630 jobs. To illustrate the company's major role in Martinsville's economic development, reports from the *Martinsville Bulletin* show that StarTek injected more than $9.5 million into the Martinsville community through its payroll and also contributed $35,000 to area nonprofit organizations between 2005 and 2007. Given these statistics, it is obvious that the closure of StarTek had a significant negative impact on the city's economy. However, in April of 2011, Governor McDonnell announced that more than five hundred new jobs in Henry County will be created from a $15 million operations center opened by ICF International. ICF International is a global professional services firm headquartered in northern Virginia. With the help from the Virginia Economic Development Partnership, and a $500,000 grant approved by Governor McDonnell from the Governor's Opportunity Fund, the Martinsville-Henry County Economic Development Corporation secured the project. Governor McDonnell's office also announced that funding and services to help support job recruitment and training will be provided through the Virginia Jobs Investment Program.

Source: http://martinsvillebulletin.com/article.cfm?ID=28089, "ICF to Bring 539 Jobs," April 12, 2011; and http://www .martinsvillebulletin.com/article.cfm?ID=28612, "StarTek to Close in July," May 24, 2011.

wherein he spent eleven days promoting Virginia products and resources in India and Israel. Acting as an economic development ambassador, Governor McDonnell's eleven-day trade mission was spent promoting Virginia wine, film, and tourism industries, as well as the Commonwealth's natural resources, such as wood products, apples, processed foods, and soybean oil.

Agencies Aiding Virginia Businesses and Workforce Development

A milestone for the state's involvement in the field of economic development was the incorporation of the **Virginia Economic Development Partnership (VEDP)** by the Virginia General Assembly in 1995. The goal of creating the partnership was to help foster economic growth in the Commonwealth. According to the VEDP, Virginia is the best state for business because of its robust economy, pro-business climate, financial advantages, quality workforce, great educational system, innovative research and development, transportation infrastructure, international investment, and overall quality-of-life. The partnership is governed by a board of twenty-one businesses, which are appointed by the governor and the General Assembly (http:// www.yesvirginia.org). By working to promote a healthy business climate across the state, VEDP's experts provide the necessary knowledge and resources to help businesses thrive. Several other agencies like VEDP aid Virginia businesses and workforce, including the Virginia Department of Business Assistance, through its Virginia Jobs Investment Program (VJIP). VJIP exists to support growth in the private sector by finding and developing a skilled workforce (Virginia.gov). Other agencies working to uphold Virginia's standing in the economy include the Virginia Small Business Finance Authority, Virginia Employment Commission, and the Virginia Department of Social Service.

In addition to the various state and local government agencies working to promote and foster economic development in the state are lobbyists, associations, business led organizations (such as the Virginia Chamber of Commerce), and federally enacted organizations. With a unique combination of assets and the support of several agencies such as the ones mentioned, the Commonwealth remains on top as one of the best states with which to do business.

Conclusion

Crafting public policies is one of government's most important undertakings. Policymaking is a complex process that involves a large number of actors and institutions both inside and outside of government. Understanding the policy process can help citizens become more engaged and better able to have input into the laws, rules, and regulations that govern their lives every day. While the media often pays more attention to policies coming out of Washington, D.C., significant policy activity occurs at the state and local levels. This includes policies generated by state legislatures, executive orders, bureaucratic rule making, and precedents set by state court decisions. Additionally, states and localities play a major role in implementing federal policies.

A state's unique history, culture, and economy produce important variation in public policies across the country. In addition to providing an overview of the policy process, this chapter has highlighted a number of major policy areas that are vital to Virginians today. Like other states, Virginia has the primary task of educating future citizens and ensuring a high-skilled workforce. This includes funding, directing, and administering schooling from preschool to higher education. The Commonwealth also administers a number of policies designed to improve citizens' health and welfare. These include policies to aid people in poverty and to expand access to health care; many of Virginia's health and social service programs are fully or partially funded by the federal government.

Virginia's energy and environmental policies, like those of most states, are highly interdependent. Virginia's Energy Plan established three primary goals: to make Virginia the energy capital of the East Coast; to expand education about energy production, consumption, and efficiency; and to improve clean energy research and development. Not unrelated to Virginia's energy and environmental policies are the state's policies and efforts as related to homeland security and emergency management. These help to ensure that Virginia is prepared for and can respond quickly and effectively to natural or human disasters.

Key Concepts

Policy Process

Distributive policies
Federalism
Focusing events
Implement
Institutional agenda
Policy evaluation

Policy process model
Public policies
Redistributive policies
Regulatory policies
Systemic agenda

K-12 Education

Achievement gap
Charter schools
Governor's Schools
Human capital
Magnet schools

National Assessment of Educational
    Progress (NAEP)
No Child Left Behind
School vouchers
Standards of Learning (SOL)

Health and Human Services

Family Access to Medical Insurance
    Security (FAMIS)
Means-tested
Medicaid
Medicare
Patient Protection and Affordable Care
    Act (PPACA)
Poverty guidelines

Poverty threshold
Supplemental Nutrition Assistance
    Program (SNAP)
Temporary Assistance to Needy
    Families (TANF)
Virginia Health Care Freedom Act
Virginia Initiative for Employment
    Not Welfare (VIEW)

Energy and Environment

Brownfields
Hydraulic fracturing
Hydrofracking
Renewable energy sources

Sustainable energy
Virginia Energy Sense
Water supply planning

Emergency Management and Homeland Security

Infrastructure
National Incident Management System

State of emergency

Economic Development Policy

Governor's Commission on Economic
Development and Job Creation
Virginia Economic Development
Partnership (VEDP)

Workforce development centers

Suggested Resources

- http://www.pewstates.org/: Explore state-centered policy research and analysis by the **Pew Center for the States**.
- http://www.ncsl.org/: The **National Council of State Legislatures** provides information on contemporary issues and state-level solutions to policy problems.
- http://jlarc.virginia.gov/: In Virginia, the **Joint Legislative Audit and Review Commission** studies emerging issues in the Commonwealth. Read Commission reports on a wide variety of policy topics.
- http://www.doe.virginia.gov/: Learn more about the **Virginia Department of Education**, including school policies and school division report cards.
- http://www.dss.virginia.gov/: Explore the Virginia Department of Social Services to find out more about programs to help strengthen the welfare of Virginia's citizens.
- http://www.famis.org/: Learn more about Virginia's health insurance programs, **FAMIS**.
- http://www.dmme.virginia.gov/: Virginia's Department of Mines, Minerals and Energy regulates the energy industry in the Commonwealth.
- http://www.virginiaenergysense.org/cue/about/energy-plan.html: Read more about the Virginia Energy Plan.
- http://www.vaemergency.gov/: Learn more about disaster preparedness at the Virginia Department of Emergency Management.
- http://www.yesvirginia.org/whyvirginia/financial_advantages/business_incentives.aspx: There are a variety of economic development incentives in Virginia. Find out more.

- http://www.ltgov.virginia.gov/initiatives/jcc/JCC_final_report.pdf: Explore the Governor's Commission on Economic Development and Job Creation.
- https://www.virginia.gov/business: Discover the benefits of and incentives for doing business in Virginia.

Notes

1. Michael E. Kraft and Scott R. Furlong, *Public Policy: Politics, Analysis, and Alternatives* (Washington, DC: CQ Press, 2010). See also Roger W. Cobb and Charles D. Elder, *Participation in American Politics: The Dynamics of Agenda Building*, 2nd ed. (Baltimore, MD: John Hopkins University Press, 1983).

2. John W. Kingdon, *Agendas, Alternatives, and Public Policies,* 2nd ed. *(White Plains, NY: Longman, 2010).*

3. This phrase, coined by Harold Laswell in his 1936 book, *Politics: Who Gets What, When, How,* is widely given as a definition of politics.

4. Virginia Constitution, Article VIII, Sec. 1.

5. Virginia Department of Education, "2011–2012 Fall Membership Data," 2011, http://bi.vita.virginia.gov/doe_bi/rdPage.aspx?rdReport=Main&subRptName=Fallmembership.

6. Virginia Department of Education, "Virginia Board of Education: Duties," 2012, http://www.doe.virginia.gov/boe/index.shtml.

7. Commonwealth Education Poll 2010–2011, http://www.cepi.vcu.edu/polls/2010-2011/CEPI%20poll%20report%20on%20K-12%20for%20release%2012-16-10.pdf, para. 1.

8. Ibid.

9. Virginia Department of Education, Division of Policy and Communications, "Virginia Students Again Rank Third in Nation in Achievement on Advanced Placement Tests: Eighth Division Recognized for Increasing AP Participation & Achievement," *Virginia Department of Education News*, February 8, 2012, http://www.doe.virginia.gov/news/news_releases/2012/feb08.pdf.

10. Virginia Department of Education. "Testing and Standards of Learning: The Standards and Sol-Based Instructional Resources," 2012, http://www.doe.virginia.gov/testing/sol/standards_docs/index.shtml.

11. Virginia Department of Education, Board of Education, "2011 Annual Report on the Condition and Needs of Public Schools in Virginia," November, 29, 2011, http://www.doe.virginia.gov/boe/reports/annual_reports/2011.pdf.

12. Patrick McGuinn, "The National Schoolmarm: No Child Left Behind and the New Educational Federalism," *Publius* 35, no. 1 (2005): 41–68, http://publius.oxfordjournals.org/content/35/1/41.short.

13. Virginia Department of Education, "Adequate Yearly Progress (AYP) Reports," November 29, 2010), http://www.doe.virginia.gov/statistics_reports/accreditation_ayp_reports/ayp/index.shtml.

14. Samieh Shalash, "Virginia Adopts New Method to Measure Students, Drops AYP," *Daily Press,* August 01, 2012, http://www.doe.virginia.gov/statistics_reports/accreditation_federal_reports/ayp/index.shtml.

15. Virginia Department of Education, Board of Education, "2011 Annual Report on the Condition and Needs of Public Schools in Virginia," November 29, 2011, http://www.doe.virginia.gov/boe/reports/annual_reports/2011.pdf.

16. Virginia Department of Education, Office of School Nutrition Programs (SNP), "School Year 2011–2012 National School Lunch Program (NSLP) Free and Reduced Price Eligibility Report," January 25, 2012, http://www.doe.virginia.gov/support/nutrition/statistics/free_reduced_eligibility/2011–2012/divisions/frpe_div_report_sy2011–12.pdf.

17. National Center for Education Statistics, "Table 2—Number of Operating Public Elementary and Secondary Schools, by School Type, Charter, Magnet, Title I and Title I," 2010, http://nces.ed.gov/pubs2010/pesschools08/tables.asp.

18. Alabama, Kentucky, Montana, Nebraska, North Dakota, South Dakota, Vermont, Washington, and West Virginia do not have charter school legislation, according to the Center for Education Reform, "Just the FAQs—Charter Schools," 2013, http://www.edreform.com/2012/03/just-the-faqs-charter-schools/.

19. Virginia Department of Education, "Instruction: Charter Schools," 2012, http://www.doe.virginia.gov/instruction/charter_schools/index.shtml; and Virginia General Assembly, Code of Virginia, n.d., http://leg1.state.va.us/cgi-bin/legp504.exe?000+cod+TOC2201000.

20. Ibid., "Virginia's Public Charter Schools," (n.d.), http://www.doe.virginia.gov/instruction/charter_schools/charter_schools.shtml.

21. Ibid., "Career & Technical Education," 2012, http://www.doe.virginia.gov/instruction/career_technical/index.shtml.

22. Ibid., "Family & Consumer Sciences," 2012, http://www.doe.virginia.gov/instruction/career_technical/family_consumer_science/index.shtml; Ibid., "Health & Medical Sciences," 2012, http://www.doe.virginia.gov/instruction/career_technical/health_medical_sciences/index.shtml; Ibid., "Marketing," 2012, http://www.doe.virginia.gov/instruction/career_technical/marketing/index.shtml; Ibid.,"Technology," 2012, http://www.doe.virginia.gov/instruction/career_technical/technology/index.shtml; Ibid., "Trade & Industrial," 2012, http://www.doe.virginia.gov/instruction/career_technical/trade_industrial/index.shtml.

23. Ibid.,"Academic-Year Governor's Schools," 2012, http://www.doe.virginia.gov/instruction/governors_school_programs/academic_year/index.shtml; Ibid., "Governor's School Programs," 2012, http://www.doe.virginia.gov/instruction/governors_school_programs/index.shtml.

24. Ibid., "College Partnership Laboratory Schools," 2012, http://www.doe.virginia.gov/instruction/laboratory_schools/index.shtml.

25. Ibid., "News Release: State Superintendent Approves Additional Virtual-School Programs," 2012, http://www.doe.virginia.gov/news/news_releases/2012/apr06.shtml.

26. U.S. Department of Education, "Characteristics of Private Schools in the United States: Results from the 2009–10 Private School Universe Survey" (Washington, DC: NCES, 2011), Table 15, http://nces.ed.gov/pubs2011/2011339.pdf.

27. "Income Tax, Corporate; Tax Credits for Donations to Non-Profit Organizations, etc. (SB131)," Richmond Sunlight, April 22, 2013, http://www.richmondsunlight.com/bill/2012/sb131/.

28. Virginia Department of Education, "Home Schooled Students and Religious Exemptions, 2011–2012," 2012, http://www.doe.virginia.gov/statistics_reports/enrollment/home_school_religious_exempt/index.shtml.

29. Home Educators Association of Virginia, "Religious Exemption Demystified," n.d., http://heav.org/va-law/religious-exemption/religious-exemption-demystified/; and The Organization of Virginia Homeschoolers, "Religious Exemption From Compulsory Schooling," n.d., http://www.vahomeschoolers.org/guide/relig ious_exemption.asp.

30. Commonwealth of Virginia, Poverty Reduction Task Force, Poverty in Virginia (2010, p. 5), http://www.dss.virginia.gov/geninfo/reports/agency_wide/poverty_long.pdf.

31. Liz Schott and Ife Finch, "TANF Benefits Are Low and Have Not Kept Pace with Inflation: Benefits Are Not Enough to Meet Families' Basic Needs," 2010, Center on Budget and Policy Priorities, http://www.cbpp.org/cms/index.cfm?fa=view&id=3306.

32. Virginia Department of Health and Human Resources, "Report of the Virginia Health Reform Initiative Advisory Council," December 20, 2010, http://www.hhr.virginia.gov/initiatives/healthreform/docs/VHRIFINAL122010.pdf;KaiserFamilyFoundation,"AverageAnnual Percent Growth in Health Care Expenditures by State of Residence, 1991–2009," http://www.statehealthfacts.org/comparemaptable.jsp?typ=2&ind=595&cat=5&sub=143&sortc=1&o=a.

33. The Urban Institute, "Profile of Virginia's Uninsured 2010," 2010, http://www.urban.org/UploadedPDF/412422-Profile-of-Virginia-Uninsured-2010.pdf.

34. Virginia Department of Health and Human Resources, "Report of the Virginia Health Reform Initiative Advisory Council," December 20, 2010, 42–43, http://www.hhr.virginia.gov/initiatives/healthreform/docs/VHRIFINAL122010.pdf.

35. Kaiser Family Foundation, "Income Eligibility Limits for Children's Separate CHIP Programs by Annual Incomes and as a Percent of Federal Poverty Level, January 2013," 2013, http://www.statehealthfacts.org/comparemaptable.jsp?cat=4&ind=204.

36. Richard Cauchi, "State Legislation and Actions Challenging Certain Health Reforms" (National Conference of State Legislatures, 2013), http://www.ncsl.org/issues-research/health/state-laws-and-actions-challenging-ppaca.aspx.

37. U.S. Energy Information Administration, "Virginia: State Profile and Energy Estimates," 2010, http://www.eia.gov/beta/state/?sid=VA.

38. Department of Mines, Minerals and Energy, "The Virginia Energy Plan," p. 1–7, July 1, 2010, http://www.dmme.virginia.gov/DE/VAEnergyPlan/2010-VEP/VEP-2010.pdf.

39. Ibid., p. §1–6.

40. Ibid. p. §8–1.

41. Ibid., p. §8–3.

42. Ibid.

43. Ibid., p. 6.

44. Ibid., p. 7.

45. Virginia Department of Criminal Justice Services, "Standards, Policy and Homeland Security: Law Enforcement Information Exchange (LInX)," n.d., http://www.dcjs.virginia.gov/cple/ohs/.

46. Mark Warner, "Executive Order No. 102," November 1, 2005, http://www.dcjs.virginia.gov/cple/documents/NIMSexecutiveOrder.pdf.

47. Virginia Department of Emergency Management, "What We Do," 2012, accessed October 17, 2011, http://www.vaemergency.gov/aboutus/what-we-do.

48. Virginia Employment Commission, "Quarterly Census of Employment & Wages," 2011, accessed October 17, 2011, http://www.alex.vec.virginia.gov/lmi/reports/industry/2011–01.pdf.

49. Robert McDonnell, Ric Brown, and David Von Moll, *A Comprehensive Annual Financial Report for the Fiscal Year Ended June 30, 2010*, accessed October 17, 2011, http://www.doa.virginia.gov/Financial_Reporting/CAFR/2010/S_Statistical.pdf.

50. Virginia Studies, "Virginia Pathways Video Series," n.d., accessed October 17, 2011, http://www.vastudies.org/episode3/path.pdf.

51. "Military Bases in Virginia," Militarybases.com, 2011, accessed October 17, 2011, http://militarybases.com/virginia/.

52. Virginia Economic Development Partnership, "A Guidebook for Local Elected Officials: 2011–12" (n.d.), accessed February 2, 2013, http://www.virginiaallies.org/assets/files/publications/ed_handbook.pdf, p. 4.

Academic achievement, 159–63
Achievement gaps, 161–62
Actual innocence, writ of, 95
Adequate yearly progress, 160
AFDC. *See* Aid to Families with Dependent
    Children
Affordable Care Act. *See* Patient Protection
    and Affordable Care Act
African Americans. *See also* Blacks
    civil rights timeline for, 27
    disenfranchisement of, 17, 26
    population statistics for, 5–6
    voting patterns, 51
    voting rights of, 26
Age
    population demographics based
        on, 5, 7
    for voting, 29
Agencies. *See* Bureaucratic agencies
Agenda setting stage, of policymaking,
    155–56
Aid to Families with Dependent
    Children, 167
Aid to localities, 127
Air quality, 177
Alabama Constitution, 12, 23
Albemarle, 146, 163
Albo, David, 99
Allen, George, 82, 84
Amendments to state constitution, 23
American Council on Intergovernmental
    Relations, 141
Amicus curiae briefs, 55
AMO. *See* Annual measurable objectives
Annexation, 143, 145–46
Annual budget, 119–20
Annual household income, 8
Annual measurable objectives, 161–62
Appalachian Plateau region, 3

Appeals, judicial, 94–96
Appellate jurisdiction, 94
Appointment of legislators, 69–70
Appropriations Committee, 121
Area Development Act, 149
Arlington, 137
Armstrong, Ward, 56
Articles, Virginia Constitution
    Bill of Rights, 19
    corporations, 22
    education, 21–22
    executive branch, 20
    finance, 22–23
    judicial branch, 21
    legislative branch, 20–21
    list of, 18
    local governments, 22, 133, 139
    taxation, 22–23
Articles of Confederation, 12
Asians, 5–6
Atkinson, Frank, 4
Attorney general
    duties and responsibilities
        of, 20, 87–89
    powers of, 88
    qualifications of, 87

Baby Boomers, 5
Balanced budget, 121
Balance of powers, 14
Ballot access, 36
Ballot initiatives, 36
Battle, William, 83
Bench trial, 92
Bicameral, 61
Biennial budget, 119–20
Bill(s)
    budget, 121
    legislative, 64, 66–67

Bill of Rights, 19
Blacks. *See also* African Americans
    civil rights timeline for, 27
    voting patterns, 51
    voting rights of, 26–28
Black suffrage, 17
Blue Ridge Mountains, 3
Board of Education, 21, 159
Bolling, Bill, 70, 87, 99, 185.
        See also Lieutenant governor
Bonds, 143
Brown v. Board of Education, 46
Brownfields, 178
Budget
    annual, 119–20
    balanced, 121
    biennial, 119–20
    development process for, 120–27
    expenditures, 126–27
    fiscal health, 127–28
    governor's role in preparing, 83, 120
    purpose of, 119
    revenue sources, 122–25
Budget surplus, 127
Bureaucracy
    description of, 80
    merit system for hiring employees,
        111–13
    organization of, 106, 108–9
Bureaucratic agencies
    economic development involvement
        by, 184
    list of, 106–7
    mission statements, 113
    performance measures for, 113
    productivity of, 114–16
    workforce development involvement
        by, 186–87
Bureaucratic power
    overview of, 105–6
    sources of, 106–9
Byrd, Harry Flood, 46, 83
Byrd Organization, 28, 45–47

Cabinet, governor's, 106, 109
Cabinet secretary, 109
California Constitution, 12
Campaign spending, 56

Candidates
    campaign spending disclosures by, 56
    fundraising by, 56
    public funding of, 56
Capitol, Virginia, 61
Career and technical education
        programs, 164
Casework, 68
Castlewood, 138
Caucus, 70
    legislative, 29, 70
    nominating, 33, 44
Charlottesville, 146
Charter, municipal, 135
Charter schools, 163
Chesapeake, 134
Chief justice, 21
Circuit courts, 17, 93–94
Cities
    expenditures by, 143–44
    governmental consolidation of,
        143, 145–46
    independent, 133–34
    revenues of, 140
    towns versus, 133
Citizen legislature, 62
Civil cases, 92
Civil rights
    of felons, 29–30
    timeline of, 27
Civil Service Commission, 112
Civil War, 4, 12
Clifton Forge, 134
Closed primaries, 33
Coal mining, 2
Coastal Plain region, 3
Coastal Zone Management
        Program, 155
Code of Virginia, 126, 146
Cognitively impaired persons, voting
        rights of, 29
Colgan, Charles J., 62
Collective good, 12
College of William and Mary
        redistricting, 32
College Partnership Laboratory
        School, 164
Commission on Constitutional Reform, 18

Commission on Local Government, 137
Committees, legislative, 64–66, 70
Commodities, revenue from sale of, 124
Common law, 13
Commonwealth, 4
Concurrent powers, 97
Confederacy system of government, 12
Confederate Congress, 4
Conference committees, 65, 122
Conservative Democrats, 28
Consolidated-city, 146
Constituents
    definition of, 62
    services for, 68
Constitutional convention, 14, 16, 23
Constitutional law, 97
Constitution (U.S.)
    equal schooling rights, 97
    federalism and, 157
    Fifteenth Amendment of, 26
    Fourteenth Amendment of, 18
    Nineteenth Amendment of, 29
    Twenty-fourth Amendment of, 28
Constitution (Virginia)
    1776, 13–15, 68
    1830, 15
    1851, 16
    1864, 16
    1870, 16–17
    1902, 17–18, 145
    1971, 18–23
    amending of, 23
    articles of. *See* Articles
    evolution of, 13–23
    governorship, 78–79
    overview of, 11
    women's voting rights ratified by, 29
Contracts, revenue from, 124
Corporations, 22
Council-manager form of government,
    134–35
Council on Virginia's Future, 5
Counties
    Article VII requirements for elected
        positions in, 139
    cities independent of, 133
    comparison of, 134
    elected officials in, 139–40

expenditures by, 143–44
governing body of, 139
population variations in, 135
revenues of, 140
County governments, 137–40, 152.
    See also Local governments
County seat, 134
Court(s). *See also* Judges
    appellate jurisdiction, 94
    circuit, 93–94
    Court of Appeals, 91, 94–96
    district, 92–93
    domestic relations, 93
    drug, 100
    general district, 92
    judicial policymaking by, 97–98
    judicial review by, 97
    jurisdiction of, 92–94
    juvenile, 93
    magistrates, 91–92
    national, 96–97
    original jurisdiction, 92, 96
    schematic diagram of, 91
    structure of, 90–96
    Supreme Court of Virginia.
        See Supreme Court of Virginia
Creatures of the state, 135
Criminal cases, 92
CTE programs. *See* Career and technical
    education programs
Cuccinelli, Kenneth, 31, 87, 116, 172

Danville, 151
Declaration of Independence, 13
Declaration of Rights, 14, 19
Delegates. *See also* House
    of Delegates
    appointment of, 69
    ethnic diversity of, 72
    number of, 62
    occupations of, 71
    racial diversity of, 72
    reimbursement of expenses, 64
    salary of, 63–64
    staff support for, 64–65
Democracy
    direct, 36–37
    representative, 13, 32

Democratic Party. *See also* Political parties
   Byrd Organization's influence on, 45–47
   government control by, 48
   governors from, 83
   history of, 45
   party platform, Virginia, 49, 50
   political values of, 49–50
   Republican Party versus, 49
   "Statement of Common Purpose," 50
   voter characteristics, 51–52
Democratic Party of Virginia's Party and
      Delegate Selection Plan, 44
Department of Defense, 182
Department of Environmental Quality,
      176–78
Department of Health, 117
Department of Homeland Security, 182
Department of Medical Assistance
      Services, 172
Department of Mines, Minerals and
      Energy, 174, 176
Department of Motor Vehicles, 113, 116
Descriptive representation, 72
Dillon's Rule, 135–36
Direct democracy, 36–37
Disclosure laws, for campaign financing, 56
Distributive policies, 157
District courts, 92–93
Divided government, 45
Dividends, revenue from, 124
Division of Legislative Services (DLS), 65
DMAS. *See* Department of Medical
      Assistance Services
DMME. *See* Department of Mines,
      Minerals and Energy
Domestic relations courts, 93
Donations, revenue from, 124
Drug courts, 100
Drunk driving, 109

Economic diversity, 8
Economy
   description of, 7–8
   economic development policy, 184–87
   impact on policy, 7, 157, 176, 187–88
Education. *See* K–12 education; Public
      education
1830 Constitution, 15

1851 Constitution, 16
1864 constitution, 16
1870 constitution, 16–17
Elected officials. *See also* Delegates;
      Senator(s)
   in counties, 139–40
   impeachment of, 69
   interest group targeting of, 54
Elections
   "candidate-centered," 44
   impact on national politics, 34–36
   primary, 32–33
   public financing in, 56
   recall, 36–37
   voter turnout rates affected by timing
      of, 34
Electoral offices, 32
Electoral seats, 69
Electorate, political parties in, 43–44
Emergency management, 180–83
Employees
   bonuses given to, 127
   merit system for hiring, 111–13
Employers
   Department of Defense, 182
   federal government as, 8
Employment Eligibility Verification,
      111–12
Energy and environmental policy
   air quality, 177
   description of, 174–77
   energy consumption, 174
   energy sources, 175
   hydrofracking, 179–80
   interdependency of, 188
   overview of, 173
   renewable energy sources, 174–75, 178
   sustainable energy, 178
   water supply planning, 177–78
   wind energy, 179
English common law, 13
Environmental Protection Agency,
      177, 179
Equal Suffrage League of Virginia, 28
Ethnic diversity, 5–6
Ethnicity
   achievement gaps and, 161
   health care coverage and, 170

of judges, 100
of legislators, 72
voting rates based on, 35
Executive branch
budget implementation by, 122
description of, 14, 20, 77
governor. *See* Governor(s)
members of, 77
structure of, 85
Executive Budget Act of 1922, 83
Executive Mansion, 80
Executive officers, 84, 86–87
Executive orders
description of, 81–82, 155
economic development focus
of, 184–85
No. 15, 113, 116
No. 40, 181
No. 41, 181
Expenditures
local government, 141, 143–44
state, 120, 126–27

Fairfax (city), 134
Fairfax County, 138
Fall Line region, 3
Family Access to Medical Insurance
Security (FAMIS), 168, 172
Federalism, 11–12, 96, 157
Felon(s)
civil rights of, 29–30
voting rights of, 29–30
Felonies, 92–94
Fifteenth Amendment, 26
Finance, Article X provisions for, 22–23
Fines, revenue from, 124
First-past-the-post system, 43
Fiscal health, 127–30
Fiscal year, 122
Florida Constitution, 13
Focusing events, 156
Forfeitures, revenue from, 124
Fourteenth Amendment, 18
Franchise, 26, 28
Funders Party, 45

Gay marriage, 19, 38
Gays, 100

General Assembly. *See also* House of
Delegates; Senate (Virginia)
administrative power of, 106
annexation legislation by, 146
appointment of members of, 69–70
Article that establishes, 20
bicameral structure of, 61
as citizen legislature, 62
committees, 64–66
creation of, 13–14
education funding determined by, 21–22
executive oversight by, 68–70
facts about, 63
fiscal oversight by, 69
history of, 60
impeachment power of, 69
judicial oversight by, 68–70
lawmaking power of, 66–68
legislative sessions held by, 62–63
majority rule, 67–68
meeting of, 20, 62–63
members of, 62, 69–70
partisan makeup of, 63
party leadership in, 44
pay, 63
public opinion about, 60
size of, 62
structure of, 61–66
support staff of, 64–65
voter qualifications established by, 33
General district courts, 92
General fund revenues, 122
General purpose government, 147
Geographical regions, 2–3
Gerrymandering
political, 31–32, 69
racial, 26, 69
Gilmore, James, 82, 84
Gingrich, Newt, 36
Godwin, Mills E. Jr., 83
Godwyn, S. Bernard, 95
Goodsell, Charles, 105
GOP. *See* Grand Ole Party
Government
branches of, 42, 68
communication in, 45
confederacy system of, 12
council-manager form of, 134–35

federalism system of, 11–12
forms of, 11–12
general purpose, 147
local. *See* Local governments
mayor-council form of, 134
political parties in, 44–45
political party control of, 48
sovereign, 12
unitary system of, 12
weak-mayor form of, 135
Governmental consolidation, 143, 145–46
Government Performance Project, 7
Governor(s). *See also* Lieutenant governor
administrative responsibilities of, 81
Article V provisions for, 20
budgetmaking power of, 83, 120
Byrd's tenure as, 83
chief appointer and administrator
    role of, 83–84
chief budgeting officer role of, 83
Constitutional provisions, 78–79
election of, 68, 78
executive office of, 84–85
executive orders from. *See* Executive
    orders
government appointments by, 83–84
history of, 78–79, 84
informal roles of, 84
lawmaking role of, 81
list of, 84
as party head, 82–84
powers of, 80–82
responsibilities of, 20, 80–81
state spokesperson role of, 84
term limits for, 78–79
veto power of, 81
Governor's mansion, 80
Governor's Schools, 164
Grand jury, 93
Grand Ole Party, 47
Grants, 124

Habeas corpus, writ of, 95
Hall, Frank, 63
Hamilton, Alexander, 97
Handgun sales, 38
Harper v. Virginia State Board of Elections, 28
Harrison, Benjamin, 84

Harrison, William Henry, 4
Harrisonburg, 134
Health and human services
    health care, 169–73
    overview of, 165
    poverty, 165–69
    social welfare programs, 166–67, 169
Health care, 169–73
Health insurance, 170
Henry, Patrick, 79, 84
Higher education, 126. *See also* Public
    education
Highland County, 139
Hiring of employees, 110–13
Hispanics, 5–6
Holley, James, 36–37
Holton, Linwood, 83, 164
Home districts, 68
Homeland security, 180–83
Homeland Security Act, 183
Homeland Security Program, 180–81
Home Rule, 135–36
Homeschooling, 165
Household income, 8
House of Burgesses, 13
House of Delegates. *See also* Delegates
    description of, 14, 20–21
    lawmaking power of, 66–67
    leadership in, 70–71
    lobbyists-to-state representatives
        ratio in, 53
    majority leader in, 71
    minority leader in, 71
    qualifications to be member of, 62
    reapportionment of seats for, 31
    standing committees in, 66, 70
    term limits for, 62
    women in, 29, 73
House of Representatives (U.S.), 69
Howell, Henry, 83
Human capital, 158
Hydrofracking, 179–80

Ideologies, 4
Ideology, 43
Immigration
    diversity caused by, 5
    population growth secondary to, 5

Impeachment
  of elected officials, 69
  of judges, 101
Income growth, 169
Incorporation, 136–38
Incumbent, 31
Independent cities
  council-manager form of government,
    134–35
  governmental consolidation to
    create, 146
  list of, 133
  loss of, 134
Industries, 182
Infrastructure, 182
Initiatives, 36
Institutional agenda, 156
Institutional revenues, 124
Interest, revenue from, 124
Interest groups, 49, 52–56, 109
Interim committees, 65
Intermediary institutions, 42
Irish Catholics, 28
Iron triangle, 54, 109–10

Jamestown, 4
Jefferson, Thomas, 1, 4, 15, 61, 84, 96
Jim Crow laws, 26
Job descriptions, Virginia government
    employees, 110
Joint legislative committees, 64
Joint Legislative Audit and Review
    Committee, 69
Judges
  compensation of, 100–101
  diversity of, 100
  impeachment of, 101
  misconduct by, 101
  qualifications of, 99–100
  retirement age for, 99
  selection of, 98–99
  tenure of, 100–101
Judicial activism, 98
Judicial branch. See also Court(s)
  description of, 14, 21
  employees of, 91
Judicial Inquiry and Review
    Commission, 101

Judicial review, 97
Judiciary, 21
Juvenile courts, 93

K–12 education. See also Public education
  academic achievement, 159–63
  achievement gaps, 161–62
  adequate yearly progress requirements
    under NCLB, 160–61
  career and technical education
    programs, 164
  charter schools, 163
  decentralization of education policy, 159
  funding for, 159
  Governor's schools, 164
  history of, 158–59
  homeschooling, 165
  magnet schools, 163
  on-time graduation rates, 162–63
  online education, 164
  schools, 163–65
  state constitution provisions
    for, 97, 157
  statistics about, 159
  test scores, 160
Kaine, Timothy, 82, 84
Kentucky, 29
Key, V. O., 45
King Charles II, 4
King George III, 14
King James I, 13
Kinser, Cynthia, 95, 100

Law Enforcement Terrorism Prevention
    Program, 180
Lawmaking, 44, 66–68, 81, 155
Legislative branch, 20–21
Legislative commissions, 65
Legislative referendum, 36
Legislators. See also Delegates; Senator(s)
  appointment of, 69–70
  demographic profile of, 71–72
  educational level of, 71
  ethnic diversity of, 72
  racial diversity of, 72
Legislature. See General Assembly
Lemons, Donald, 95
Lesbians, 100

LETPP. *See* Law Enforcement Terrorism Prevention Program
Lieutenant governor. *See also* Bolling, Bill
  legislative role of, 70–71, 87
  power of, 81, 84, 86–87
  qualifications of, 87
  responsibilities of, 20, 70–71, 77
Limited English proficiency students, 161–63
Line-item veto, 81
Liquor stores, 38
Literacy tests for voting, 28
Lobbying
  definition, 49–52
  regulations, 53
Lobbyists, 53–54
  growth in, 53
Local governments
  annexation by, 143, 145–46
  Article VII provisions for, 22, 133
  economic development by, 186
  education expenditures by, 141, 143–44
  establishment of, 22
  expenditures by, 141, 143
  facts about, 145
  growth of, 136–43
  incorporation of, 136–38
  number of, 132
  overview of, 151–52
  revenues of, 140–43
  special districts, 147
Local income tax, 143
London Company, 4
"Lottery Proceeds Fund," 22
Loupassi, G. Manoli, 101

MADD. *See* Mothers Against Drunk Driving
Madison, James, 4, 15, 55
Magistrates, 91–92
Magnet schools, 163
Majority leader, 70
Majority opinion, 96
Majority rule, 67–68
Male suffrage, 17
Manchester, 134
Mandamus, writ of, 94

Marriage, 19
Marshal, John, 15
Martin, Thomas, 46
Martin Organization, 46
Maryland Constitution, 13
Mason, George, 14, 18
"Massive resistance," 46–47
Mayor-council form of government, 134
McCain, John, 34, 47
McClanahan, Elizabeth, 95
McDonnell, Bob, 70, 78, 81–82, 112, 127, 155, 173, 181, 184
McEachin, Donald, 70–71
Means-tested social welfare programs, 166–67
Medicaid
  expenditures for, 126
  fraud associated with, 116
  health care provided by, 171
Medicare, 171
Merit system, 110–13
Metro area, 149
Metropolitan Planning Organizations, 147–48
Metropolitan Statistical Areas, 149–51
Micropolitan Statistical Areas, 151
Miller, Yvonne B., 73
Millette, LeRoy, Jr., 95
Minority leader, 70
Misdemeanor, 92
Mission statements, 113
Monroe, James, 4, 15, 79, 84
Mothers Against Drunk Driving, 109
Motor Voter laws, 34
MPOs. *See* Metropolitan Planning Organizations
MSAs. *See* Metropolitan Statistical Areas
Municipal charter, 135
Municipal governments, 133–36

National Assessment of Educational Progress (NAEP), 160
National Association for the Advancement of Colored People (NAACP), 55
National committees, 44
National courts, 96–97
National Incident Management System, 181

National politics, state voting impact on, 34, 36
"Negro Constitution," 16
New England Constitution, 13
New Hampshire, 62, 165
Newport News, 134
New York
    Civil Service Commission, 112
    Constitution of, 13
1902 Constitution, 17–18, 145
1971 Constitution, 18–23
Nineteenth Amendment, 29
No Child Left Behind Act, 50, 160
Non-general fund revenues, 124–26
Northern Virginia, 8, 125, 165
Northern Virginia Transportation
    Authority, 98
Nuclear power, 175–76

Obama, Barack, 34, 47, 88, 172
Occupy movement, 37
Office of the Executive Secretary for the
    Supreme Court of Virginia, 92, 96
Offshore oil drilling, 175–76
"Old Dominion State," 4–5
Open primaries, 33
Original jurisdiction courts, 92, 96
Overseas trade missions, 185–86

PACs. See Political action committees
Party conventions, 44
Party realignment, 47
Patient Protection and Affordable Care
    Act, 88, 97, 172
Patronage, 46
PDOs. See Planning District Commissions
Performance measures, 113
Perry, Rick, 36
Personal Responsibility and Work
    Opportunity Reconciliation Act, 167
Piedmont region, 3
Planning District Commissions, 147–49
Poindexter, Charles, 56
Policy evaluation, 156
Policymaking, 97–98, 155–56. See also
    Public policies
Policy process model, 155–56
Political action committees, 56

Political culture
    description of, 4
    state constitutions influenced by, 12–13
    traditionalist. See Traditionalist political
    culture
Political gerrymandering, 31–32, 69
Political participation
    by blacks, 26, 28
    conventional, 37
    gerrymandering effects on, 31–32
    importance of, 25
    by Irish Catholics, 28
    national politics affected by, 34, 36
    redistricting effects on, 30–32
    unconventional, 37–38
    by women, 28
Political parties. See also Democratic Party;
    Republican Party
    conventions held by, 44
    in electorate, 43–44
    in government, 44–45
    government control by, 48
    history of, 45–49
    as organization, 44
    primaries held by, 43
    purpose of, 42–45
    realignment of, 47
    responsible party model, 43
    as "umbrella" organizations, 43
    in voting, 43
Politics
    direct democracy, 36–37
    history of, 4–5
    public input into, 42
    voting rights. See Voting rights
Pollard, Fred C., 83
Poll taxes, 26, 28
Popular referendum, 36
Population
    age demographics of, 5, 7
    distribution of, 5
    ethnic diversity of, 5–6
    growth of, 5, 16, 70, 151
    racial diversity of, 5
Pork barrel spending, 157
Poverty
    in Northern Virginia, 8, 165
    measurement, 168

social welfare programs for, 166–67, 169
statistics regarding, 165–66
Temporary Assistance to Needy Families
for, 167, 169
Poverty guidelines, 168
Poverty threshold, 168
Powell, Cleo Elaine, 95
Preparedness planning, for
emergencies, 182
President pro tempore, 71
Presidents, 4
Primaries
description of, 32–33
by political parties, 43
open, 33
closed, 33
hybrid, 33
Primary elections, 33
Prince William County redistricting, 32
Private schools, 164
Progressives, 17
Prohibition, writ of, 94–95
Property, revenue from sale of, 124
Property tax revenue, 141
Prosecutors, 93
PRWORA. *See* Personal Responsibility and
Work Opportunity Reconciliation Act
Public demonstrations, 37
Public education
academic achievement, 159–63
achievement gaps, 161–62
adequate yearly progress requirements
under NCLB, 160–61
Article VIII provisions for, 21–22
attainment levels, 158
career and technical education
programs, 164
charter schools, 163
funding for, 21, 159
Governor's Schools, 164
history of, 158–59
local government expenditures for,
141, 143–44
magnet schools, 163
merit-based pay for teachers, 112–13
on-time graduation rates, 162–63
revenues for, 122
schools, 163–65

state constitution provisions for, 97, 157
statistics regarding, 5
test scores, 160
Public financing in elections, 56
Public opinion, 38
Public policies
distributive, 157
economic development policy, 184–87
education. *See* K–12 education; Public
education
emergency management, 180–83
energy and environmental policy. *See*
Energy and environmental policy
evaluation of, 156
health and human services. *See* Health
and human services
homeland security, 180–83
impact of, 154
implementation of, 156
process of, 155–57
reasons for creating, 157
redistributive, 157
regulatory, 157
summary of, 187–88
types of, 155
Public School Charter Fund, 163
Putney, Lacey, 62

Race
achievement gaps and, 161
diversity of, 5
health care coverage and, 170
of judges, 100
of legislators, 72
voting rates based on, 35
voting rights and, 26
Racial disenfranchisement, 17, 26
Racial gerrymandering, 26, 69
Racial segregation, 26
Readjuster Party, 45
Reapportionment, 15–16, 31, 70
Recall elections, 36–37
Receipts, revenue from, 124
Recession, 7
Reconstruction, 17, 26
Redistributive policies, 157
Redistricting, 30–32, 69–70
Referendum, 36

Regional Cooperation Act, 149
Regionalism, 146–51
Registration for voting, 26
Regulatory policies, 157
Renewable energy sources, 174–75, 178
Rents, revenue from, 124
Representative democracy, 13, 32
Representatives
    salary of, 63
    term limits for, 62
Republican Party. *See also* Political parties
    "Creed" of, 50
    Democratic Party versus, 49
    government control by, 48
    governors from, 83
    "loyalty oath," 33
    political values of, 49–50
    post–World War II resurgence of, 47
    voter characteristics, 51–52
Responsible party model, 43
Revenues
    description of, 120
    general fund, 122
    local government, 140–43
    non-general fund, 124–26
    sources of, 122–25
Reynolds v. Simms, 31, 69
Richmond, 16, 134
Right-to-work legislation, 159
Robb, Chuck, 83

Salary
    of delegates, 63–64
    of judges, 101
    of senators, 63–64
Sale of property and commodities, revenue
    from, 124
Same-sex marriage, 19, 38
SCHIP. *See* State Children Health
    Insurance Program
Schofield, John, 16
Schools, 163–65
Schools of democracy, 1
School voucher programs, 164
Secretary of Administration, 108
Secretary of Agriculture and Forestry, 108
Secretary of Commerce and Trade, 108
Secretary of Education, 108

Secretary of Finance, 108
Secretary of Health and Human
    Services, 108
Secretary of Natural Resources, 108
Secretary of Public Safety, 108
Secretary of Technology, 108
Secretary of the Commonwealth, 108
Secretary of Transportation, 108
Secretary of Veteran Affairs and Homeland
    Security, 108
Senate (Virginia)
    description of, 14, 20–21
    lawmaking power of, 66–67
    leadership in, 70–71
    lobbyists-to-state representatives
        ratio in, 53
    reapportionment of seats for, 31
    standing committees in, 66
    women in, 29
Senator(s)
    description of, 21
    ethnic diversity of, 72
    number of, 62
    qualifications to be, 62
    racial diversity of, 72
    salary of, 63–64
    staff support for, 64–65
    term limits for, 62
1776 Constitution, 13–15, 68
Single member plurality, 43
Slavery, 16
Smith, George William, 79
Social welfare programs,
    166–67, 169
SOL. *See* Standards of Learning
Solvency, 127
South Boston, 134
Southern Virginia, 8, 125
Sovereign, 96
Sovereign government, 12
Speaker of the House, 64–65, 70
Special districts, 147
Split-ticket voting, 43, 47
Spoils system, 110
Standards of Learning, 160
Standing committees, 64, 66, 70
State Children Health Insurance
    Program, 172

State constitutions, 12–13. *See also* Constitution (Virginia)
State Convention of the Republican Party of Virginia, 44
State of emergency, 181
Statewide Mutual Aid Program, 181
Status offenses, 93
Statutory law, 97
Street-level bureaucrats, 109
Substantive representation, 72
Suffolk, 134
Suffrage
  universal male, 17
  women's, 28–29
Superintendent of Public Instruction, 159
Supermajority, 68
Supreme Court of Virginia
  appeals to, 95–96
  chief justices of, 100
  majority opinion of, 96
  opinions by, 100
  original jurisdiction of, 96
  power of, 21
  state constitution creation of, 90, 95
  term limits for, 100
  women on, 100
Supreme Court (U.S.), 91
Sustainable energy, 178
Swing voters, 43
Systemic agenda, 156

TANF. *See* Temporary Assistance to Needy Families
Taxes/taxation
  Article X provisions for, 22–23
  local income, 143
  revenue from, 122–23, 141
Taylor, Zachary, 4
Teachers, 112–13
Tea Party, 37, 48
Temporary Assistance to Needy Families, 167, 169
Term limits
  for governor, 78–79
  for legislators, 62–63
  state comparisons of, 79
Texas, 12

Thorne-Begland, Tracy, 100–101
Tidewater region, 145
Towns
  cities versus, 133
  governmental consolidation of, 143, 145–46
  growth of, 139
  incorporation of, 136–38
Traditionalist, 4
Traditionalist political culture
  description of, 12–13
  voting rights influenced by, 25, 28
Transfers, revenue from, 124
Transportation
  energy consumption for, 174
  planning of, 147
Trustee model, 62
Twenty-fourth Amendment, 28
Tyler, John, 4, 84
Tysons Corner, 138–39

Underwood Constitution, 16–17
Unemployment rates, 7
Unitary system of government, 12
Universal male suffrage, 17
Urban Areas Security Initiative (UASI), 182–83

Valley and Ridge region, 3
VCERC. *See* Virginia Coastal Energy Research Consortium
VEEP. *See* Virginia Environmental Excellence Program
Vermont Constitution, 12
Veto
  of bills, 68, 81
  line-item, 81
  overriding of, 81
  of redistricting plans, 69
Victim's Rights Amendment, 19
Virginia Beach redistricting, 32
Virginia Black Caucus, 29
Virginia Citizen Defense League, 38
Virginia Coastal Energy Research Consortium, 178–79
Virginia Company of London, 13
Virginia Department of Education, 106, 159–60

Virginia Department of Emergency
    Management, 181
Virginia Division of Legislative Services, 64
Virginia Economic Development
    Partnership (VEDP), 186–87
Virginia Energy Plan, 174, 176, 188
Virginia Energy Sense, 178
Virginia Environmental Excellence
    Program, 178
Virginia Farm Bureau, 55
Virginia Health Care Freedom Act, 172
Virginia Jobs Investment Program
    (VJIP), 187
*Virginia Law Enforcement Anti-Terrorism
    Pocket Guide,* 180–81
Virginia Municipal League, 54
Virginia Performs Program, 128–30
Virginia Personnel Act, 110
Virginia Retirement System, 127
Virginia State Corporation Commission, 22
Virginia Workforce Council, 184
Voter(s)
    characteristics of, 51–52
    Democratic, 51–52
    eligibility requirements for, 29
    General Assembly establishment of
        qualifications for, 33
    identification requirements for, 29
    local turnout for, 34
    registration of, 26, 34
    Republican, 51–52
Voter turnout, 33–35
Voting
    age requirements, 29
    declining rates of, 39
    disenfranchised groups, 26, 28
    literacy tests for, 28
    political parties' role in, 43
    poll taxes for, 26, 28
    purposes of, 33
    redistricting effects on, 30–32, 69–70
    registration for, 26, 34

split-ticket, 43, 47
statistics regarding, 33–34
Voting rights
    age requirements, 17
    of blacks, 26–28
    of cognitively impaired persons, 29
    of felons, 29–30
    history of, 26–29
    individuals not allowed, 26
    race and, 26
    1776 Constitution provision
        for, 14–15
Voting Rights Act
    description of, 28
    oversight exemptions, 31

Wallace, Robert Daniel, 105
Warner, Mark, 82, 84
Warwick, 134
Washington, George, 4
Washington–Arlington–Alexandria
    metropolitan statistical area, 151
Water supply planning, 177–78
Weak-mayor form of government, 135
Webb, Jim, 84
Wilder, L. Douglas, 83–84, 86
Wilson, Woodrow, 4
Wims, William, 95
Wind energy, 179
Women
    in House of Delegates, 73
    political participation by, 28–29
    suffrage movement by, 28–29
    on Supreme Court of Virginia, 100
    ultrasound requirements before
        abortion, 37–38
    voting rights, 26, 28–29
Workforce development centers, 184
World War II, 47
Writ of habeas corpus, 95
Writ of mandamus, 94
Writ of prohibition, 94–95

SAGE research**methods**

The essential online tool for researchers from the world's leading methods publisher

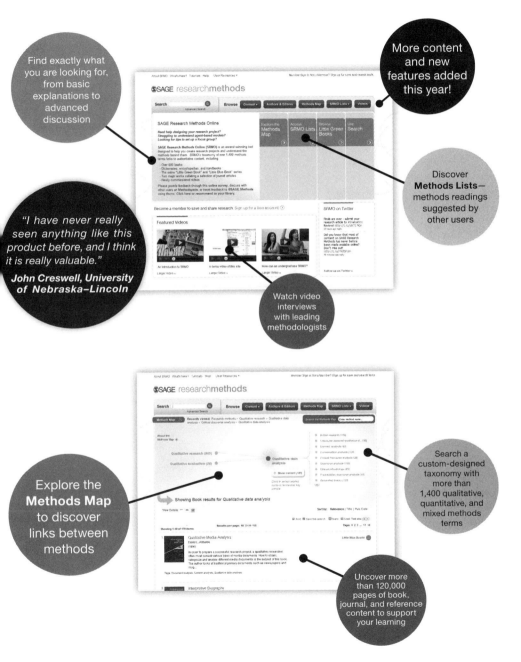

Find exactly what you are looking for, from basic explanations to advanced discussion

More content and new features added this year!

Discover **Methods Lists**— methods readings suggested by other users

"I have never really seen anything like this product before, and I think it is really valuable."
John Creswell, University of Nebraska–Lincoln

Watch video interviews with leading methodologists

Explore the **Methods Map** to discover links between methods

Search a custom-designed taxonomy with more than 1,400 qualitative, quantitative, and mixed methods terms

Uncover more than 120,000 pages of book, journal, and reference content to support your learning

Find out more at
www.sageresearchmethods.com